Electronic Projects

made easy

Stewart Dunn

CollinsEducational

An imprint of HarperCollins*Publishers*

First published by Unwin Hyman 1990
This edition published 1991 by
CollinsEducational
77–85 Fulham Palace Road
Hammersmith London W6 8JB

ISBN 0 00 322268 3

Illustrated by Stewart Dunn
Cover photograph Martyn Chillmaid
Typeset by RDL Artset Ltd.
Printed in Great Britain by Martin's of Berwick
Bound by Hunter & Foulis Ltd, Edinburgh

CONTENTS

Preface to Teachers   v
General Introduction   vii
Using this book with the National
    Curriculum   ix
What are these?   xi
Worksheet   xiii

Getting Started
Circuit Training   1
Will it Conduct?   2

Simple Control
Controlling Voltage   3
Bulb Control by Light   4

Work with Bulbs
Lots of Lights   5
Bulbs in Series   6

Work with Switches
Making Switches   7
Switch Types/Simple Switch Logic   8
Magic Magnet Switch   9
Magnet Controlled Buggy   10
Flashing Light   11

Vehicles/Buggies
Simple Vehicles   12
Steerable Buggy   13
Parts for Buggy   14
A Simple Crane   15

Simple Projects
Quiz Maker   16
One-Way Only Diodes   17
Boat – Air Propelled   18
Traffic Lights (Cams)   19
Walking Robot/Washing Machine   20

Computer Control   21
Logo – Getting Going   22
Flashing Lights   23
Computer Show   24
Computer Show (continued)   25
Computer Buggy   26
Car Park Barrier   27

Electronics Introduction
Other Outputs to Try/Capacitors   28
Measuring Voltage   29
Measuring Current   30
Batteries in Series   31
Fun Jewellery/Badge   32

Relays   33
Motor Reversing – 1   34
Motor Reversing – 2   35
Alarm – Latched   36

Sensing Circuits   37
Light/Temperature Switching   38
Liquid Level Indicator   39
Sensitive Switching   40
Very Sensitive DC Amplifier   41
Thermometer   42
Light Follower   43
Thyristor Latch   44
Plant Waterer/Automatic Door/
    Window Opener   45

Multivibrators   46

Clock Astable
Flashing Lights   47
Flasher or Siren   48
Music Organ   49
Good Motor Control   50

Timers
Timer   51
Time Delay   52
Display Ideas/Flashing Transport   53
Car Alarm or Disco/
    A Quiz Indicator   54

Sound Amplifiers
AC Amplification   55
Sound Amplifier   56
2-Watt Audio Amplifier   57
Disco – Sound Operated   58

Radio   59

Digital Electronics   60
Light/Temperature Sensing   61
Touch Latching Switch   62
Multivibrator 'Clock'   63

Seven Segment Display
A Counting Circuit   64
Lap Counter   65
0 to 9 Counter   66
Stop-Watch   67

Electronic Symbols   68
Symbols to Cut Out   69
Soldering Shapes   70
Making a PCB   71
PCB Circuit Examples   72

Appendix: Equipment;
    Useful Addresses   73
Project List   75
Index   77

PREFACE TO TEACHERS

Electronic Projects Made Easy is written by an experienced technology teacher, also the author of the successful books *'CDT – A Complete Course for GCSE'* and *'An Introduction to CDT'*. This book was written to make electronics projects both easy and fun to make and test. The book will appeal to anybody teaching or making electronic circuits, whether for individual projects, courses in electronics, design and technology, or science. Electronic construction kits that use international symbols, including the EZI–DUN and Locktronics kits, or can be assembled on spring boards, printed circuit boards, or perforated boards with pins (or even pieces of wood with nails and drawing pins).

Electronic Project pages contain topic heading with brief explanation and circuit diagram drawn with **input**, **process** and **output** parts clearly shown. Beneath this is a photograph showing a practical realisation of the circuit, and the smaller text explains how each circuit works and can be used. Structured learning activities are provided, generating many project ideas.

The section on computer control is written using a Logo type language suitable to students already using Logo in other parts of their school work. Computer control using BASIC is provided next to the Logo programs for those who prefer it.

The book gathers hundreds of ideas and comes complete with worksheets, electronic symbols, soldering instructions, printed circuit board construction technique with examples, and an informative appendix.

The book follows the progression normally seen in schools but can be used in any way the user chooses. Most pages are independent from one another and all circuits have been tried, tested and photographed. The book has been designed with maximum flexibility for student and teacher alike. It was originally written with examination students in mind but lends itself to any student interested in electrics, electronics, or computer control.

Some schools may wish to use the book solely for the simple yet useful electric projects, perhaps with some computer control using the Logo control examples given. Other schools with examination classes might use the book by first revising basic electrics, then moving on to electronics and more complex circuits, before making printed circuit boards and linking circuits together with Logo or BASIC control work.

AUTHOR'S NOTE

I hope your enjoyment of the book is as great as I had when I tested ideas with students and developed the EZI–DUN contruction system. This book should be particularly welcome to the busy teacher who needs time to teach effectively. I would welcome any comments and ideas for my next book which aims to develop similar ideas further. *Stewart Dunn*

GENERAL INTRODUCTION

This book has been written so that electronic projects are easy, fun and reliable. The book is multipurpose and not dedicated to any particular kit. It may be used with any electronic construction kit or system which uses international electronic symbols.

The book can be used as a project book for examination courses, a BASIC computer control book, an ideas book, an examination and project reference book, or to encourage open ended problem solving linking up with mechanisms and structures.

Schools introducing this book may choose to start with the electrics section at the front and progress to the work with transistors, timer chips etc and then on to more complex circuits making printed circuit boards which could be linked up with computer control work.

HOW TO USE THIS BOOK

Because this book is copyright free within an institution, it may be used in a variety of ways including:

photocopying the circuit and using it as a **paper template** through which connecting wires can be pushed;

handing out **photocopies** (and worksheets) of the circuit to be made;

cutting out **electronic symbols** from the 'symbols to cut out' page to stick onto the worksheets provided, before making the circuit;

making up **booklets** for the students to work at their own pace.

POWER SUPPLIES

Use batteries when making and testing circuits rather than using power supplies which supply too much current and may damage the more sensitive components. Four to six volts can be used for nearly all the circuits. Most circuits are tolerant up to nine volts.

POSSIBLE CONSTRUCTION METHODS

SPRING BOARD

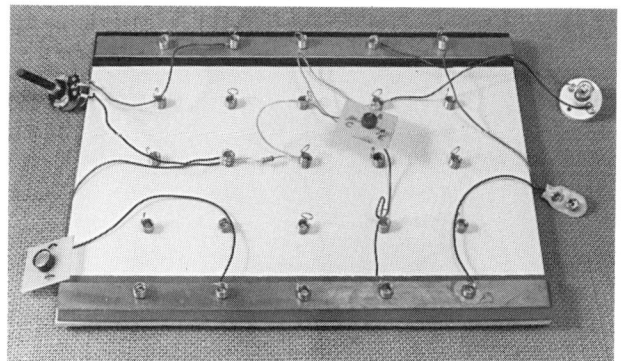

EZI–DUN BOARD

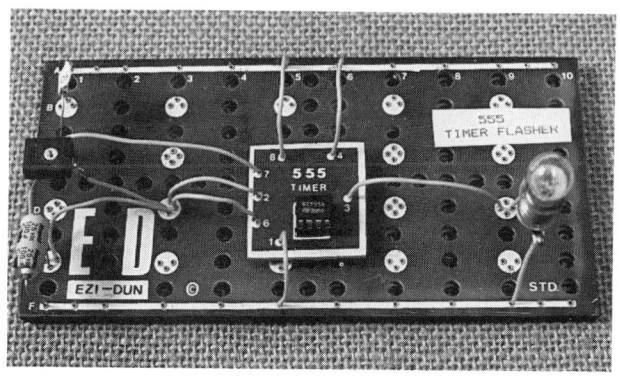

MATRIX BOARD

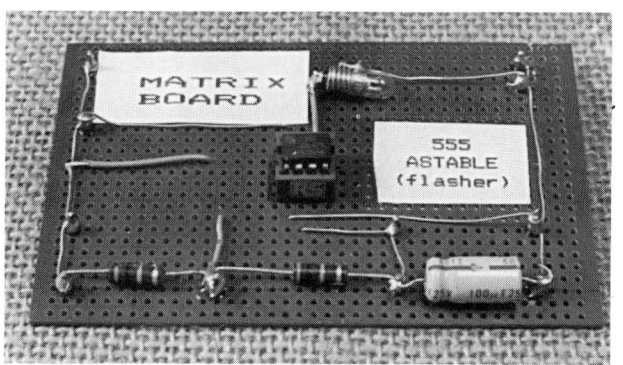

PRINTED CIRCUIT BOARD

USING THIS BOOK WITH THE NATIONAL CURRICULUM

DESIGN AND TECHNOLOGY

The material is suitable for all attainment targets covering 5 to 16 year olds. The book covers just about everything needed during a pupil's period at school concerned with the use of electric, electronic, microelectronic and digital electronic systems as well as some computer control work to solve problems.

The design and technology programmes of study do not specify how design and technology should be taught but provide a basic framework. This book is written so that the relevant page or pages can be photocopied and used as required to help a particular activity, lesson or project to be carried out.

Examples from the National Curriculum for Design and Technology

To design and make systems, including open loop and closed loop systems (Level 7)

To design and implement systems, within specified boundaries, in which control is maintained without the need for human intervention (Level 9). To operate, process and transmit information to establish control over another system (Level 10).

SCIENCE

The material is suitable for all the key stages of Attainment Target 11, electricity and magnetism.

Examples from the National Curriculum for Science

Experience simple activities using bulbs, buzzers, batteries and wires.
(Key Stage 1, 5-7 years).
Construct simple electrical circuits. Vary the flow of electricity in a simple circuit and observe the effects. Describe and record diagrammatically simple electrical circuits.
(Key Stage 2, 7-11 years).
Investigate a wider range of electrical components. Be provided with opportunities to investigate and test ideas.
(Key Stage 3, 11-14 years)

INFORMATION TECHNOLOGY

The material is also suitable for Attainment Target 12, the scientific aspects of information technology including microelectronics.

ACKNOWLEDGEMENTS

I would like to thank all those who have helped in any way with the production of this book. Thanks go in particular to Maja Dunn, Mark Dunn, Jennifer Dunn, Jan Shimmin, Hugh Morgan, Timothy Coote of Commotion, and staff at Unwin Hyman publishers who have assisted in various ways, from checking text to helping with photographs. Thanks also to the many teachers, advisers and others who have encouraged me. I would like particularly to thank Commotion who sell this book and the EZI–DUN kits. For their address and other useful addresses and component parts etc, see the appendix on page 73.

WHAT ARE THESE?

CAN YOU NAME THESE PARTS USED IN ELECTRONICS?

ANSWERS AT THE BOTTOM OF PAGE

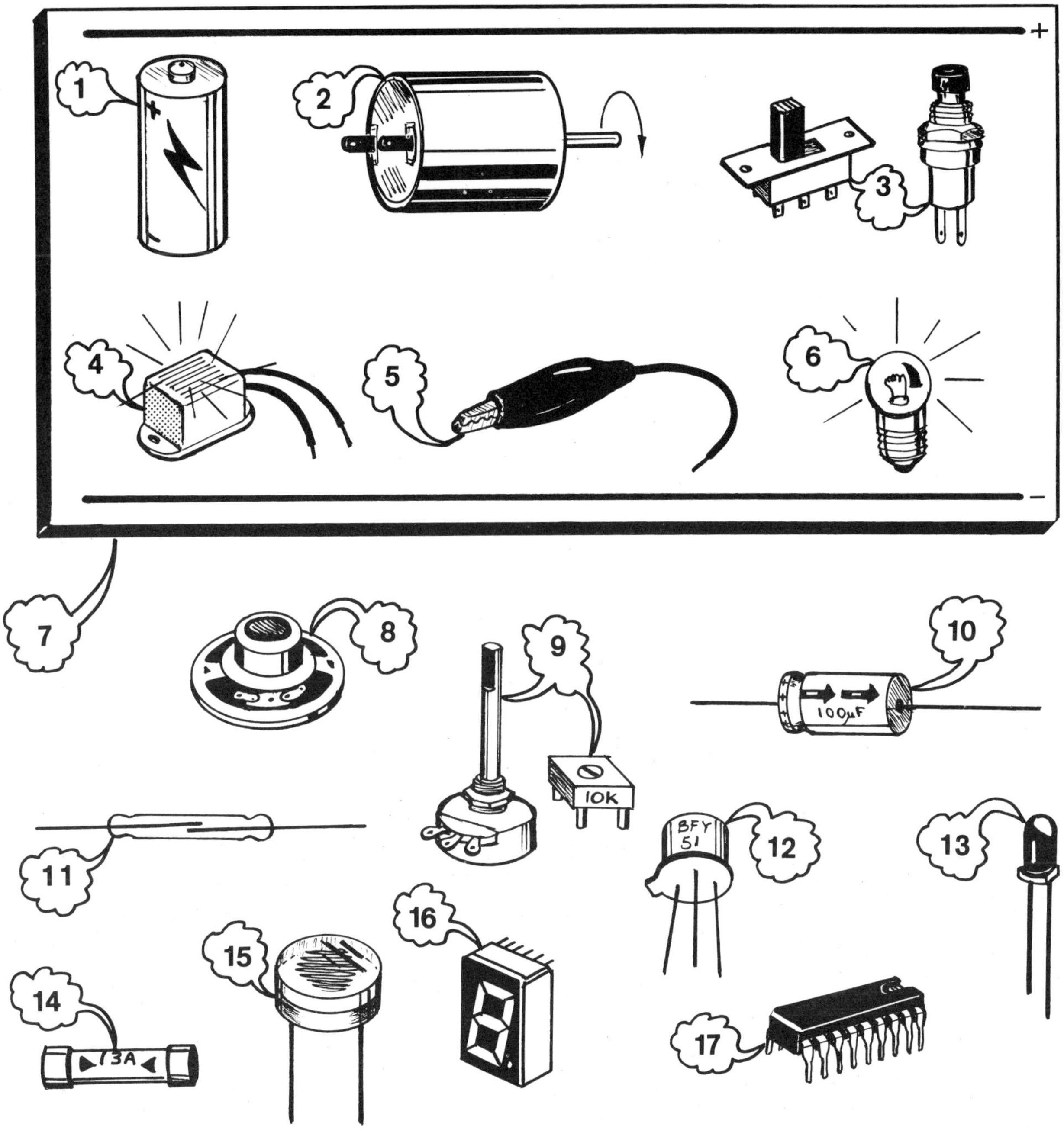

ANSWERS

(1) Battery (2) Motor (3) Switches (4) Buzzer (5) Clip (6) Bulb (7) Board (to mount circuit on)
(8) Loudspeaker (9) Variable resistor (or Potentiometer) (10) Capacitor (11) Reed switch
(12) Transistor (13) LED (Light Emitting Diode) (14) Fuse (15) LDR (Light Dependent Resistor)
(16) Seven segment display
(17) Microchip (Integrated circuit).

WORKSHEET

AND TEMPLATE
BOARDS ARE DRAWN FULL SIZE

MOTOR M

NAME(S) _____

FORM_____ GROUP_____ DATE / /

TITLE	

A ————————————————————————————— +

	1	2	3	4	5	6	7	8	9	10
B	○		○		○		○		○	
C	○		○		○		○		○	
D	○		○		○		○		○	
E	○		○		○		○		○	

F ————————————————————————————— −

(COPY CIRCUIT DIAGRAM ON HERE CAN ALSO BE USED AS TEMPLATE)

OBSERVATIONS/RESULTS/IDEAS _____
_____
_____
_____

TITLE	

A ————————————————————————————— +

	1	2	3	4	5	6	7	8	9	10
B	○		○		○		○		○	
C	○		○		○		○		○	
D	○		○		○		○		○	
E	○		○		○		○		○	

F ————————————————————————————— −

MIC

OBSERVATIONS/RESULTS/IDEAS _____
_____
_____
_____

b c e

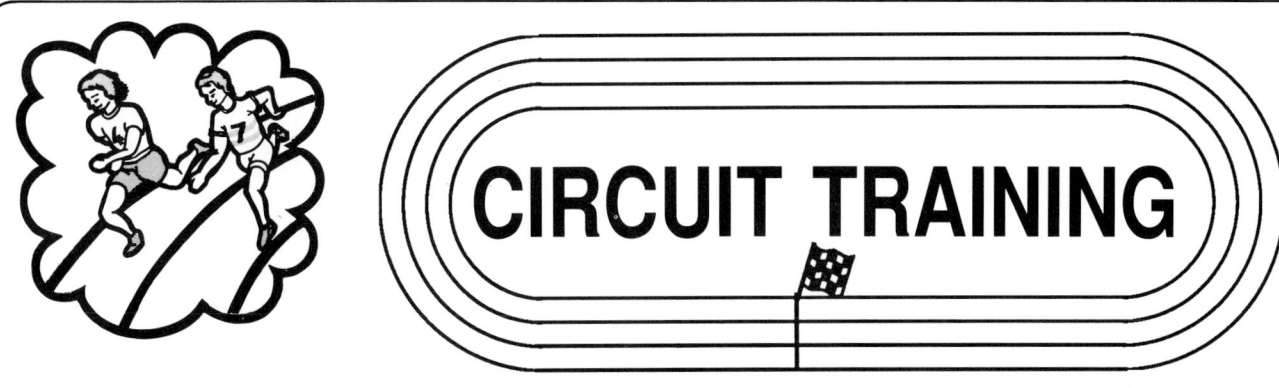

CIRCUIT TRAINING

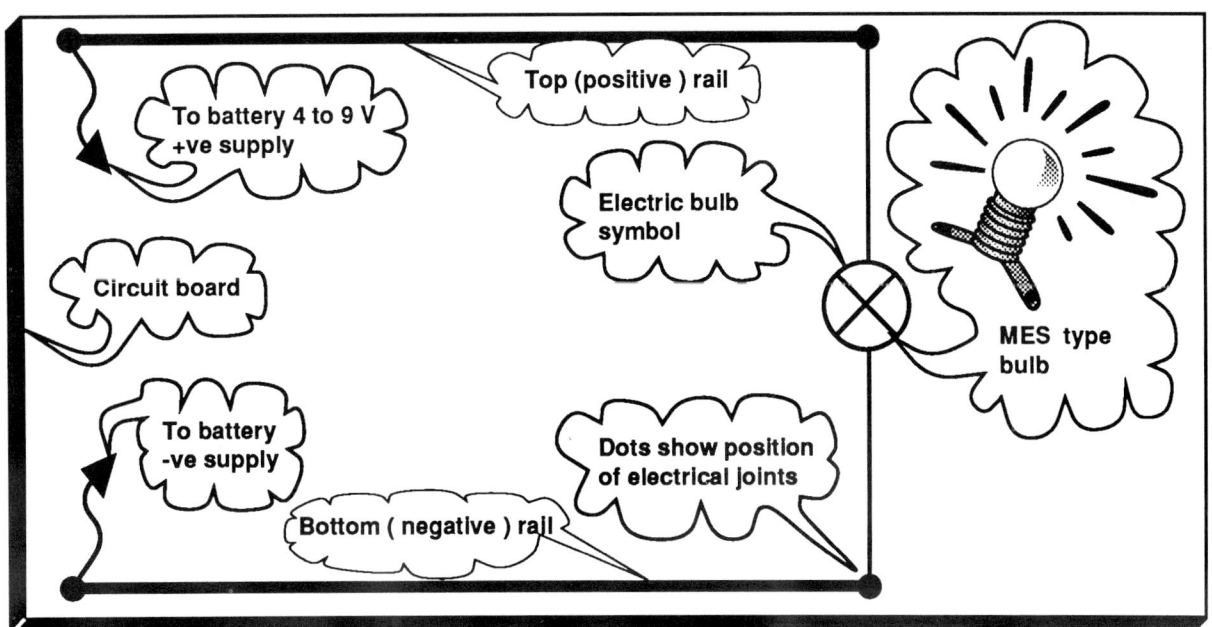

- To battery 4 to 9 V +ve supply
- Top (positive) rail
- Electric bulb symbol
- Circuit board
- MES type bulb
- To battery -ve supply
- Dots show position of electrical joints
- Bottom (negative) rail

An electrical circuit allows electricity to flow round the circuit rather like a runner going round a running track or a racing car going round a racing circuit. Electricity can only flow through **electrical conducting materials** like copper wire. It cannot flow through **electrical insulators** such as the plastic sleeving on the copper wire or air.

Circuits can be drawn diagrammatically like the drawing below. It is a symbolic drawing using agreed international symbols.

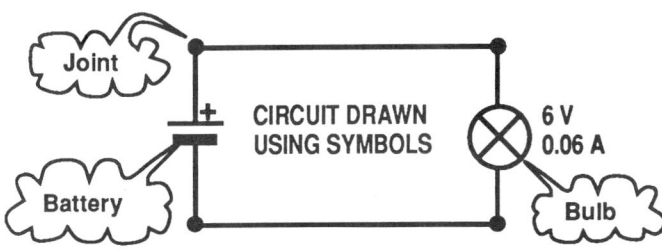

- Joint
- CIRCUIT DRAWN USING SYMBOLS
- 6 V 0.06 A
- Battery
- Bulb

ACTIVITIES

(1) Make a **bulb glow** by connecting it up as in the drawing above. The bulb can be connected either way round.
(2) Extend the circuit above using two more lengths of wire to connect it up. Does it make any difference to the bulb's brightness?
(3) Make the bulb flash ON and OFF by touching wires together by hand. Is it possible to send a 'morse code' message like this?

(4) Replace the bulb with a motor and make a note of the direction it turns round. Which way is it turning — clockwise or anticlockwise?
(5) Now see if you can reverse the direction of the motor. How was this done?
(6) Take the bulb out of its holder and see if you can connect the bulb directly onto the battery. Some batteries may not allow this.
(7) Does the bulb get hot when it glows?

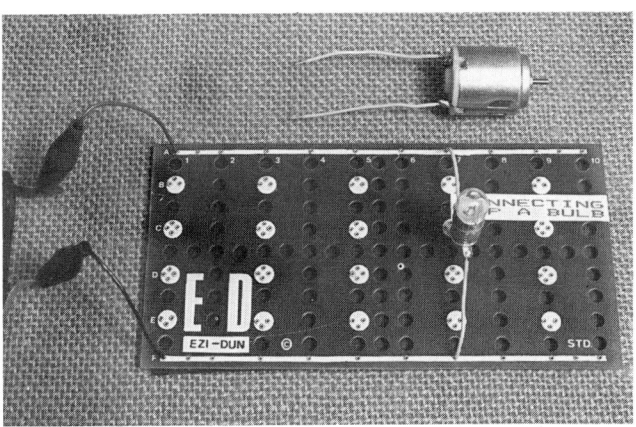

The bulb and battery can be connected as shown. The motor can then be connected in place of the bulb.

Safety

Low voltage batteries are safe but mains electricity is very dangerous and can kill.

Bulb glows – CONDUCTOR
Bulb out – INSULATOR

WILL IT CONDUCT?

Do you know which materials allow electricity to flow through them? Find out by connecting up test pieces to the crocodile clips. If the bulb lights up, the material is said to be **conducting**. If the bulb does not glow, the material is an **insulator**.

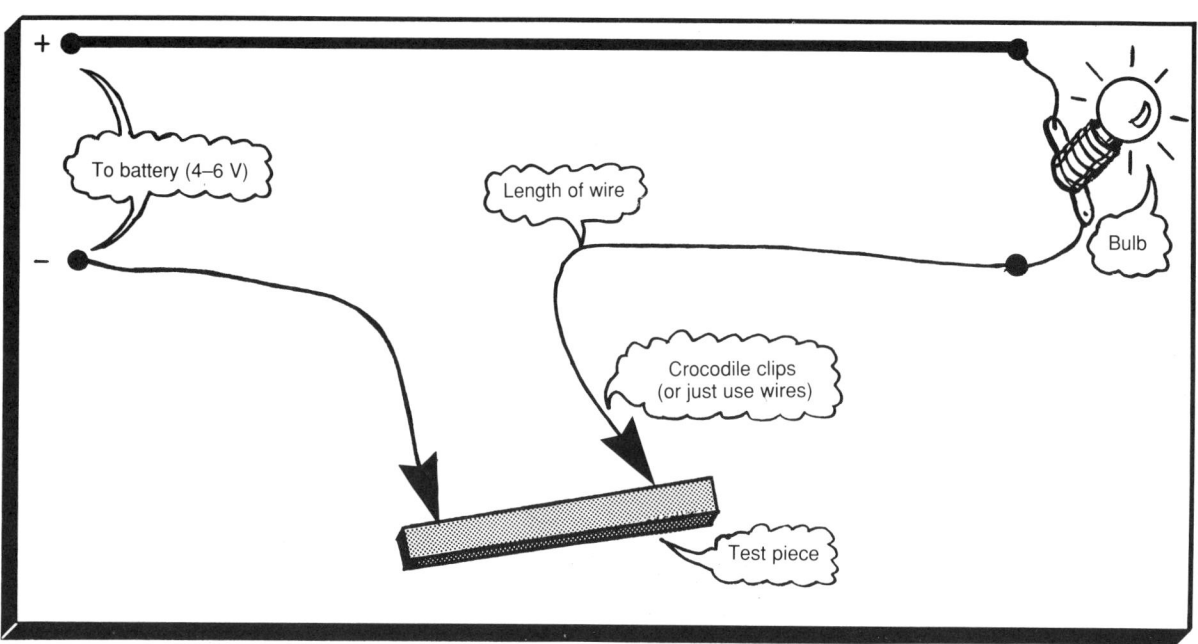

+

To battery (4–6 V)

Length of wire

–

Bulb

Crocodile clips
(or just use wires)

Test piece

INPUT	PROCESS	OUTPUT
ELECTRIC POWER	CONDUCTOR OR INSULATOR USED	BULB 'ON' OR 'OFF'

JUST TESTING ! ! !

Connect up the circuit above (including a 4.5 or 6 V battery) and test the circuit by touching the crocodile clips together. The bulb will glow if it works.

ACTIVITY

Collect various **test pieces** such as those shown below and then test them, keeping a written record of which were **insulators** and which **conductors**.

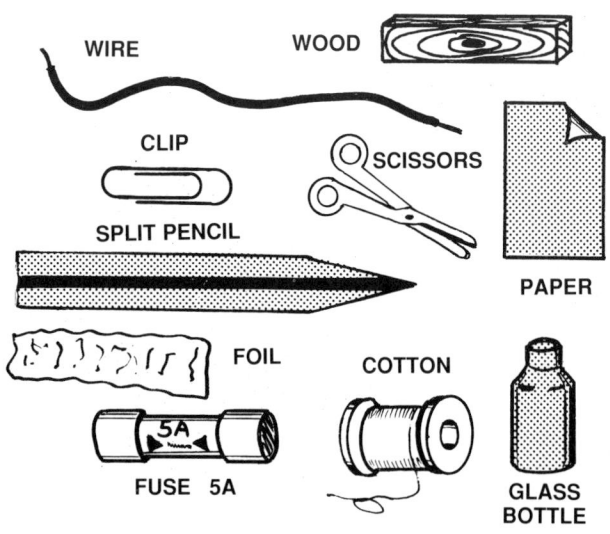

WIRE

WOOD

CLIP

SCISSORS

SPLIT PENCIL

PAPER

FOIL

COTTON

FUSE 5A

GLASS BOTTLE

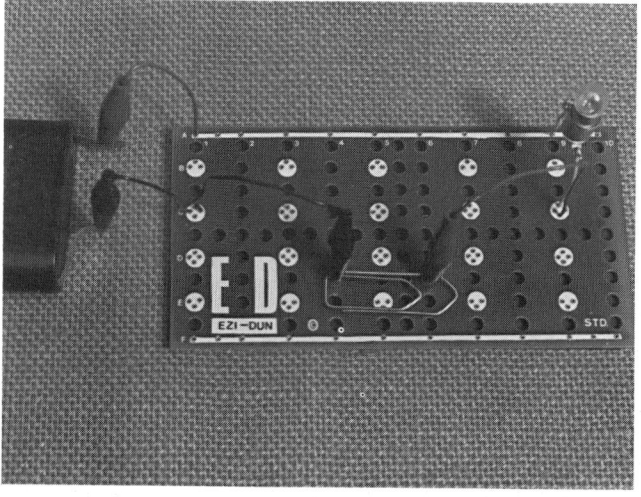

Testing a paper clip to see if it conducts electricity.

Now . . .

Make your circuit into a working display that other people can use, giving instructions such as:
Is it an insulator or conductor?
Connect each test piece in turn between the crocodile clips to find out.

This page may be copied for use in the classroom (see page ii). Electronic Projects – made easy.

3

CONTROLLING VOLTAGE

The **speed of motors** and the **brightness of bulbs** etc can be altered if the voltage supply is changed. Batteries are supplied with a fixed voltage so we need something that can vary the flow of electricity like a water tap controls water flow. A **variable resistor** or **potentiomenter** can do this.

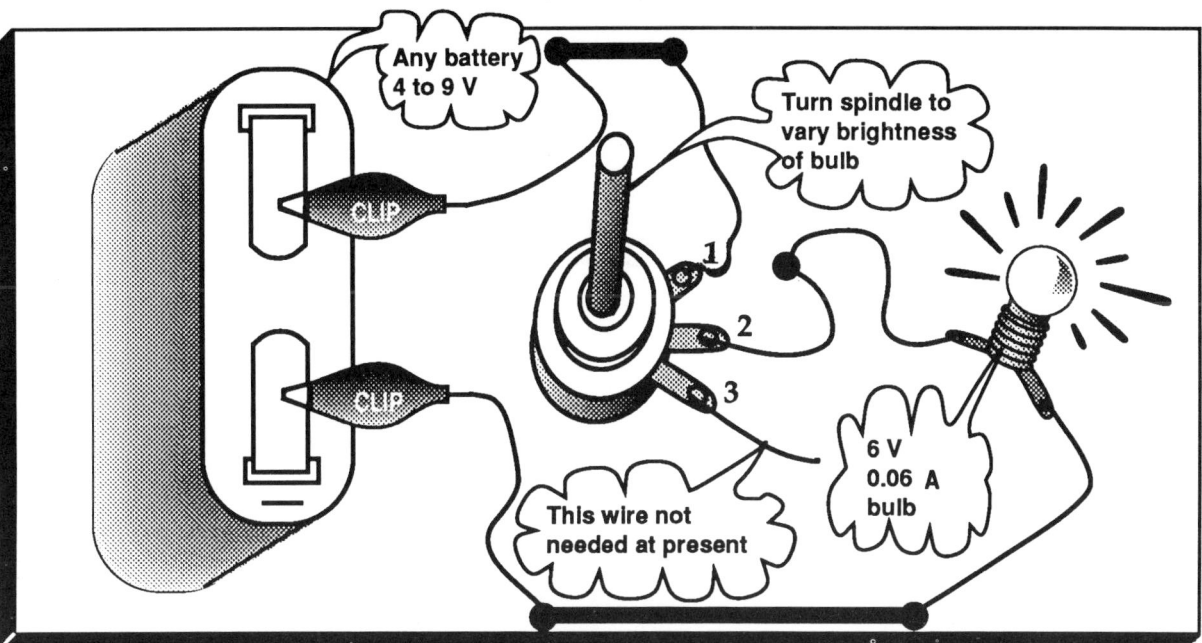

Any battery 4 to 9 V

Turn spindle to vary brightness of bulb

1

2

3

This wire not needed at present

6 V 0.06 A bulb

CLIP

CLIP

INPUT	PROCESS	OUTPUT
Fixed battery voltage	Vary voltage	Light (variable)

The flow of electricity can be controlled like the flow of water through a tap. The 1 kΩ (1000 ohms) **variable resistor** can be varied from a few ohms to 1000 ohms when the spindle is turned.

Below are the **connections** and **symbol** for the **variable resistor**, the connections are labelled 1,2,3 for our convenience.

1 Variable
2 resistor
   connections
3

2 1 Symbol
   3

ACTIVITIES

(1) Using the centre **wire 2** of the variable resistor and outer **wire 1**, connect up the circuit as shown above. What happens to the bulb as the spindle is turned?

(2) What happens if **wire 1** is replaced by **wire 3**?

(3) What happens if only **wire 1** and **wire 3** are connected up?

(4) Now connect up two bulbs, as shown in the picture, using all three wires on the variable resistor. What happens to the two bulbs as the spindle is turned from one extreme to the other?

(5) Replace the bulb with the electric motor and vary the speed.

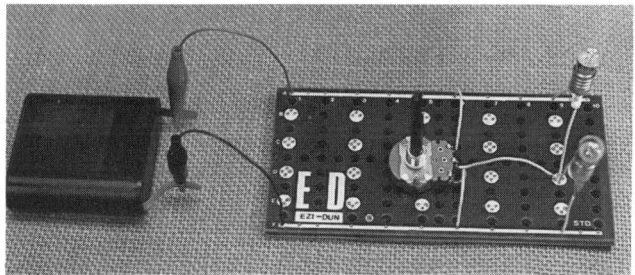

Varying the brightness of the two bulbs using the variable resistor (or potentiomenter).

Now . . .

Apply the knowledge you have gained and make one of the following:

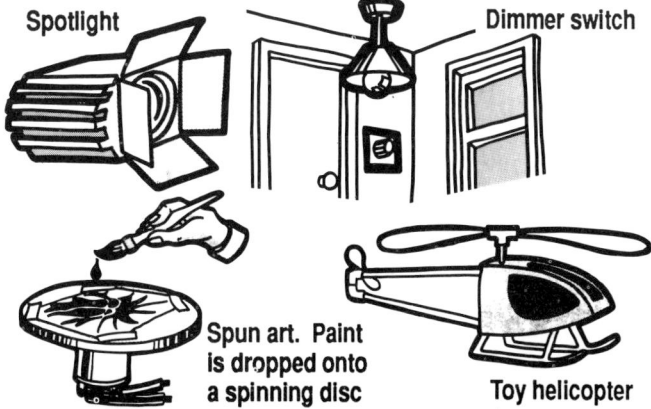

Spotlight

Dimmer switch

Spun art. Paint is dropped onto a spinning disc

Toy helicopter

BULB CONTROL BY LIGHT

NOTE: **Works best on sunny days.**

Place the **light dependent resistor (LDR)** in the sunshine and its resistance is lowered. More electricity can then flow causing the **bulb to glow**, or a **motor to speed up**.

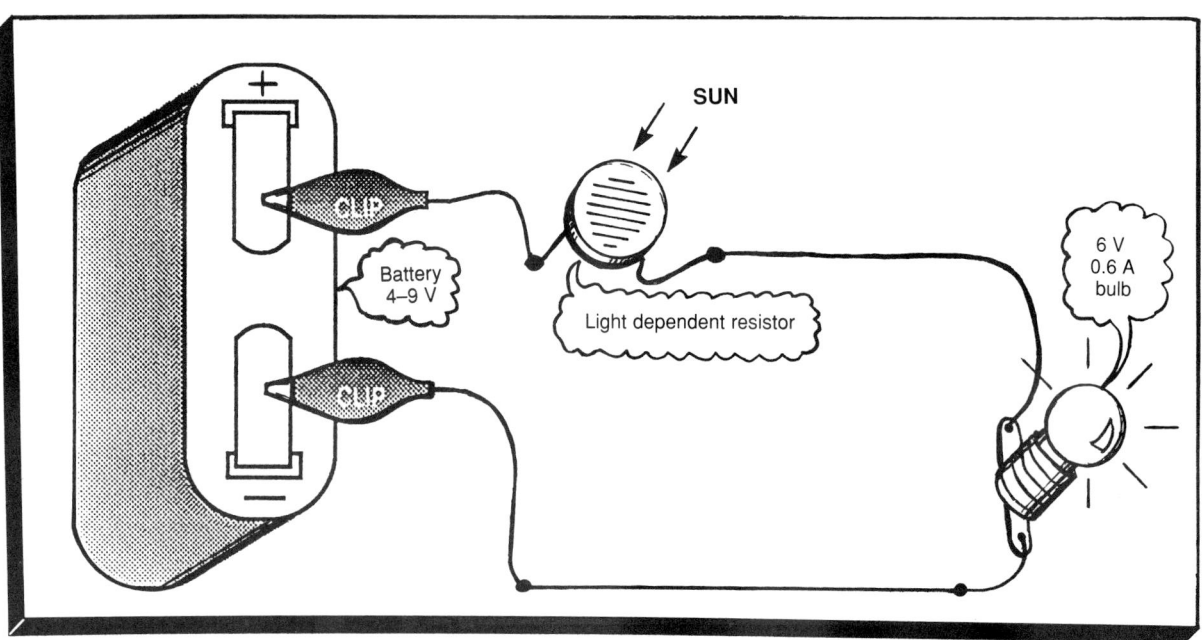

 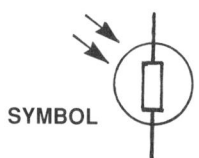

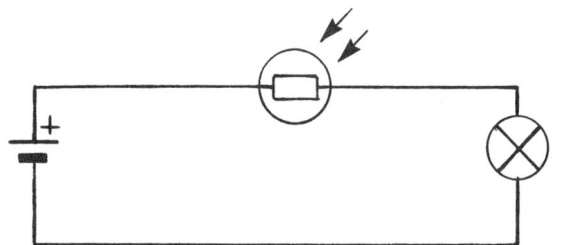

When the LDR is placed in the **sunlight**, the resistance of the LDR is reduced. This allows the electricity to flow through it easily and light the bulb or drive a small electric motor.

Note: A light emitting diode (LED) works better than a bulb if available. Amplified circuits using an LDR can detect very small changes in light level.

The **symbol** for a **light dependent resistor** is given below. The two arrows represent light.

SYMBOL

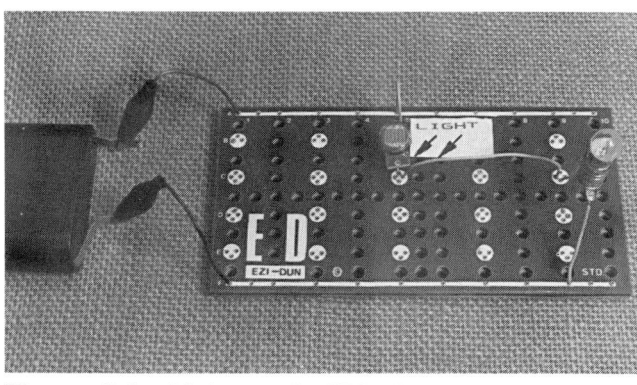

The spotlight shining on the LDR allows electricity to flow more easily, so the bulb glows.

CIRCUIT DRAWN USING SYMBOLS

The circuit below is the same as the one above except it is drawn using agreed international **electrical symbols**.

Can you see the similarity between the two drawings?

ACTIVITIES

(1) Connect up the circuit above. Nothing will happen until you allow bright **direct sunlight** or a **very** bright light to shine on the LDR.

(2) Replace the bulb with the electric motor and see how fast it turns.

Note: The motor is only supposed to work off 1.5 to 4.5 V. **Don't** burn it out on a higher voltage.

(3) Try reflecting a beam of light with a mirror onto the LDR. Does it still work?

(4) Copy out the circuit using agreed international symbols.

LOTS OF LIGHTS
CONNECTING UP IN PARALLEL

When they are connected in **parallel**, lots of light bulbs in the same circuit can work as if each bulb were connected in a separate circuit. If connected in **series**, the result is very different (see next page).

To battery 4 to 9 V +ve supply

All bulbs 6 V 0.06 A

Add motor here – question (4) only

MOTOR

To battery -ve supply

INPUT	PROCESS	OUTPUT
Electric power	All connected up in parallel and all working normally	

If a large battery is being used, at least four bulbs, or other output devices such as motors, can be used off the one battery. If a bulb is added or taken away the circuit works the same.

If the battery can supply enough electrical current, a variety of bulbs and other output devices such as motors can be used at the same time.

ACTIVITIES

(1) Connect the circuit shown above and connect the battery. Are all the bulbs the same brightness?

(2) Disconnect one of the bulbs. Has anything happened to the other two bulbs?

(3) Disconnect a second bulb. Has anything noticeable happened to the last bulb?

(4) Connect the three bulbs again and then add an electric motor in parallel. Are the bulbs still bright?

(5) Add a **buzzer** to the above circuit, ensuring the **red wire** is connected to the **positive** (+) line. Has anything happened to the brightness of the bulbs?

(6) Model the **ring mains** found in houses using the **ring main diagram** to help you. Why do you think it is called a **ring main**?

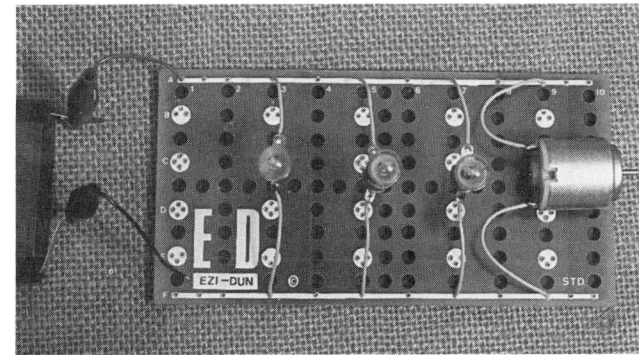

Three bulbs and a motor being operated from one battery. If the battery is powerful enough, the bulbs and motor will all work normally.

(7) Where would a **switch** or **switches** be needed to turn off (a) **all the bulbs**, (b) **each bulb separately**?

Clue – pull out wires to find out.

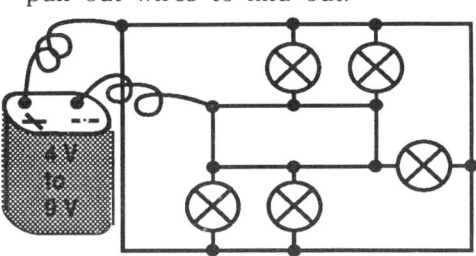

House ring main diagram.
Add bulbs around the circuit as required

CHRISTMAS TREE LIGHTS

BULBS IN SERIES
THIS ALSO APPLIES TO OTHER COMPONENTS

Connecting up bulbs in **series** always reduces the brightness of **bulbs**. If one bulb is removed, it acts like a switch and all the bulbs go out. Unlike connecting up in **parallel** (see previous page), each bulb or component affects the others.

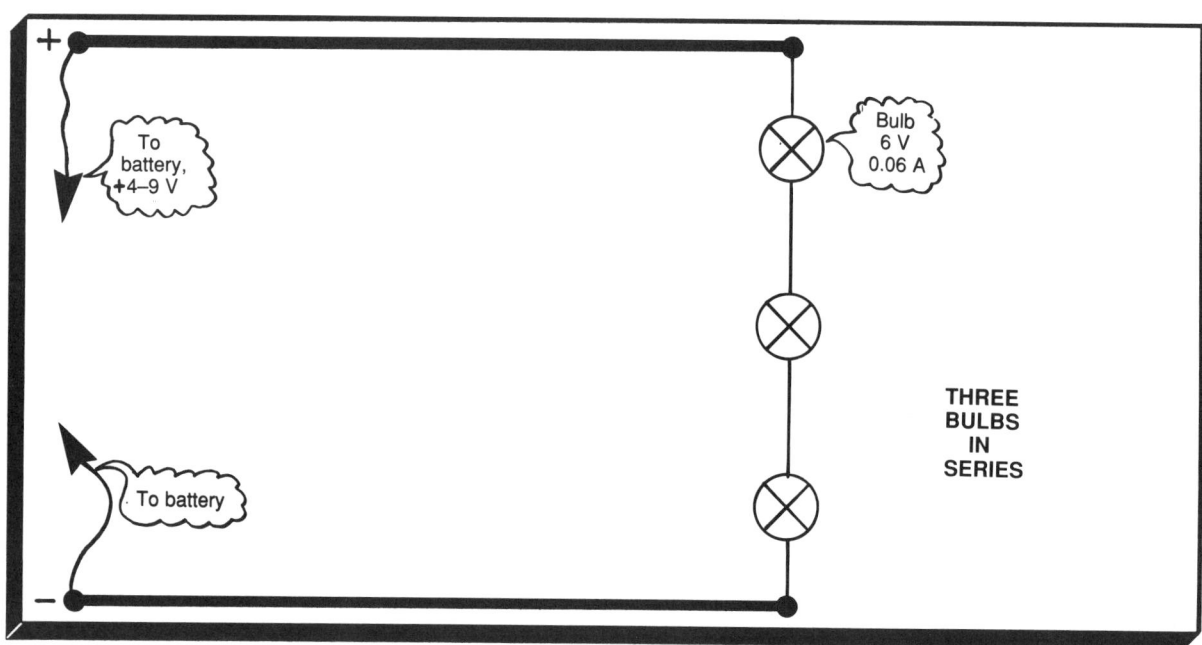

INPUT	PROCESS	OUTPUT
BATTERY VOLTAGE	INCREASED RESISTANCE REDUCES THE BULBS' BRIGHTNESS	

In a circuit, current passing through components connected in **series** is rather like a runner having to run over a series of high hurdles; they slow the runner down. **Series circuits** share out the voltage according to the **resistance of each component**. Christmas tree lights are connected this way. Small low voltage bulbs share out the 240V **mains electricity**. **NEVER CONNECT YOUR CIRCUITS TO THE MAINS ELECTRICITY.**

The total resistance of a **series circuit** is the **total of all the resistances (in ohms)** in the **series circuit**.

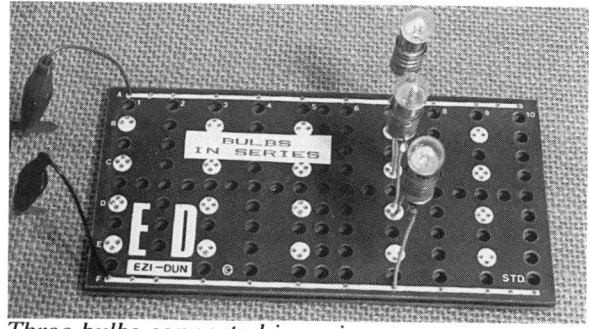

Three bulbs connected in series

Now . . .

Using the knowledge gained about **series** and **parallel** circuits, predict what will happen to the two circuits (1) and (2) below; then build them and see if you are right.

ACTIVITIES

(1) Connect the circuit shown in the diagram above and notice how weak the brightness of the bulbs is.

(2) Remove **Bulb 1** and the bulbs go out. Does this happen if any of the bulbs are disconnected?

(3) Connect two bulbs in series, **Bulb 1** from A to C and **Bulb 2** from D to F. Are the bulbs brighter?

(4) Remove **Bulb 2** and replace it with a **buzzer**. (Black wire goes to negative rail.)

(5) Remove the **buzzer** and replace it with the **motor**. Which works – the bulb or the motor?

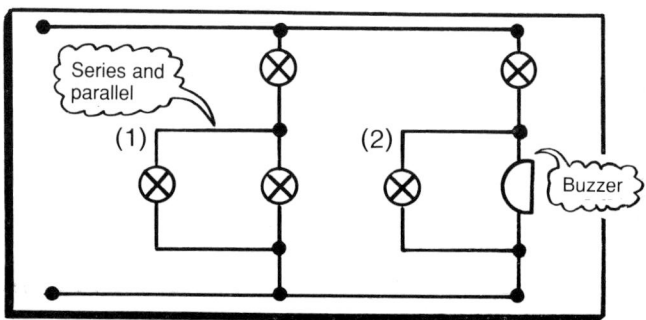

MAKING SWITCHES

This page shows ways of making cheap switches. The three switches shown on the **EZI-DUN** **circuit board** are all made from **plastic sheet** with **aluminium foil** glued underneath. The **membrane switch** also uses **aluminium foil**.

**INSTRUMENT USING
MEMBRANE SWITCHES**

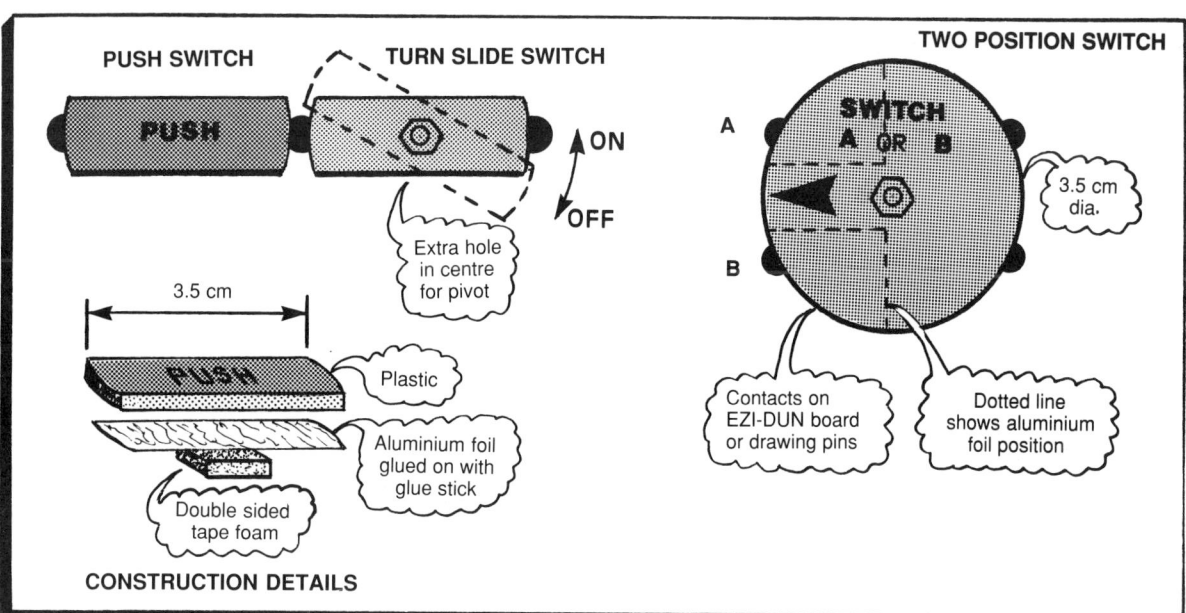

PUSH SWITCH　　　**TURN SLIDE SWITCH**

ON
OFF

Extra hole
in centre
for pivot

3.5 cm

Plastic

Aluminium foil
glued on with
glue stick

Double sided
tape foam

CONSTRUCTION DETAILS

TWO POSITION SWITCH

SWITCH
A OR B

A

B

3.5 cm
dia.

Contacts on
EZI-DUN board
or drawing pins

Dotted line
shows aluminium
foil position

*Three switches made from odds and ends: a push
switch, a turn switch and a two–position switch.*

ACTIVITIES

(1) Make a simple **push switch** which is pushed
down onto **two contacts**.
(2) Make one of the other switches shown.
(3) Use one of your switches to operate a bulb
to make a fun face, for instance using card.

MEMBRANE PANEL SWITCH

The making of a **membrane switch** is a good
project by itself, with opportunity for graphic
design on the card switch front.　All that is
needed is thin card, aluminium cooking foil,
glue stick, stapler and scissors.　Try making
one about 6 cm x 6 cm with a hole of about 1.5
cm in the centre piece.

ASSEMBLED MEMBRANE PANEL SWITCH

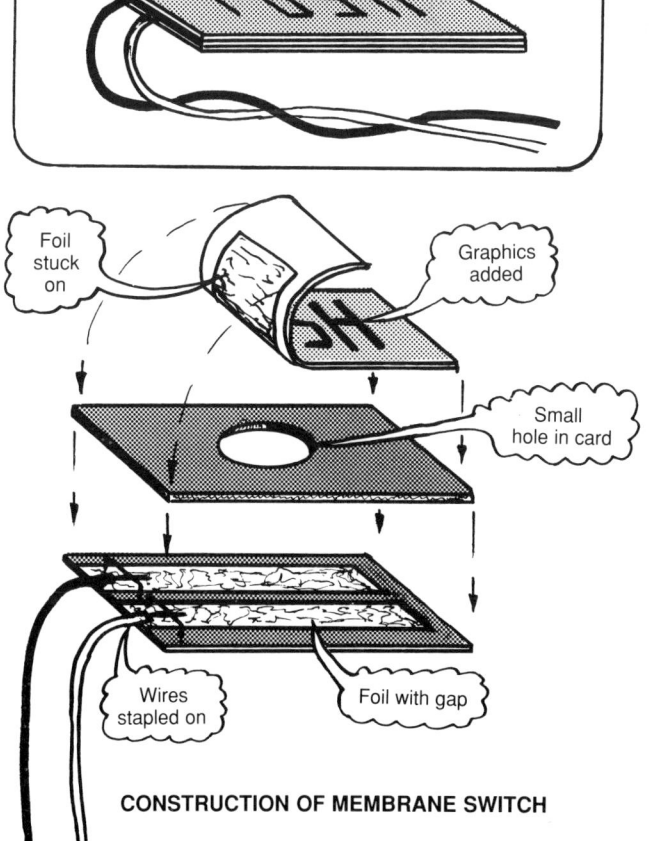

Foil
stuck
on

Graphics
added

Small
hole in card

Wires
stapled on

Foil with gap

CONSTRUCTION OF MEMBRANE SWITCH

SWITCH TYPES

EMERGENCY SWITCH

There are many varieties of switches. You will be using most of the ones shown on this page. Below are sketches of switches often used with their **symbols**. The symbol refers to the **electrical contacts** and not the switch shape.

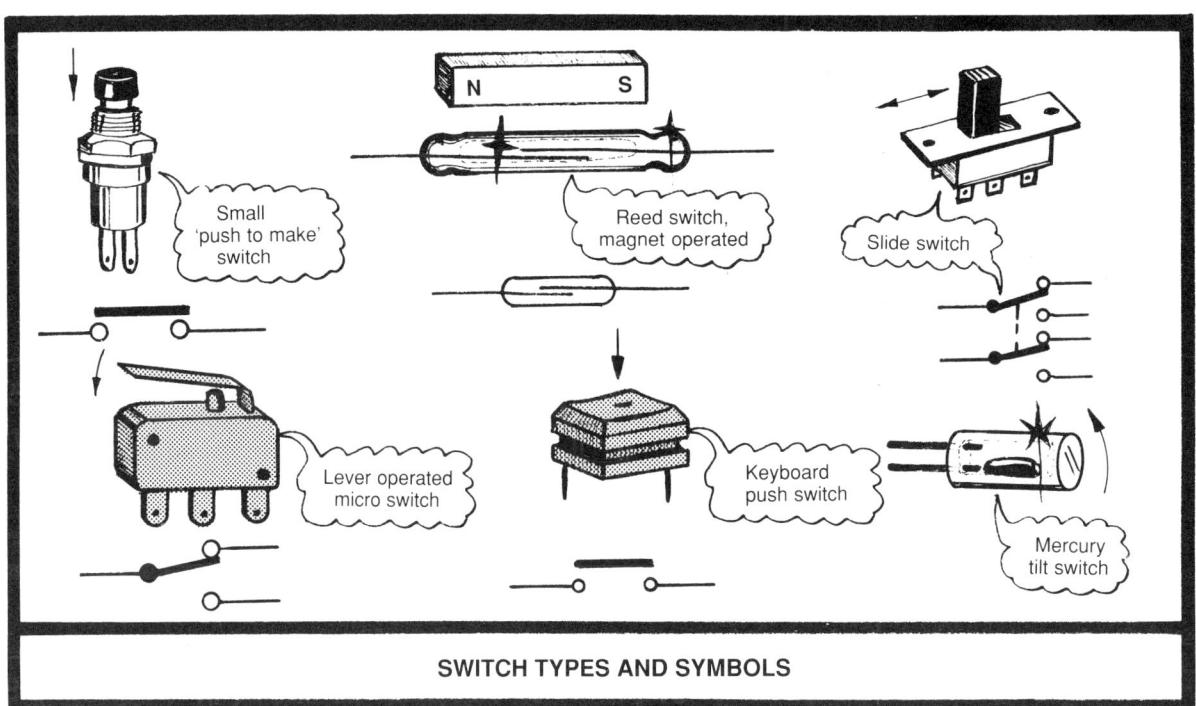

Small 'push to make' switch

Reed switch, magnet operated

Slide switch

Lever operated micro switch

Keyboard push switch

Mercury tilt switch

SWITCH TYPES AND SYMBOLS

SIMPLE SWITCH LOGIC

Logic problems involving **AND** or **OR** logic arrangements can easily be assembled as shown below.

Simple logic is like everyday language, for example:

(1) Using **OR logic**
A house bell must ring if operated at the **front** or the **back door** (notice the **OR** in the sentence).

A practical circuit that has two switches connected with **OR** logic is given below.

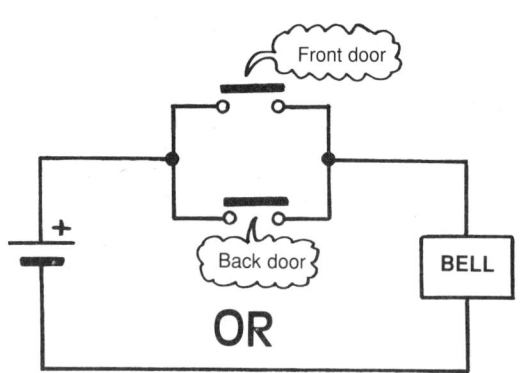

Front door

Back door

BELL

OR

(2) Using **AND logic**
A machine can only start if the **safety guard AND** the **start switch** are operated.

A practical circuit that has two switches connected with **AND** logic is given below.

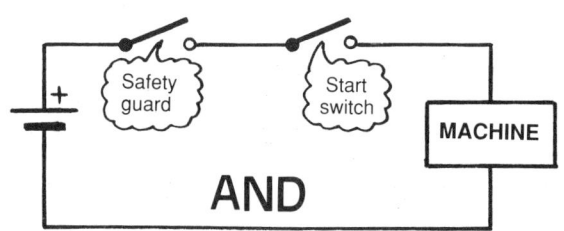

Safety guard

Start switch

MACHINE

AND

ACTIVITIES

(1) Construct a circuit that lets a visitor know, by operating a **bulb**, whether their day museum ticket *or* yearly card is still usable.

(2) Construct a circuit that works a **buzzer** if John *and* Jane arrive for work.

This page may be copied for use in the classroom (see page ii). Electronic Projects – made easy.

9

MAGICIAN'S WAND

'MAGIC' MAGNET SWITCH

USING REED SWITCHES

Using a **magnet** to operate a **reed switch** gives the appearance of **magic**. The magnet can operate through paper and thin card, enabling the switch to be hidden.

To battery positive

MAGNET

S
N

REED SWITCH

Glass tube   Steel contacts

To battery negative

Bulb
6 V
0.06 A

INPUT	PROCESS	OUTPUT
ELECTRIC POWER	MAGNET OPERATES SWITCH	LIGHT ON/OFF

A **reed switch** consists of a glass tube with two steel contacts inside. When a **magnet** is placed next to the reed switch the contacts are magnetised and attract each other. This turns the switch on.

Various seemingly **magic effects** can be produced because the switch does not need to be touched by hand.

ACTIVITIES

(1) Connect up the **circuit** shown above and make the light operate by holding a **magnet** next to the **reed switch**. How far away in **centimetres** can the magnet be, yet still work the switch?
(2) Slide the **magnet** along the **reed switch**. Can you find a position where the magnet does not operate the reed switch?
(3) How many pieces of paper, or card, can the **magnet** operate through?
(4) Replace the **bulb** with the a **buzzer**, connect it the correct way round. How can the bulb be added again so the buzzer and bulb work together?
(5) Remove **bulb** and **buzzer** and operate the **motor** instead.

Now . . .

Using the knowledge gained, make one of the following, or something of your choice.

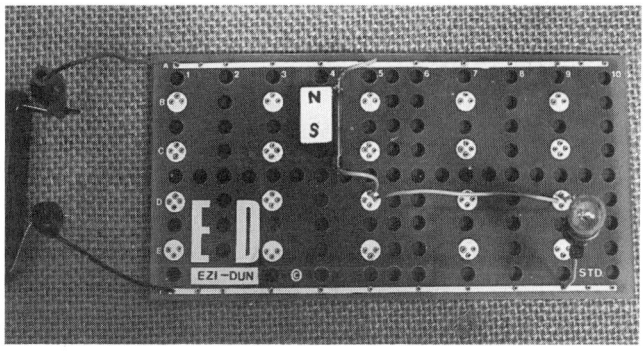

The bulb glows when the magnet is placed next to the reed switch.

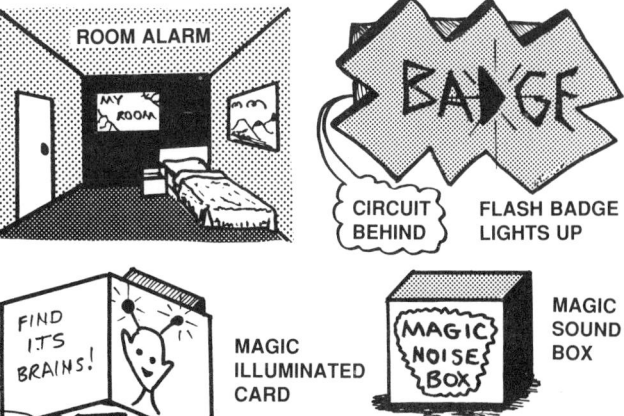

ROOM ALARM

CIRCUIT BEHIND

FLASH BADGE LIGHTS UP

MAGIC ILLUMINATED CARD

MAGIC NOISE BOX

MAGIC SOUND BOX

MAGNET CONTROLLED BUGGY

This buggy can be controlled by placing a **magnet** next to the **reed switch**. Once made the vehicle can form the basis of many projects. Other switch types etc could then be tried.

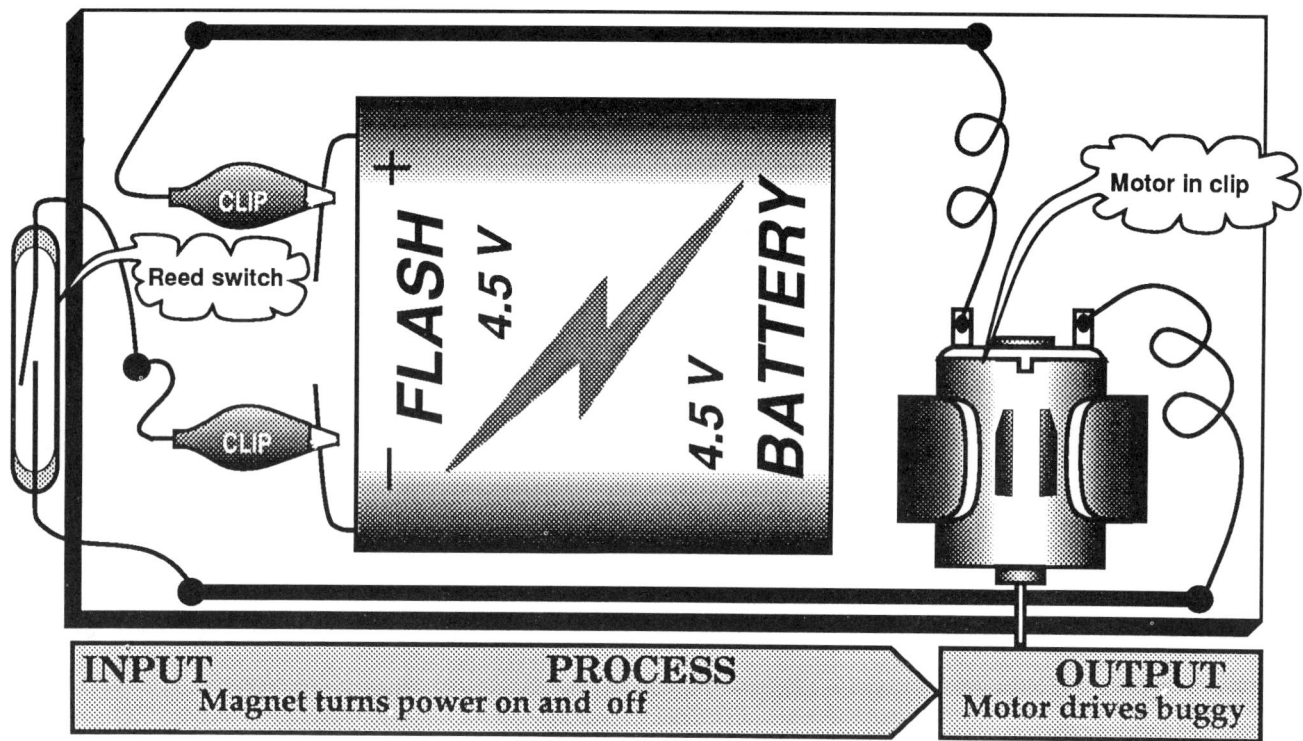

INPUT	PROCESS	OUTPUT
Magnet turns power on and off		Motor drives buggy

The buggy's speed should be slow, so some form of gearing is needed like that shown in the photo. The wheel and pulley **support pieces** used in the photograph were made from strips of plastic with holes. The **EZI–DUN board** can be used as a **drilling jig** to do this. Some kits already include suitable parts. NOTE: If a **geared-down motor** is available only one **pulley** is needed.

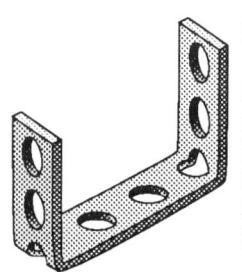

MAKING WHEEL SUPPORTS

No measurement needed, just count holes.
If the support is made of metal bend in a vice, if plastic use a strip heater.
Bolt to EZI-DUN board

The magnetic buggy moves along when the magnet is placed near the reed switch. A rectangular magnet is being used here.

ACTIVITIES

(1) Connect up the circuit as shown above. The motor is shown held in clips provided.
(2) Add the **wheels** and **drive pulley**. Use construction kit parts if you have them, such as LEGO®, PLAWCOTECH, MECCANO, FISCHERTECHNIK etc. The wheel support pieces can be made as shown.

(3) Make the buggy travel along with the magnet attached to the reed switch.
(4) Make the buggy **stop after travelling 4 metres**. Cotton attached to the magnet may help.
(5) Make the buggy **stop at the edge of the table**. A micro switch may help if available.
(6) Make the buggy stop when it **tips over more than about 30 degrees** to the left. A microswitch or tilt switch may help if available.

FLASHING LIGHT
A BUZZER CAN ALSO BE ADDED

By fixing a **magnet** on a **disc** and turning it round by hand or using an electric motor a **reed switch** can be made to switch **ON** and **OFF**. The effects produced can be varied by altering the position of the **reed switch** and the **speed** of the disc.

LIGHTHOUSE

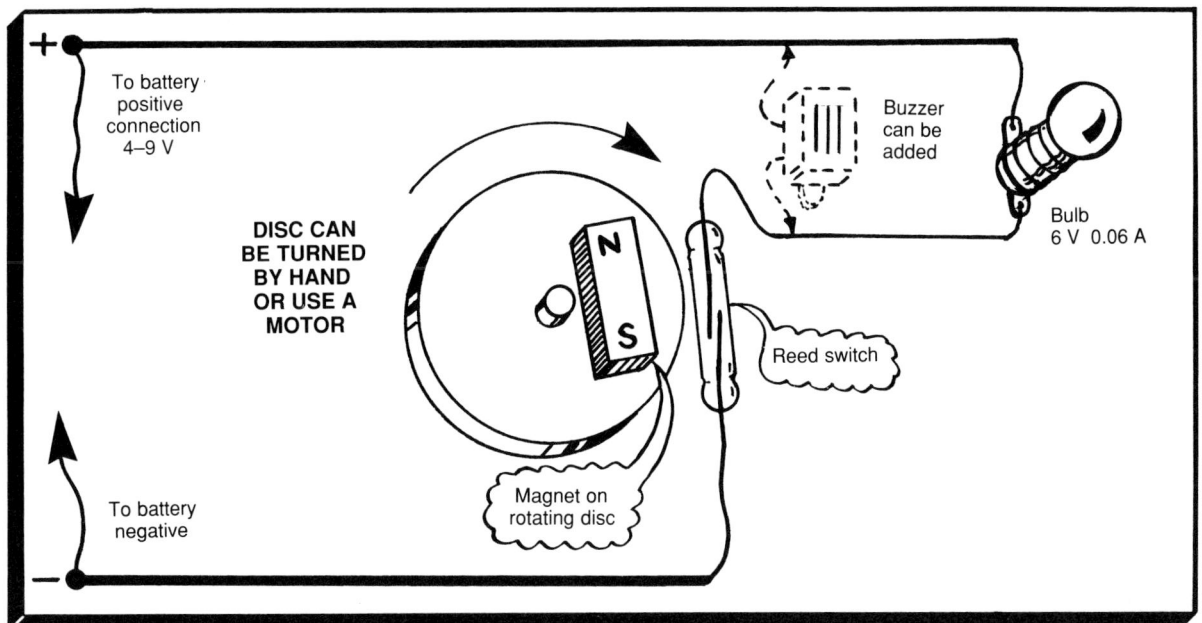

INPUT	PROCESS	OUTPUT
ELECTRIC POWER	SWITCHING	LIGHT ON/OFF

The disc can be turned by hand but if required an electric motor can be added as shown in the photograph. One problem is getting the disc to turn slowly enough. Only about 1.5 V is required for the motor. This can be obtained by using a **1.5 V battery** or a 100 Ω **variable resistor** in **series** with the motor.

When the magnet goes past the reed switch it turns it ON and OFF. The disc can be motorised as shown.

ACTIVITIES

(1) Connect up the circuit shown above. The **disc** needs a **shaft** that passes through one of the holes in the EZI–DUN board. The **magnet** can be stuck on with Blu Tack. The **reed switch** needs to be placed within about half a centimetre of the **magnet**. When operated, is the bulb ON more than it is OFF?

(2) Vary the position of the magnet and speed of the disc by hand. Is it possible to keep the bulb on all the time?

(3) Add a **buzzer across the bulb** as well. Does the **buzzer** work when the bulb comes on?

Other things to try

(A) See if you can make a program (or sequence) of flashes by adding **other magnets** on the disc.

(B) See what effects you can get by adding **another reed switch and bulb**.

(C) **Motorise the disc**. A simple way is shown in the photograph but other methods can be used.

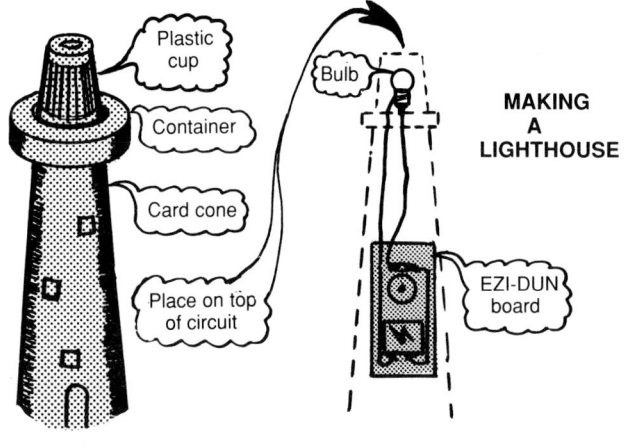

MAKING A LIGHTHOUSE

SIMPLE VEHICLES

A simple vehicle that moves forward when the switch is operated can be converted into a **van, lorry, tip–up truck, mobile crane, train** etc. The **switch** is best held about 2 metres away from the vehicle.

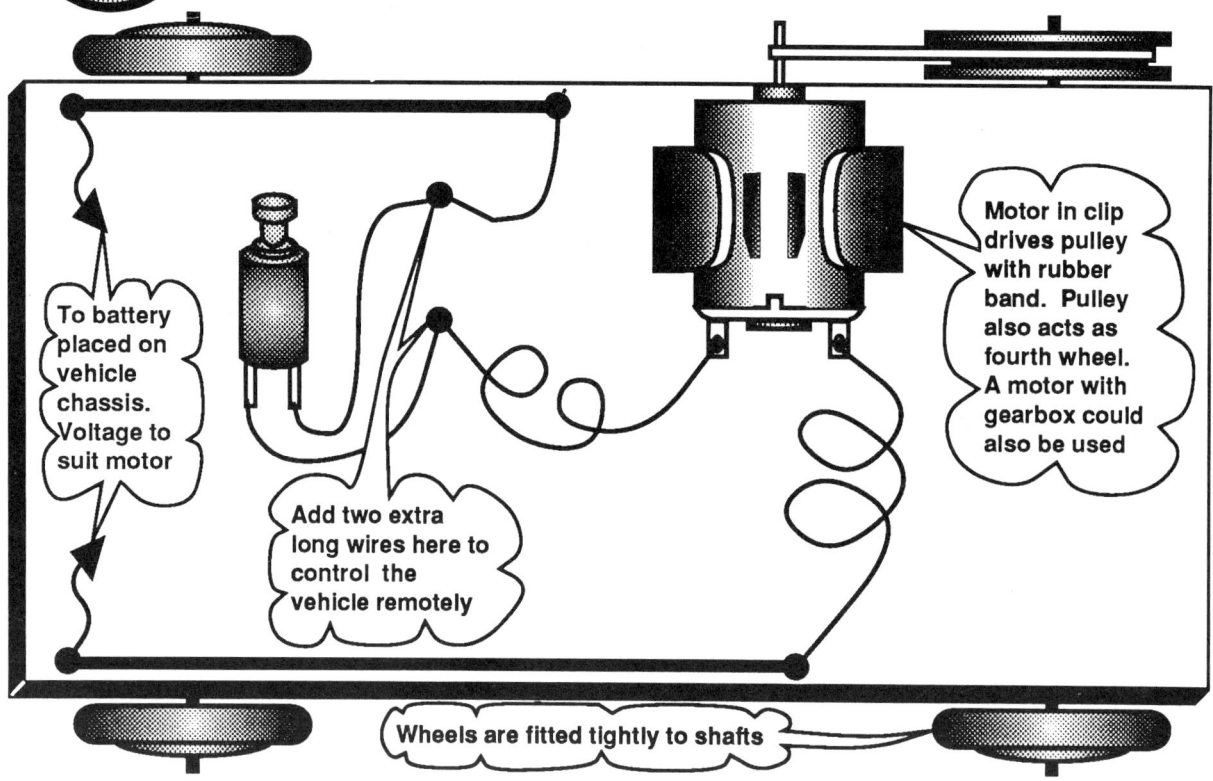

To battery placed on vehicle chassis. Voltage to suit motor

Add two extra long wires here to control the vehicle remotely

Motor in clip drives pulley with rubber band. Pulley also acts as fourth wheel. A motor with gearbox could also be used

Wheels are fitted tightly to shafts

INPUT	PROCESS	OUTPUT
Battery	Switch on / off	Motor on / off

The **wheels** can be held in place using the same 'bent strip of plastic idea' as the **magnet controlled buggy** on the previous page. The wheels can be from any kit you have such as LEGO®, PLAWCOTECH, MECCANO, wood or plastic pulleys etc. A 1.5 V battery provides the best speed but any voltage up to 6 V can be used.

A vehicle being controlled by a remote switch.

ACTIVITIES

(1) Connect up the **electric circuit** as shown above. How can you reverse the direction of the motor?

(2) Add the **wheels** and **connect the motor** to the wheels using the elastic band. Does the vehicle move too fast when empty?

(3) Can the vehicle climb slopes? Do the driving wheels need more grip?

(4) Add headlights etc as you want.

(5) Convert the present chassis into something that looks like a real vehicle such as a lorry or milk float.

POSSIBLE IDEAS

Tipper truck with lights

Railway engine with glowing smoke and firebox

STEERABLE BUGGY

Try your hand at **steering round objects**, **having time trials** etc.

Two switches and two motors are needed. Each wheel is free to turn around the axle by itself. If **both motors** are working, the buggy goes **straight**. If **only one motor** is working the buggy **turns**.

STEERABLE BUGGY–IN A HURRY!

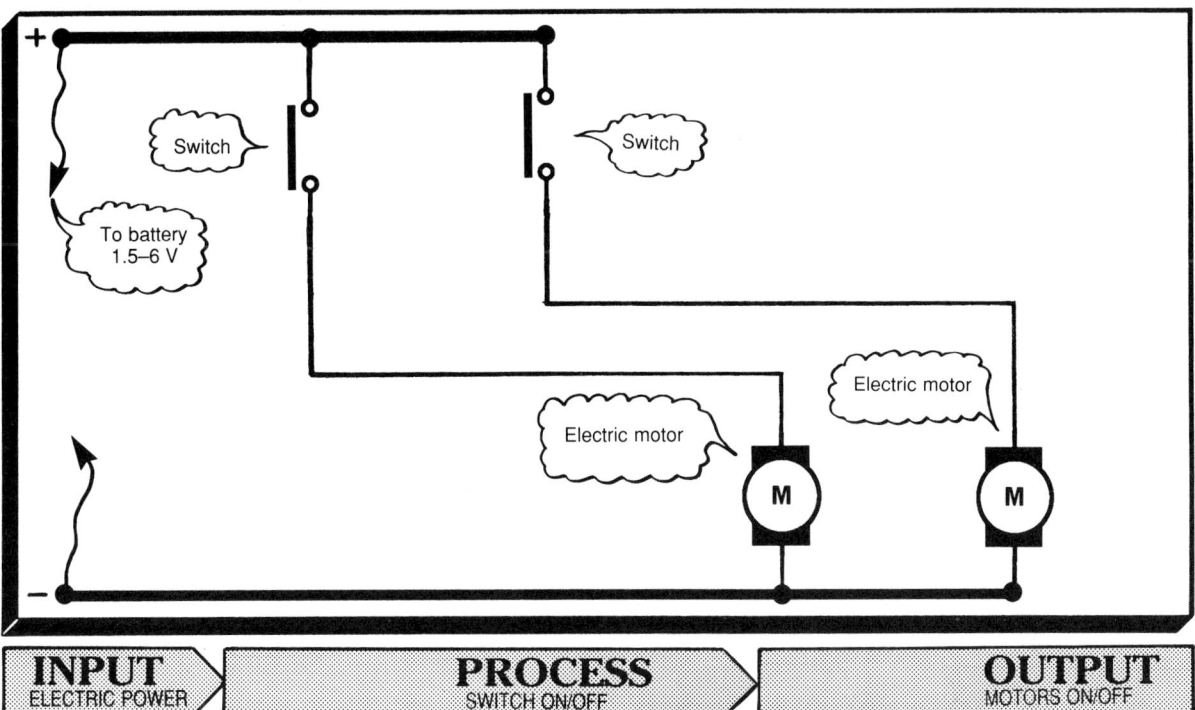

INPUT	PROCESS	OUTPUT
ELECTRIC POWER	SWITCH ON/OFF	MOTORS ON/OFF

The basic electrical circuit used is quite easy to make as shown above. It requires **one battery** which both motors share.

An understanding of **how the buggy works** is quite important in its success or failure.

The position of the wheels should be near the **half–way position** so that very little weight is resting on the back support. The **battery** is heavy and should also be placed near the centre. The **back support** shown in the photograph is very simple. A **caster wheel** would be better. The two wheels used also act as pulleys. The buggy goes slower if a **1.5 V battery** is used.

A simple manually–controlled buggy with one switch for turning left and another for turning right.

ACTIVITIES

(1) Connect up the circuit above and make the motors work. What happens if both switches are pushed down together?

(2) Add the **wheel support** and **wheels** (for possible ideas see next page).

Press both switches down and see if the wheels turn in the same direction. If they turn in opposite directions, switch over one pair of wires. How can you change the direction of **both** motors at once by switching over one pair of wires?

(3) Add a '**back support**' (see next page for ideas). Now try out the vehicle with the battery riding on the EZI–DUN board. Does it tip up when starting or stopping?

(4) To make the buggy more controllable, the switches need to be away from the buggy. Extend the distance the switches are from the buggy (see next page for ideas).

(5) Adjust the buggy to work properly, for example, alter **balance**, **threading wires** through holes to stop them pulling out, improve **support piece**.

(Continued on next page)

PARTS FOR BUGGY

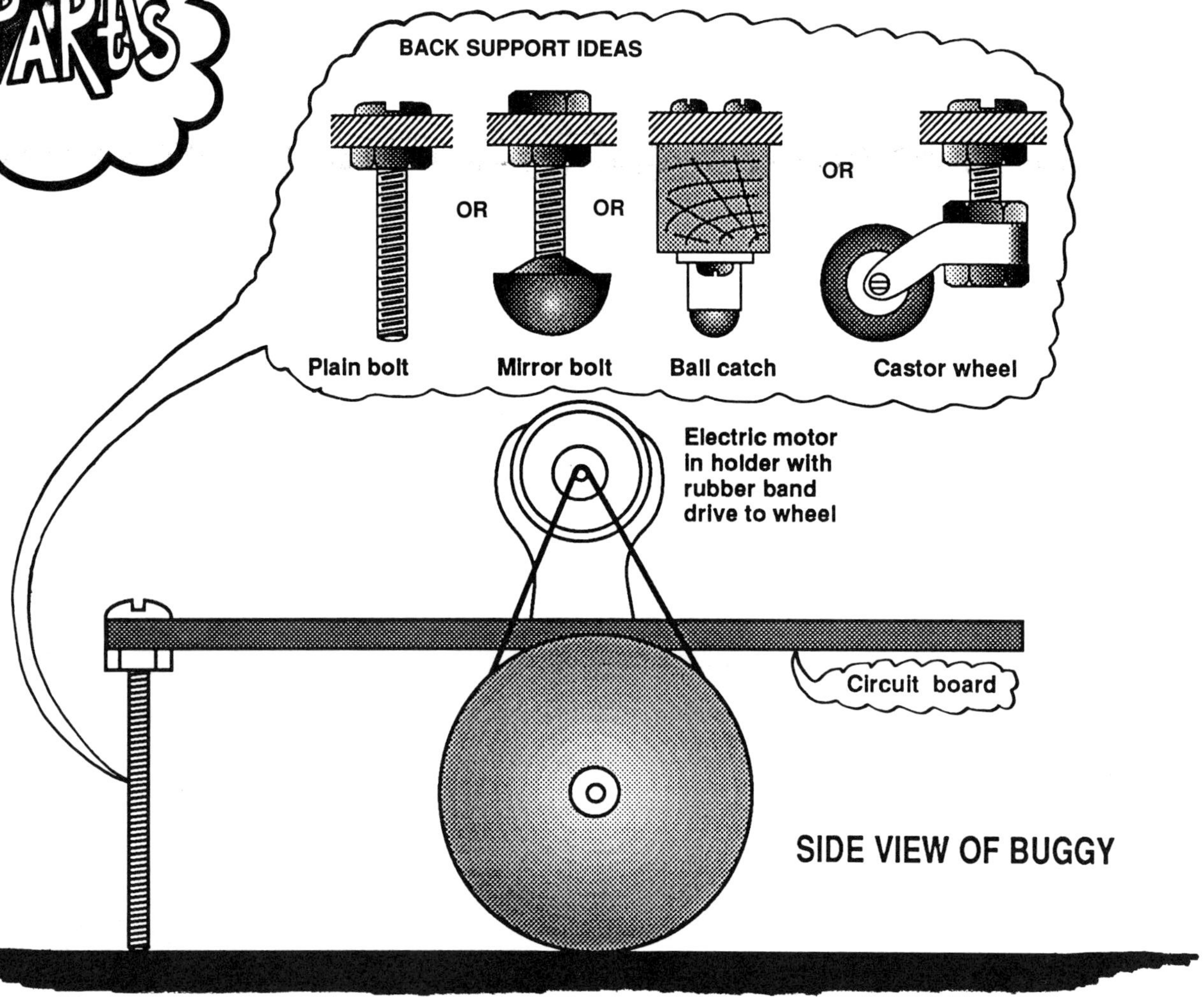

PARTS

BACK SUPPORT IDEAS

Plain bolt   OR   **Mirror bolt**   OR   **Ball catch**   OR   **Castor wheel**

Electric motor in holder with rubber band drive to wheel

Circuit board

SIDE VIEW OF BUGGY

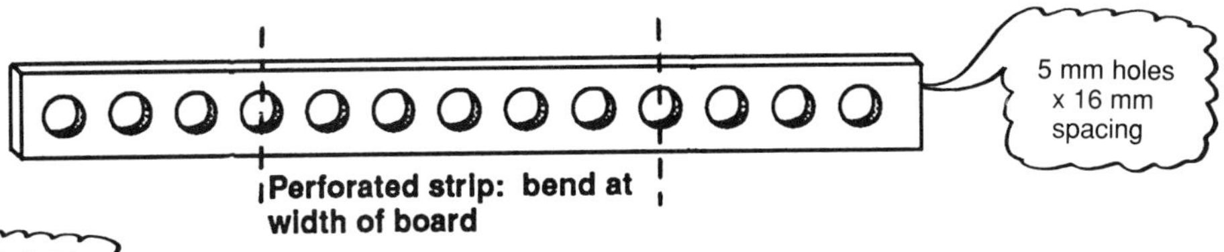

5 mm holes x 16 mm spacing

Perforated strip: bend at width of board

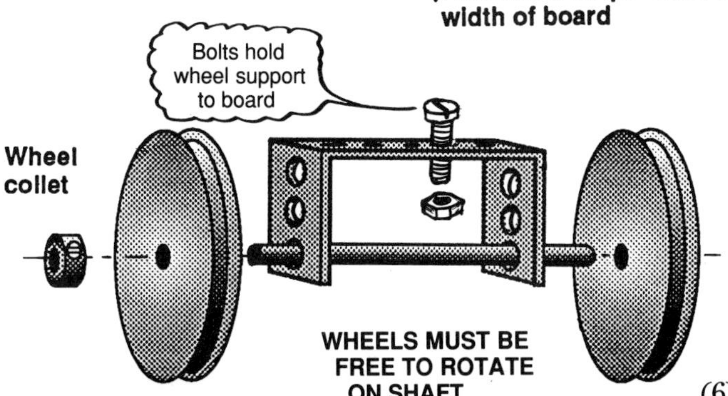

Bolts hold wheel support to board

Wheel collet

WHEELS MUST BE FREE TO ROTATE ON SHAFT

Wheels can be plastic, wood or made from three card discs

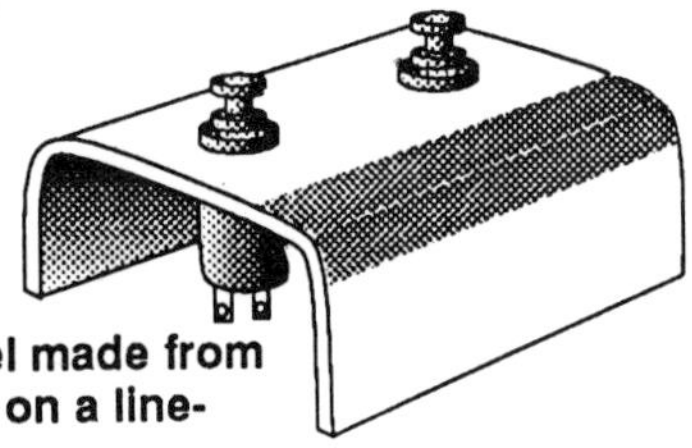

Switch panel made from acrylic bent on a line-bender

Now the buggy works properly

(6) **Steer** the buggy round an object such as a book in the fastest time.

(7) Mark out a **figure of eight** and see how well you can travel round it.

(8) **Decorate** your buggy. (Be careful not to affect its performance.)

(9) Think of further improvements you can make. One great improvement is to add tyred wheels next to the pulleys to ensure better grip.

A SIMPLE CRANE

This **crane** uses one **motor** to lift the load up. To lower the load the motor can be **reversed** if a special switch is available (see below), or the **worm gear** can be moved allowing the load to drop.

Note: A method of gearing down is needed like that shown.

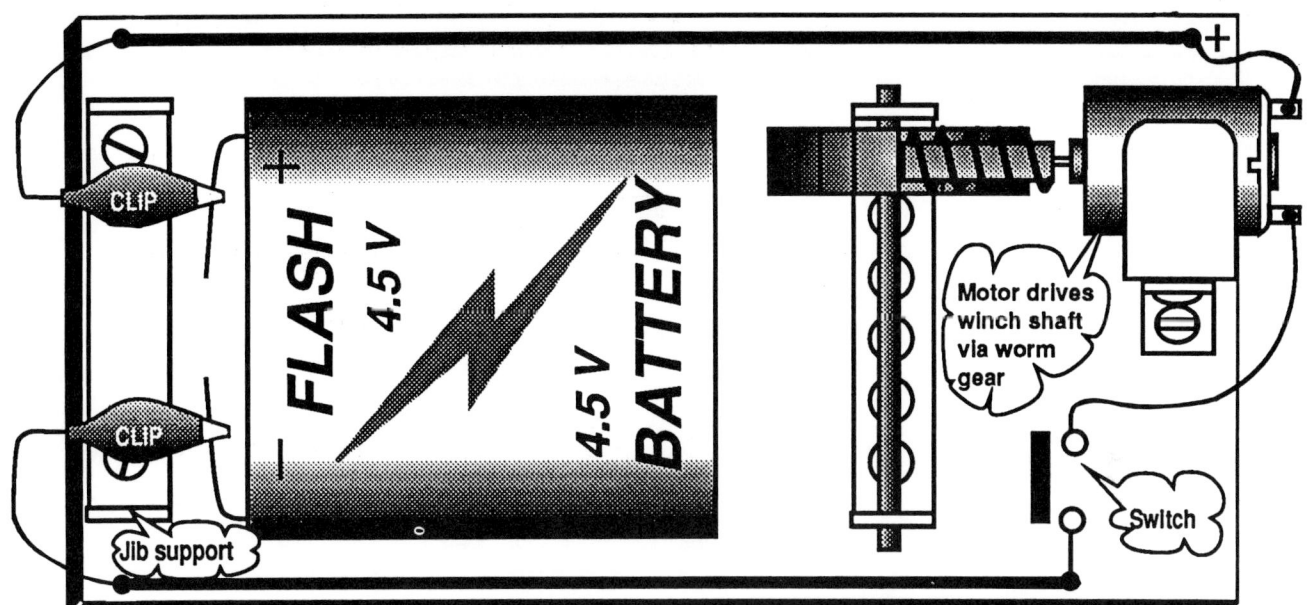

Motor drives winch shaft via worm gear

Switch

Jib support

A **simple electric circuit** is all that is needed to make the **motor** turn ON and OFF. To make it **reverse** is more difficult and requires a Double Pole Double Throw (DPDT) switch. The load on the crane needs to be lifted slowly. Using a **geared–down electric motor** is the easiest way, but the worm-and-wheel mechanism shown gives a good spindle speed reduction of about 50 to 1.

ACTIVITIES

(1) Connect up the motor circuit only, for the crane similar to the one shown in the photograph. The drawing above gives the start of the layout. If you have other construction kit parts, use them instead.
(2) Add the wheels etc. The back wheels can be made to steer.
(3) How much can the crane carry before it tips up or the load slips?
(4) How can the load be lowered very quickly?

Reversing the motor with a DPDT switch

A Double–Pole Double–Throw (DPDT) switch can be connected up as shown opposite. The **circuit diagram** shows the theory, but the **practical circuit** is the one to follow when soldering up a **DPDT switch**.
  Start by soldering the two short wires from 1 to 4 and another from 6 to 3; then add battery to connections 2 and 5. Complete by adding the motor to conections 3 and 4.

A crane with a separate ON/OFF switch and an up and down switch.

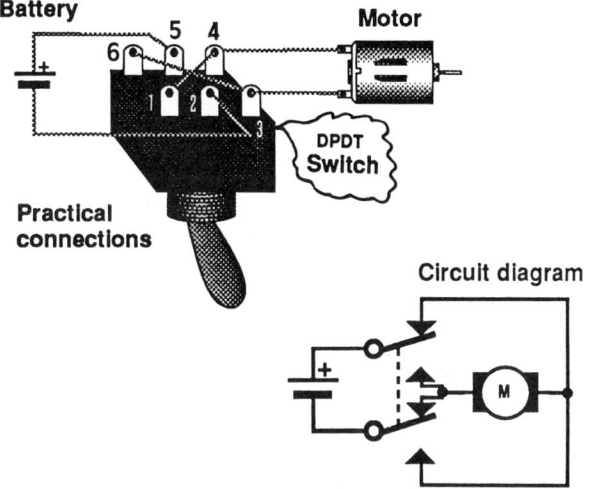

Battery

Motor

DPDT Switch

Practical connections

Circuit diagram

QUIZ TIME

QUIZ MAKER
SET A QUIZ AND TEST A FRIEND

This simple **quiz maker** indicates that answers are correct when the bulb glows. The **question probe** is placed on the **question position**, then the **answer probe** is placed on the **answer connections** until the correct one lights up.

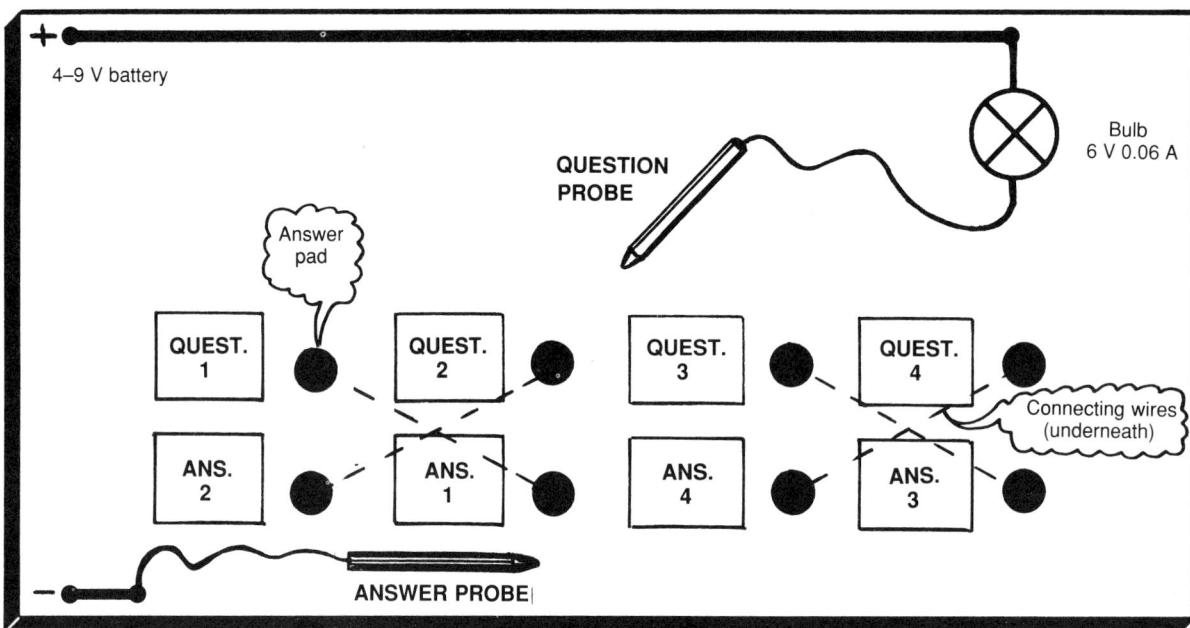

The **dashed lines** are links of wire that are hidden. When making the circuit, the wires should be positioned as shown to start with, then altered later as required. The holes in the board allow wires to hide underneath it quite easily.

Below you can see how the bulb is connected up when **Question 4** is being answered correctly.

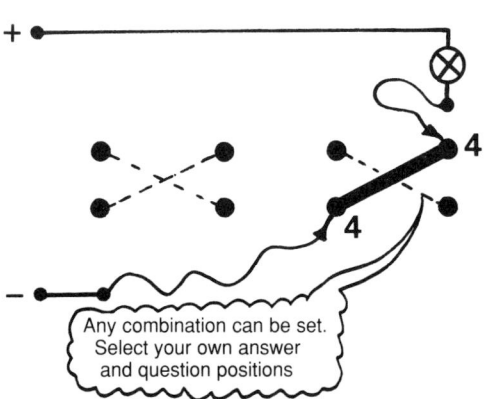

THE THEORETICAL CIRCUIT USED

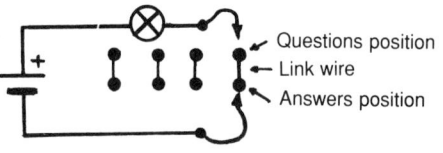

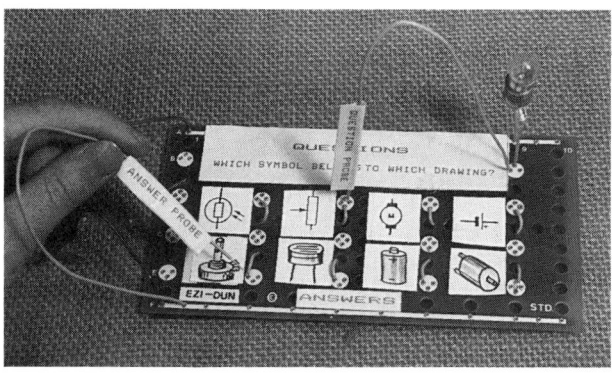

The answer probe being used. The question probe is connected to the question being asked.

ACTIVITIES

(1) **Connect up the circuit** as shown above, then plug the question probe into Question 1 position and the answer probe into Answer 1 position. If the bulb works, check the other question positions.

(2) Add **Questions** and **Answers** next to the **connecting points**, use Pritt Stick or similar glue.

(3) Add a **buzzer** across the bulb. Do you prefer this?

(4) **Test a friend**. Was it too easy for them?

(5) **Make a quiz relating to your topic.**

ONE–WAY ONLY DIODES

Diodes are like a **'one–way' gate**, allowing electricity to flow in one direction only. They are used to protect equipment or redirect current flow.

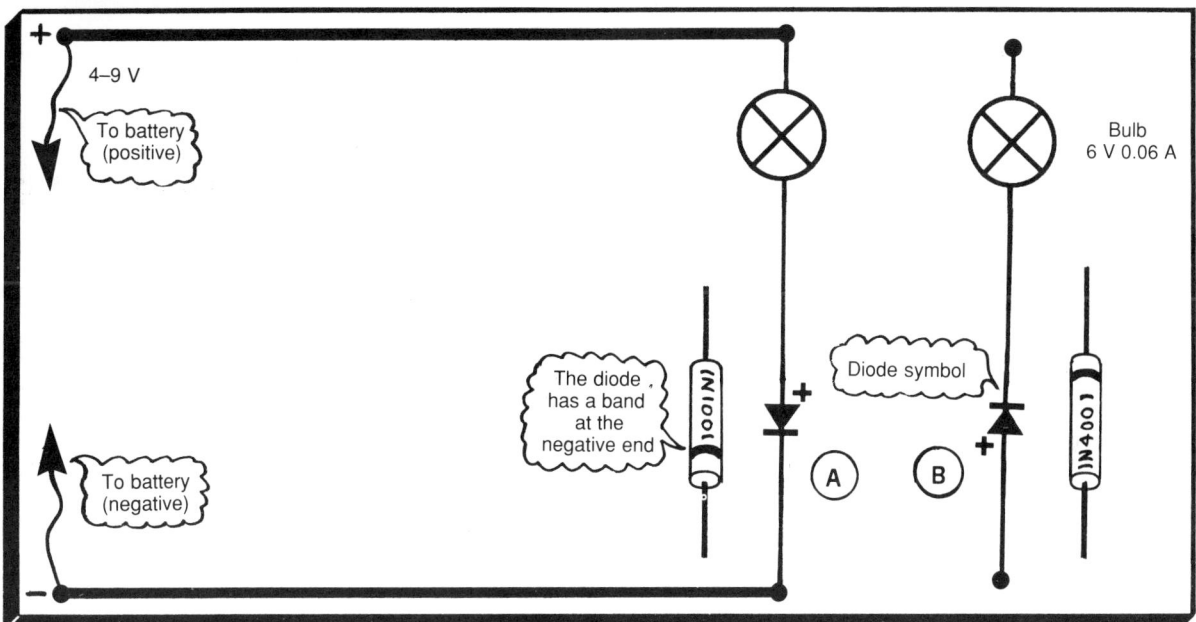

Diodes are made from 'p' type and an 'n' type **semiconductor** material joined together.

A variation of the **diode** is known as the **Light Emitting Diode** (LED). They are coloured and often used instead of small light bulbs.

The **negative** (–) end of the diode is the end with the band round it. If the **negative** end is connected to the **negative** of the battery, **electricity** flows through it.

ACTIVITIES

(1) **Connect up the circuit A** as shown above. Does the bulb glow?

(2) **Reverse the diode**, as shown in B. Does the bulb glow or not?

(3) **Connect two bulbs**, as shown in C below. What happens?

(4) **Reverse the diode**, as shown in D below. What happens?

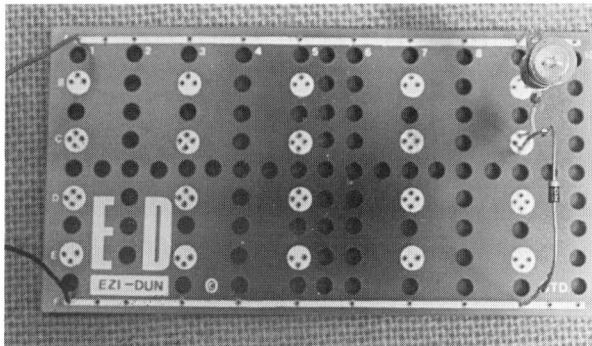

This circuit is being used to find out which way round a diode will conduct electricity.

An LED alternative to the diode and bulb used

An LED connected up with a **protection resistor** as shown can be used instead of the **diode** and **bulb**.

An example is given below of a **polarity testing circuit** using **two** LEDS and **two resistors**. By placing the **flying leads** across the battery (1.5–9 V) the circuit indicates which way round the battery is.

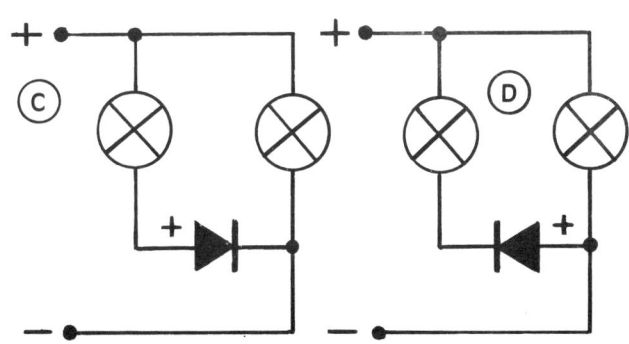

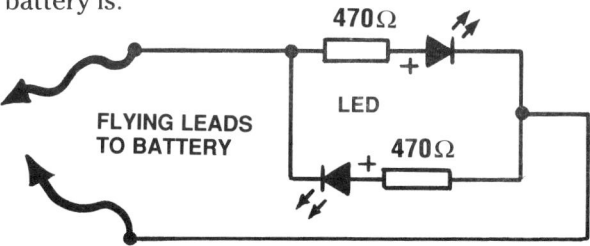

BOAT – AIR PROPELLED

Have fun making a boat move through the water. If the hull shape is good it can usually be made to go quite fast. Bought propellers are usually the best, but you can make your own.

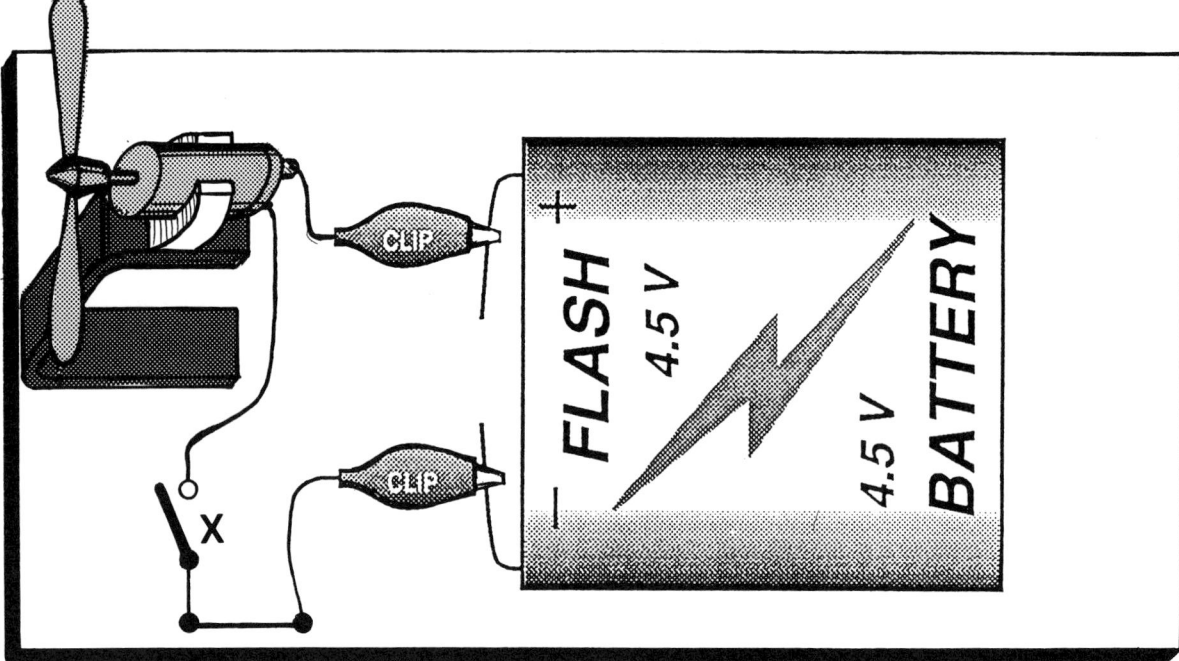

A good fan can be produced by connecting a propeller directly onto the electric motor. The boat's **balance** will have to be considered carefully to prevent the motor and battery tipping the boat over. The design shown is fairly stable.

ACTIVITIES

(1) Make a **support** for the motor, then **connect up the circuit** as shown above. The best sort of switch, at position X, is one that **stays on** – if necessary a reed switch and magnet could be used. The propeller should now work.

(2) Make a **hull** for the boat out of light materials such as foam and **fix the circuit** on top. Does it float?

(3) Experiment with the positioning of the propeller. Does it move faster when pointing forwards or backwards?

(4) See how fast you can make the boat go by improving the hull shapes. See ideas shown.

(5) **Decorate** the boat and add something else electrical to make it more interesting.

Remember: that the boat and all the materials, glues etc used will have to withstand the **effects of water**. The EZI–DUN board is waterproof, but do not use in sea water or leave in water for long.

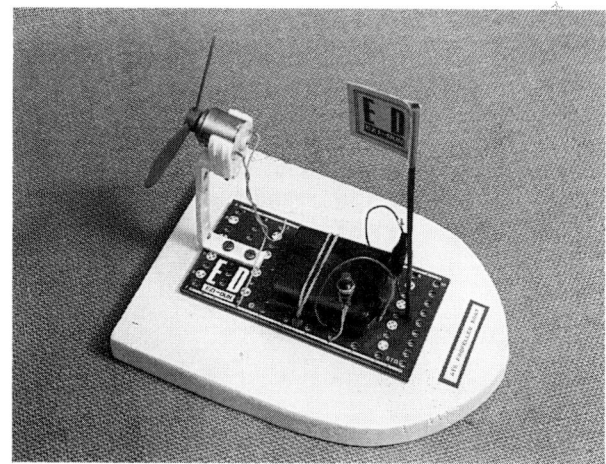

A foam boat propelled by an electric motor with a propeller.

HULL IDEAS

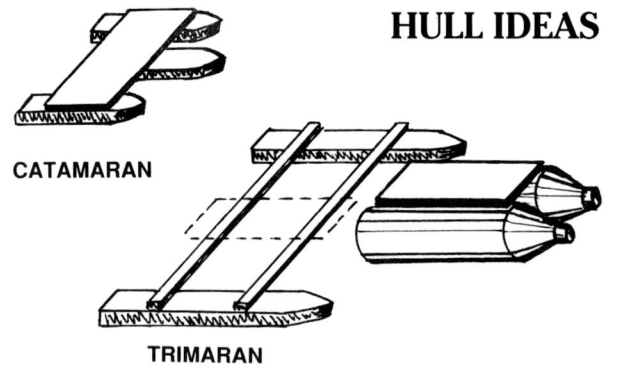

CATAMARAN

TRIMARAN

**TWO SETS OF
TRAFFIC LIGHTS**

TRAFFIC LIGHTS
★CAMS★

Traffic lights can be made using **three bulbs** that are operated by **cams**. The cam shaft can be operated by hand as shown, or **turned** by a slow motor.

Note: A cam is a rotating cylinder with an irregular shape that is used to alter the movement of the '**follower**'.

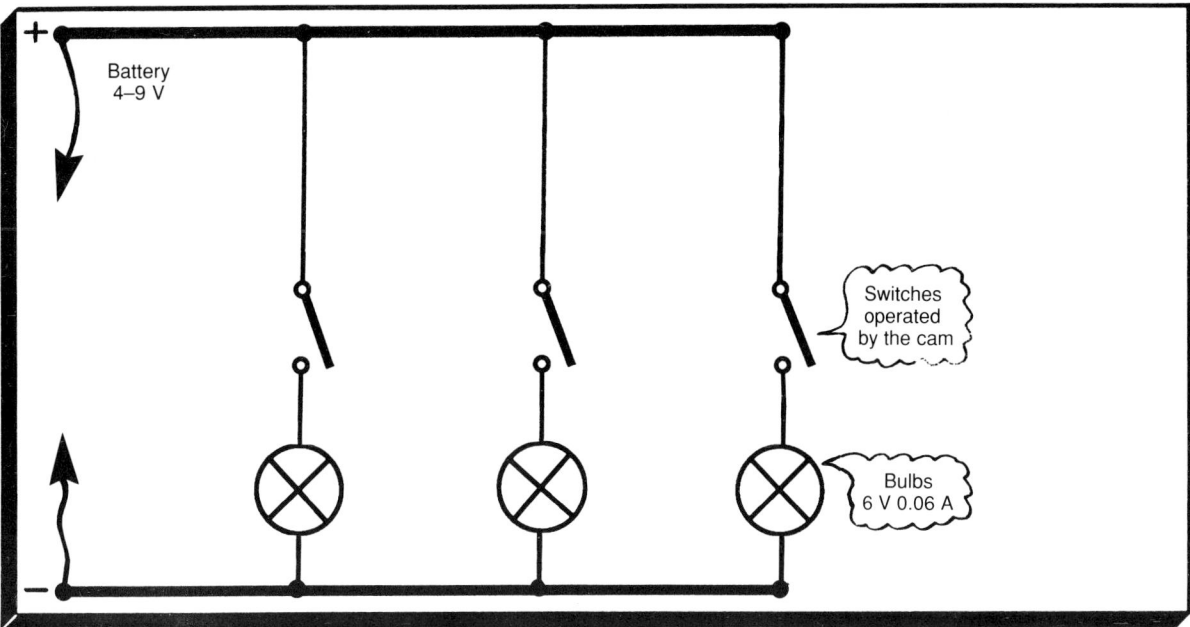

When making, allow for adjustments.
The bulbs look better if mounted on the back of the EZI–DUN board or mounted separately. Use tubes and coloured bulbs etc.

ACTIVITIES

(1) Make three **simple switches** which the **cams** will be able to operate easily. Use the EZI–DUN board connecting points as the contacts.
(2) Bolt the switches, just made, on the EZI–DUN board so that they have one end touching the rails.
(3) Connect up the circuit shown above, without the cams, and test that the switches work when operated with a finger.
(4) Make **three cams** that can be altered later if need be (see ideas below), then mount them on a **shaft**.
(5) Alter the cams to obtain the **traffic light sequence.**

Model traffic lights operated by cams which trigger aluminium foil switches as required.

Three cam ideas

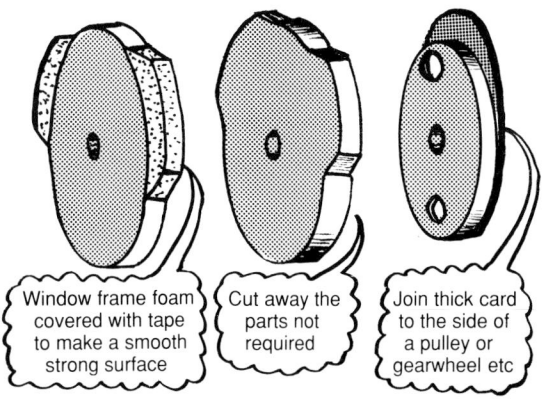

Window frame foam covered with tape to make a smooth strong surface

Cut away the parts not required

Join thick card to the side of a pulley or gearwheel etc

Switch ideas

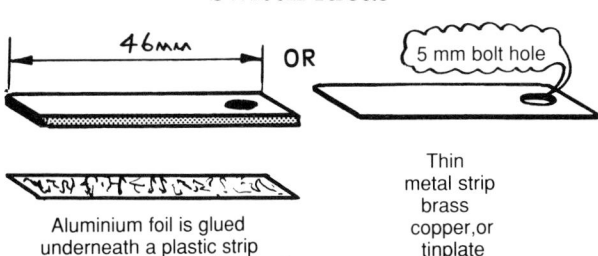

Aluminium foil is glued underneath a plastic strip
(Pritt Stick or double sided tape)

Thin metal strip
brass
copper,or
tinplate
etc

ROBOT 'PLODS' FEET

WALKING ROBOT

Make a **walking robot** that plods along and is fun to watch. It needs six gears, two feet and a motor with a worm gear.

To keep the robot light, the large battery should be kept separate from the body. The feet need to be large to stop the robot falling over when it is moving.

To battery and switch

PLOD

Glowing eyes

EZI-DUN board decorated

Gear layout

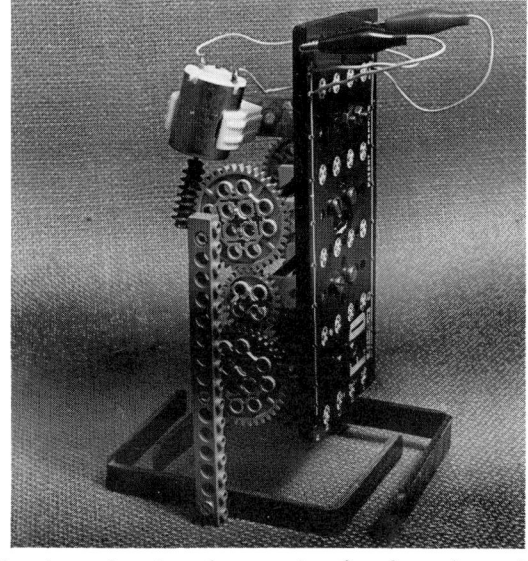

Side view showing the gearing for the robot which walks along using its U–shaped feet.

WASHING MACHINE

A circuit that switches an **alarm on** if the **washing machine door** is **opened** when it is actually washing.

Normally a **reed switch** turns ON when a **magnet** is placed next to it. By placing an **extra magnet** next to the reed switch it can turn ON when the door is opened rather than when it is closed – clever!

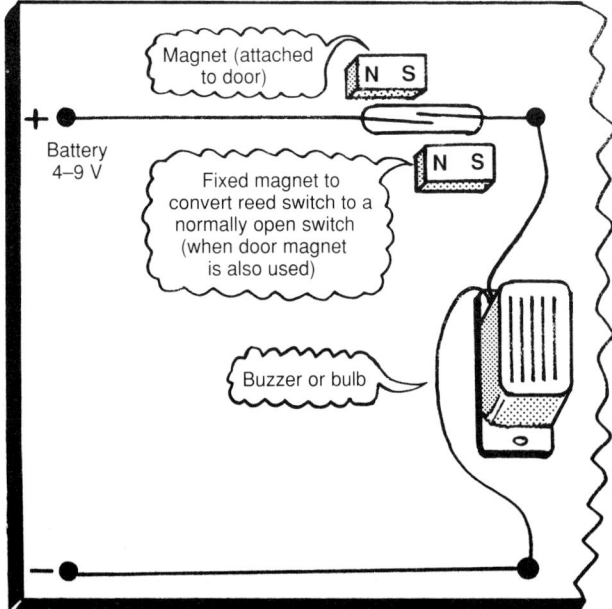

Magnet (attached to door) N S

+

Battery 4–9 V

N S

Fixed magnet to convert reed switch to a normally open switch (when door magnet is also used)

Buzzer or bulb

–

When the washing machine door is opened the alarm buzzes.

COMPUTER CONTROL
USING 'LOGO' AND 'BASIC' LANGUAGES

Computer control is fun and can be used in all sorts of ways. The next few pages show some possibilities. All examples show programs in **LOGO** and **BASIC** but the text relates mainly to beginners using **LOGO**.

TURNING BULBS ETC 'ON' AND 'OFF'

The devices we want to control such as **bulbs, buzzers, motors** etc, need more power than a computer can give from its power supply. This is achieved by having a suitable **control interface** which is controlled by the computer. There are many types on sale. The ones used in this book were obtained from **Commotion**. The **Barnet 'Control It'** interface comes with its own **'Control It' LOGO** language software and is used in this book, but full versions of **Control LOGO** can also be used. LOGO is easier to use because it uses words like 'SWITCH OFF ALL' when we want to switch everything off. Using BASIC it would be ?65120=0. The BASIC provided in this book uses the **'user port'** of a BBC computer. The **Beasty Plus interface** is suitable for programs written in **BASIC** which addresses the **user port**, or it can be used for control using LOGO.

  Warning: There are various versions of LOGO around.

Using interfaces with the EZI–DUN board

Most interfaces are supplied with 4 mm plugs and flexible wires. These can be converted for use on the **EZI–DUN boards** in various ways. Three ideas are shown below. They all require the normal 0.6 mm single strand wire.

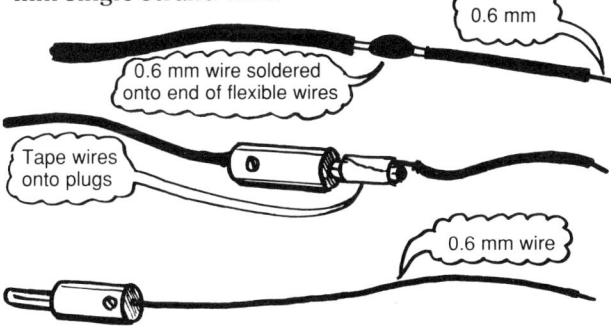

0.6 mm

0.6 mm wire soldered onto end of flexible wires

Tape wires onto plugs

0.6 mm wire

CONTROLLING BUGGIES

There are **two** ways of controlling normal two motor buggies. If the motors can only be turned ON and OFF, the buggy pivots on the stationary wheel as shown below. But if one wheel reverses while the other goes forward, it can 'spin on the spot' and is more useful.

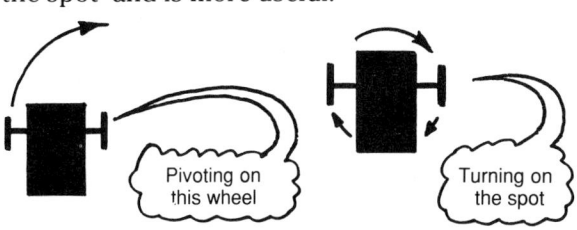

Pivoting on this wheel

Turning on the spot

SETTING UP A BUGGY

The buggy will not work properly unless it is **connected up** properly and the **correct codes** are used.

Setting up for 'Control It' LOGO

Type: MOTOR A ON < then press RETURN>
Then connect wires, from 'Output A' to the motor, so one wheel turns forward.
Type: MOTOR B ON < then press RETURN>
Then connect the other motor, from 'Output A' to the motor, so the other wheel turns forward.
Now check motors reverse by typing:
MOTOR A REVERSE <+RETURN>   and
MOTOR B REVERSE <+RETURN>

Setting up using BASIC

Make a note of which codes are useful as you test them out as shown below. You need to **record the codes** that make the buggy move:– FORWARDS, BACKWARDS, TURN LEFT (on the spot) TURN RIGHT (on the spot) and REVERSE.

Type: ?65122=255 <then press RETURN>
Then Note: what happens as you type the following:

CODE		RESULT
?65120=1	(+RETURN)	
?65120=2	(+RETURN)	
?65120=3	(+RETURN)	
?65120=4	(+RETURN)	
?65120=5	(+RETURN)	
?65120=6	(+RETURN)	
?65120=7	(+RETURN)	
?65120=8	(+RETURN)	
?65120=9	(+RETURN)	
?65120=10	(+RETURN)	
?65120=11	(+RETURN)	
?65120=12	(+RETURN)	
?65120=13	(+RETURN)	
?65120=14	(+RETURN)	
?65120=15	(+RETURN)	

If the buggy can be made to go FORWARD with the code ?65120=3 and turn when ?65120=5, the program called Circle on page 26, COMPUTER BUGGY, will work.

  If your codes are different, the program codes of Circle will need altering to match your codes in lines 40 and 60.

Note: For further help and more BASIC programs see the book **Craft, Design and Technology – a complete course for GCSE**, by Stewart Dunn.

LOGO – GETTING GOING

LEARNERS START HERE

LOGO is an easy-to-use computer program language but is capable of very complex work. This page gives practice in entering simple **commands** and observing the results. A program built up using a **procedure** is also given.

Note: BASIC programs are also given on the next few pages.

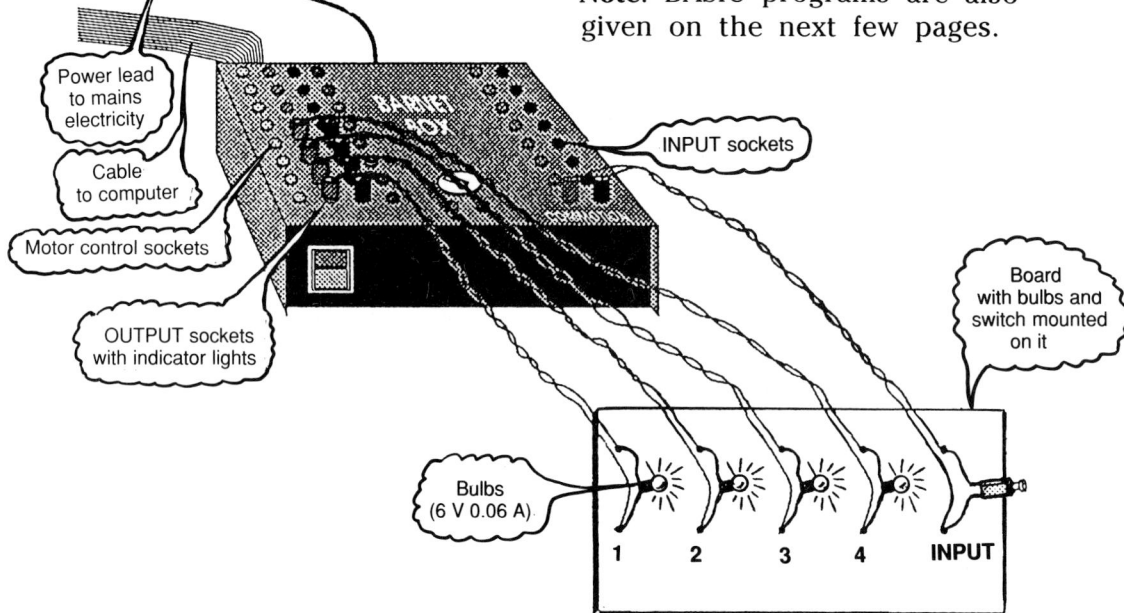

The bulbs can be connected to the EZI-DUN board as shown above. Four bulbs are used for the **outputs** and one **input switch**. If more outputs are required they can be added quite easily.

If using other LOGO languages, check the variations. Some do not have a gap between the words.

Changes to programs can be made by adding lines or deleting lines. Some use the word CHANGE to get into the editing mode (such as 'Control It').

It is assumed that the interface is connected up ready to use.

(1) **Load the LOGO program**. This is usually done by pressing the BREAK key and the SHIFT key, then letting the SHIFT key go first.

(2) Type: `SWITCH ON 1 <+RETURN>`

The Output Number 1 on the Control Interface should now be glowing.

(3) Type: `SWITCH OFF 1 <+RETURN>`

(4) Now try entering the following, remembering to press RETURN after each line.

```
SWITCH ON 1,2
SWITCH OFF 1,2
SWITCH ON 1,2,3
SWITCH OFF 1,2,3
SWITCH ON ALL
SWITCH OFF ALL
```

(5) You can now **build up a procedure** and then **call** it up as you want.
Type:

```
BUILD FLASH        <+RETURN>
REPEAT 4           <+RETURN>
SWITCH ON ALL      <+RETURN>
WAIT 2             <+RETURN>
SWITCH OFF ALL     <+RETURN>
END REPEAT         <+RETURN>
END PROCEDURE      <+RETURN>
```

Now call it up by typing:

`FLASH <+RETURN>`

then the procedure name, and it should work.

(6) Now see if you can make the program:
    (A) REPEAT 6 times instead of 4.
    (B) SWITCH OUTPUT 1 and 2 ON
    (C) Make it FLASH faster
    (D) Make use of INPUT 1 using the line of the program as follows:

`WAIT FOR 1 ON`

by inserting it after the REPEAT 4 line. Then press switch (INPUT 1).

(7) Connect **bulbs, buzzer or motors** to outputs as you want. Experiment and think of at least three ways the programs could be used.

ROBOT!!

FLASHING LIGHTS
USED ON A ROBOT

The program on this page makes the **lights flash** ON and OFF in the sequence shown below, but can easily be altered to suit your own requirements. A robot can be based around the EZI–DUN board.

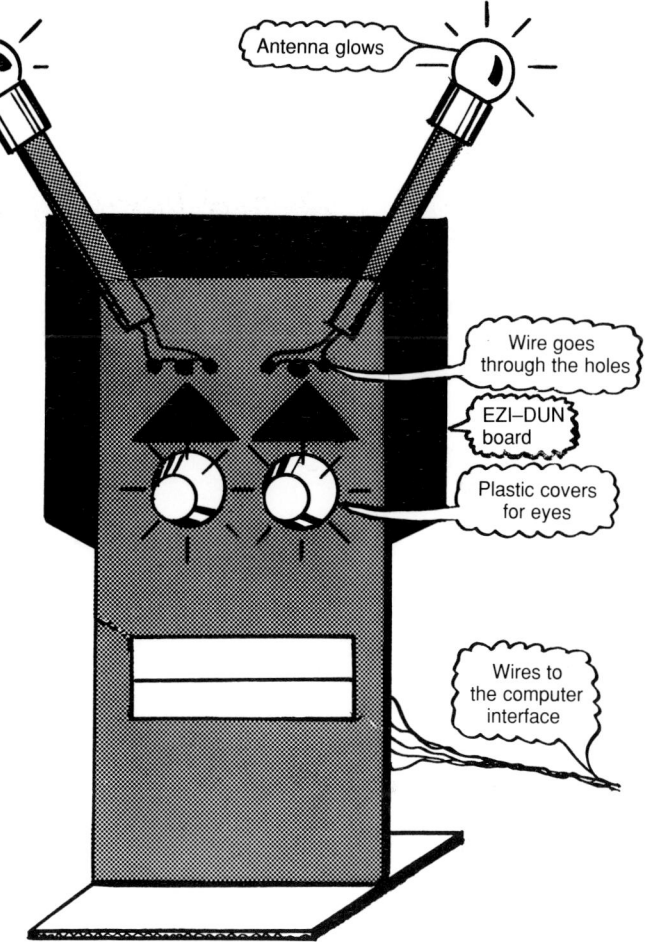

Antenna glows

Wire goes through the holes

EZI–DUN board

Plastic covers for eyes

Wires to the computer interface

To make the robot with flashing parts you need an EZI–DUN board, a **computer interface**, **four bulbs** on longish wires, **four wire leads** to the computer and parts to decorate the robot.

ACTIVITIES

(1) Connect up the **computer interface** and then copy out carefully either the **LOGO program** or the **BASIC program** and SAVE it after checking it works. The interface lights will show if it is working properly.
(2) Connect up **four bulbs to the interface** using ports 1,2,3 and 4. Check they work.
(3) Design and make the robot's face, eyes, mouth etc, testing out possible positions for the bulbs as you go along. Put some ideas down on paper first.
(4) Make the bulbs on the robot light up, then alter the program to make the bulbs **flash faster**.
(5) Make the lights work in a **different sequence**.

LIGHT SEQUENCE PLAN

TIME	PORTS			
	4	3	2	1
5 SEC				■
10 SEC			■	
15 SEC	■	■		
20 SEC	■			

'LOGO PROGRAM'

```
BUILD FLASH
REPEAT 20              Repeats program 20 times
SWITCH ON 1            Turns 1 ON
WAIT 5                 5 sec time delay
SWITCH ON 1,2          Turns ON 1 and 2
WAIT 5                 5 sec time delay
SWITCH OFF 1,2         Turns OFF 1 and 2
SWITCH ON 3,4          Turns ON 3 and 4
WAIT 5                 5 sec time delay
SWITCH OFF ALL         Switches all OFF
WAIT 5                 5 sec time delay
END REPEAT
END PROCEDURE
```

'BASIC PROGRAM'

Notes

```
10  REM CALLED B.FLASH
20  ?65122=255              Sets 'User Port'
30  ?65120=1                Turns ON Port 1

40  FOR D=1 TO 5000
50  NEXT D                  5 sec delay
60  ?65120=3                Port 1 and 2 ON
70  FOR D=1 TO 5000
80  NEXT D                  5 sec delay
90  ?65120=6                Port 2 and 3
100 FOR D=1 TO 5000
110 NEXT D                  5 sec delay
120 ?65120=0                Ports all OFF
130 FOR D=1 TO 5000
140 NEXT D                  5 sec delay
150 GOTO 30                 Makes program repeat
```

COMPUTER SHOW
BULBS, BUZZERS AND MOTORS

Putting on a grand **computer show** is impressive and great fun. Only one idea is given here but you can adapt the show quite easily. The **LOGO program** controls **four bulbs** which are used for the lighting effects, and a **motor** which spins the ballerina first one way then the other. This all operates when the **switch** is pressed.

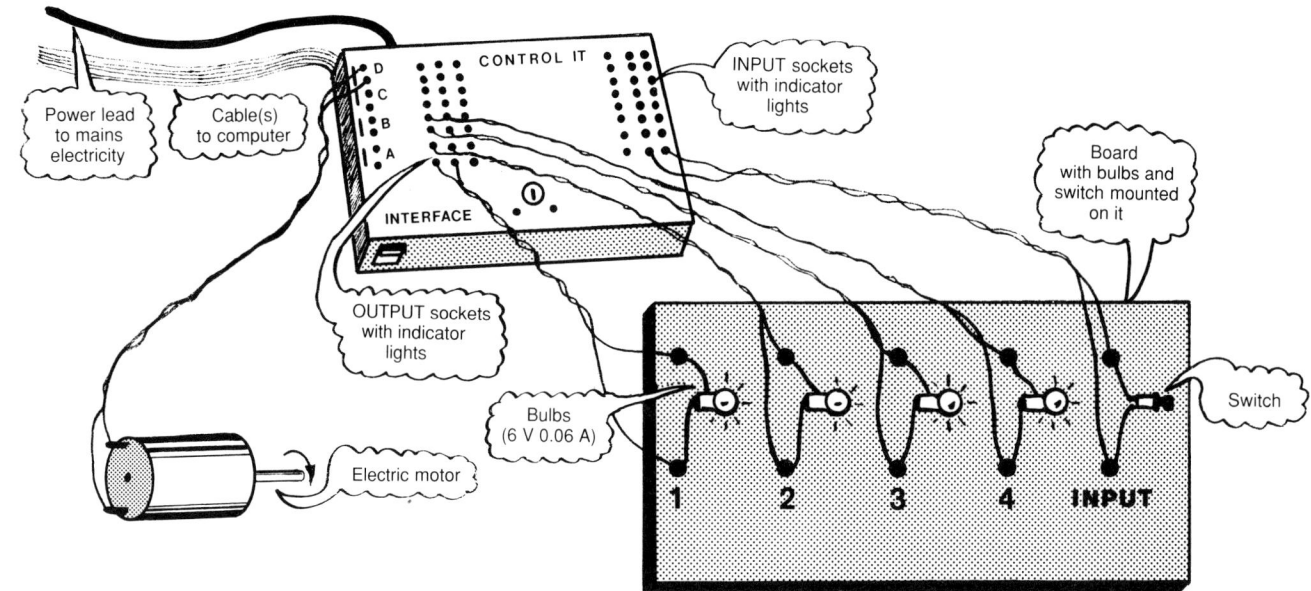

Electric connections using EZI–DUN board

ASSEMBLING THE STAGE

The EZI–DUN board is best used upside down so the stage is flat.

Long leads are needed on the bulbs to allow them to reach where required.

The numbers relate to the ones used in the LOGO program

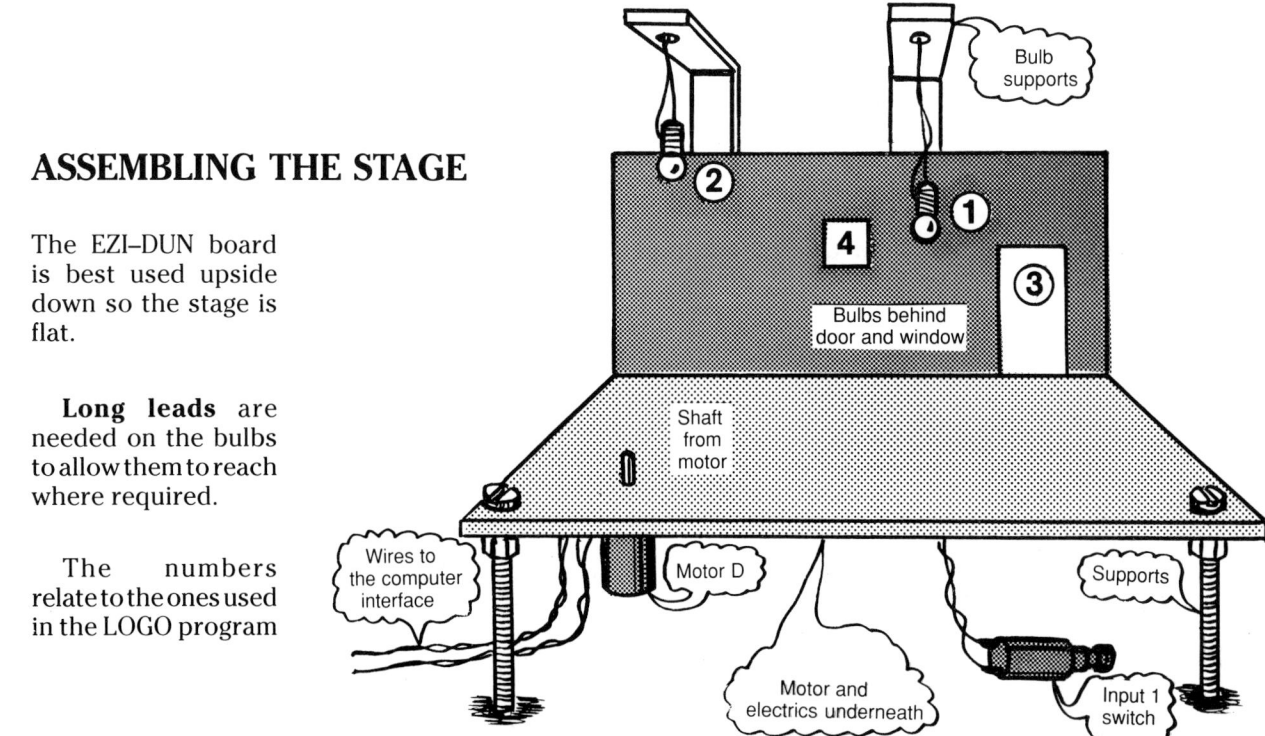

COMPUTER SHOW
(CONTINUED)

ACTIVITIES

(1) Turn an EZI–DUN board over and support it to raise it about 40 mm (using construction kit parts), then bolt a backpiece on with holes to allow bulbs to shine through.

(2a) You may need to solder extra–long wires on to the bulbs etc, so that they can reach where you want them to go.

(2b) Attach the **bulbs, motor** and **switch** as required to the EZI–DUN board (which is upside down).

(3) Connect the **computer interface** to the EZI–DUN board and test the program works as you want.

(4) **Enclose the stage**. A simple way is to add an old shoe box or similar.

(5) **Decorate** as you want, adding lamp covers, doors, curtains etc using card and other odds and ends.

(6) Alter the program **timings** and **sequence** to suit your requirements.

'LOGO' program sequence plan

TIME	8	7	6	5	4	3	2	1
2 SEC								■
4 SEC								■
6 SEC		■					■	■
8 SEC	■							■
10 SEC	■			■	■			
12 SEC					■	■	■	■

← Input 1

Now . . .

(7) Write a story that could be told using your computer show.

(8) Make sound effects on a tape recorder and then give your presentation to an audience.

(9) You may like to control the tape recorder via the computer as well.

FINISHED SHOW

The **ballerina spins**, the **chandelier** (and other lights) go ON and OFF. When the switch is pressed, the program starts. It must already be running on the computer.

● PUSH

Push switch mounted

Note: The BASIC program below only controls bulbs.

'LOGO' program (Control It)

```
BUILD THEATRE
REPEAT 20              Repeats program 20 times
SWITCH ON 1            Turns bulb 1 ON
WAIT 2                 2 sec time delay
WAIT FOR INPUT 1       Waits for Input 1 ON
SWITCH ON 2            Turns bulb 2 ON
WAIT 2                 2 sec time delay
MOTOR D ON             Motor starts
WAIT 2                 2 sec time delay
MOTOR D REVERSE        Motor reverses direction
WAIT 2                 2 sec time delay
MOTOR D OFF            Motor is turned OFF
SWITCH OFF 1,2         Turns OFF bulbs 1 and 2
SWITCH ON 5,6          Turns ON bulbs 5 and 6
WAIT 2                 2 sec time delay
SWITCH ON 1,2,3,4      Turns ON bulbs 1,2,3,4
WAIT 2                 2 sec time delay
SWITCH OFF ALL         Turns OFF all bulbs
END REPEAT
END PROCEDURE
```

'BASIC' program

```
10    REM CALLED "THEATRE"
20    ?65122=255              REM turns on ports
30    FOR R = 1 TO 20         REM 20 repeats
40    PROCaction
45    NEXT R
50    END
1000  DEFPROCaction           REM proc. starts
1010  ?65120=1                REM Port 1 ON
1020  FOR D=1 TO 2000:NEXT    REM 2 sec delay
1030  ?65120=2                REM Port 2 ON
1040  FOR D=1 TO 2000:NEXT    REM 2 sec delay
1050  ?65120=192              REM Port 6+7 ON
1060  FOR D=1 TO 2000:NEXT    REM 2 sec delay
1070  ?65120=0                REM all ports
1080  ?65120=48               REM ports 4+5 ON
1090  FOR D=1 TO 2000:NEXT    REM 2 sec delay
1100  ?65120=15               REM Port 1+2+3+4
1110  FOR D=1 TO 2000:NEXT    REM 2 sec delay
1120  ?65120=0                REM all ports OFF
1130  ENDPROC
```

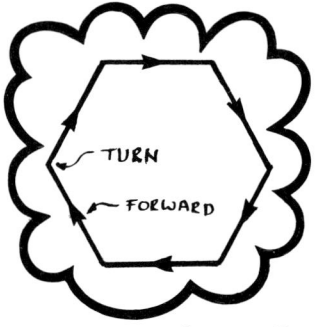

COMPUTER BUGGY
GOING ROUND IN CIRCLES

This is an easy-to-make **buggy** that can move around the floor, based on the EZI–DUN board. The programs provided allow the buggy to move about, tracing polygon shapes. The more sides a polygon has, the nearer it gets to a circle. Drawings can also be made if a pen is added.

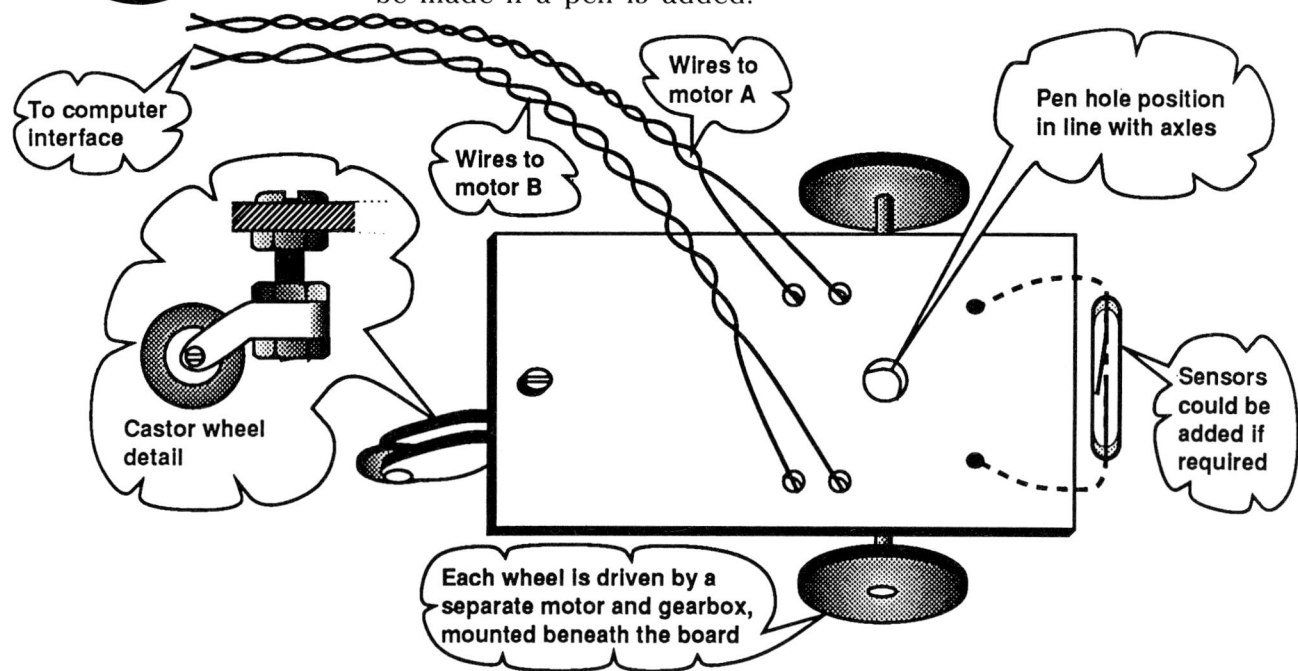

This is an easy-to-make **buggy**. Bought **geared-down motors** are best if accurate work is important, but a cheap alternative is shown on page 13 '**Steerable Buggy**'. Shapes can be drawn if a **pen is placed centrally** between the motors. Extras can be added as required, such as a **reed switch sensor** on the front.

ACTIVITIES

(1) Assemble the buggy as shown above. The Output A and Output B ports are used – see page 21, 'Computer Control' for help if needed.
(2) LOAD one of the programs given below and RUN it. How does the buggy move? Draw its path.
(3) **Alter** the program (the TURN time) and notice the effect. Now make it draw a **hexagon**, or a ten sided polygon if using the BASIC program.
(4) Make it trace a square, a triangle, a figure of eight (this is more difficult).

A computer–operated buggy using two geared–down motors. A castor wheel at the back allows it to turn easily.

'LOGO' program

```
BUILD POLY          Called POLY
REPEAT 6            Repeats 6 times
MOTOR A ON         Buggy goes forward
MOTOR B ON
WAIT 0.5           Forward 5 sec
MOTOR B REVERSE    Buggy turns
WAIT 0.1           Turning 0.1 sec
END REPEAT
MOTOR A OFF
MOTOR B OFF
END PROCEDURE
```

'BASIC' program

```
10 REM CALLED "CIRCLE"
20 ?65122=255           REM set up 'user port'
30 FOR X=1 TO 10        REM 10 repeats
40 ?65120=3             REM forward code
50 FOR D=1 TO 2000:NEXT REM 2 sec delay
60 ?65120=5             REM turn code
70 FOR D=1 TO 2000:NEXT REM 2 sec delay
80 NEXT X
90 ?65120=0:PRINT "END" REM motors off
```

Note: Also see p.21, 'Computer Control' for details of setting up a buggy.

CAR PARK BARRIER
OPERATED BY AN 'INPUT' SWITCH

The **car park barrier** needs an **'input switch'** which once triggered, allows the **motor**, via gears, to lift the **barrier**, which stops in the air, allowing the car to pass . Then the barrier returns to its original position.

A **'push' switch** and a **motor** are all the electric parts required. Connect the motor to the **Motor A** sockets and the switch to the **Input 1** sockets.

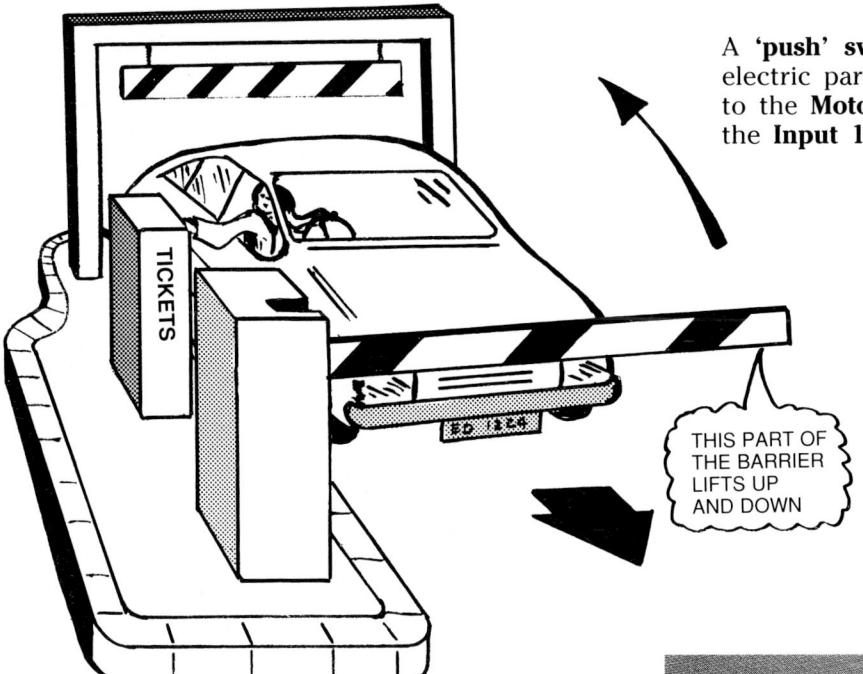

THIS PART OF THE BARRIER LIFTS UP AND DOWN

ACTIVITIES

(1) Make the **car park barrier mechanism** to your own design or like the photograph. (A geared-down motor makes it a lot easier.)

(2) Connect the **car park barrier** motor to **Motor A** on the **interface**, then copy the **procedure** called 'ACTION' below. After testing, alter the timings to match your own requirements.

(3) Copy out and run the **'BARRIER' procedure**. The barrier can now be controlled by the **'INPUT' switch**, connected to **Input 1** on the **interface**.

(4) Improve your design by making it more realistic and reliable.

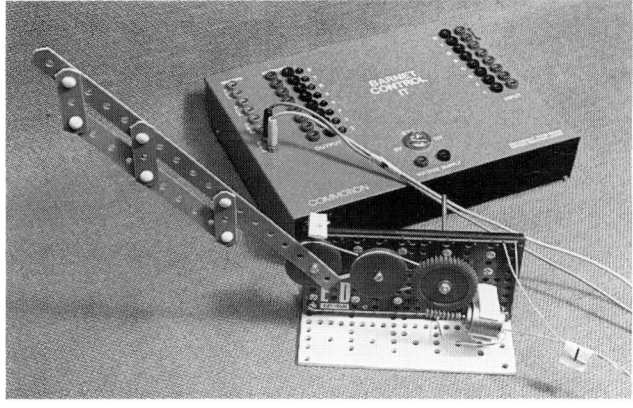

A car park barrier model operated by computer. Note the use of a computer–controlled interface.

'LOGO' program

The barrier operates when the **car** (or the driver) triggers **'Input 1'**. Two procedures can be used as shown below. The **'ACTION'** procedure can be used separately for testing purposes and then made to operate using the **'BARRIER'** procedure which links the procedures up.

Note: The LOGO program used is 'Control It'. Other programs may need slight modifications.

```
BUILD ACTION        Called 'ACTION'
MOTOR A ON          Barrier up
WAIT 5              5 sec
MOTOR A OFF         Barrier stays up
WAIT 4              4 sec
MOTOR A REVERSE     Barrier down
WAIT 3              3 sec
MOTOR A OFF         Barrier stops
END PROCEDURE
```

```
BUILD BARRIER               Called 'BARRIER'
REPEAT FOREVER
IF INPUT 1 ON THEN ACTION   *

END REPEAT                  Waiting for car
END PROCEDURE               to approach
```

*This line waits for car to approach input 1

INPUT READY TO TURN ON BARRIER

 **OTHER OUTPUTS TO TRY**

ACTIVITIES

Connect up the following and record what they do, eg "**The bulb glowed brightly**".
(1) **A bulb**
(2) **A motor** (can it be reversed?)
(3) **A buzzer** (what happens if wires are switched over?)

(4) **A solenoid** (6 V type) (if available)
(5) **A counter** (6 V type) (if available)
(6) **A relay** (does it click on and off?)
– connect to the coil of the relay only.
Any problems? – Check that the voltage of the device and the battery match.

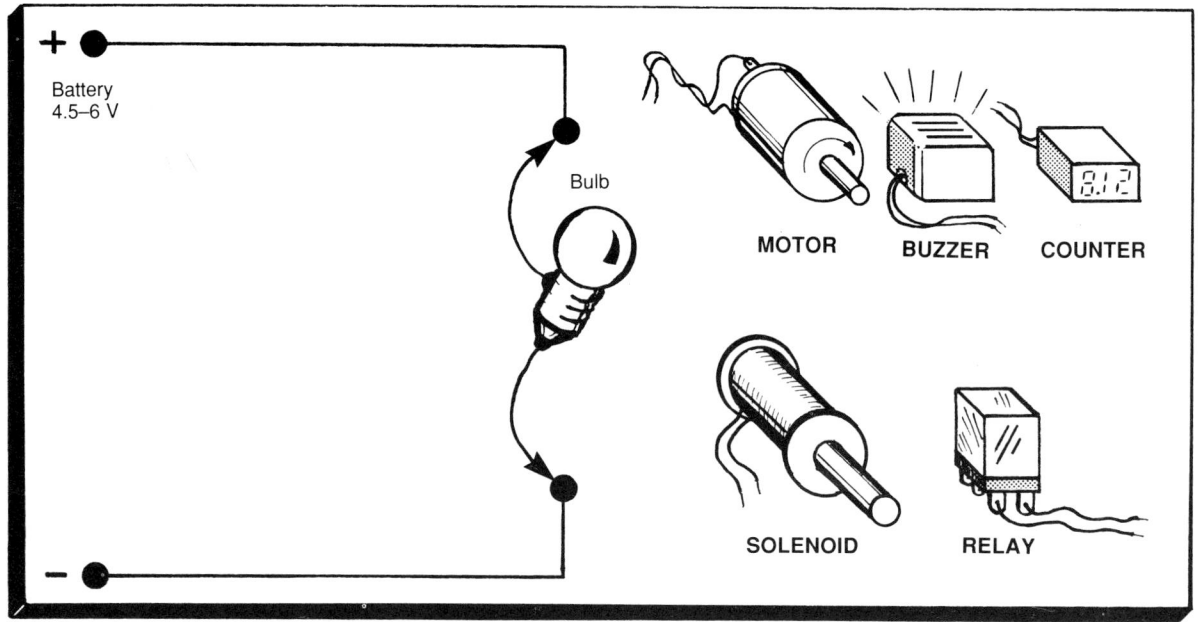

CAPACITORS

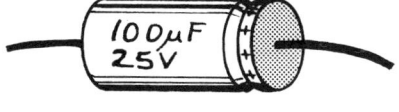 

Capacitors come in all shapes and sizes but they all **store electricity** and can be used to:
(a) Provide a **time delay** in electronic circuits.
(b) **Filter out unwanted frequencies** (eg tone controls or an amplifier circuit).
(c) Allow **alternating current** (AC) to pass but block the **direct current** (DC) in audio amplifier circuits.
There are two types of capacitor and symbol:
1. Ordinary (non–electrolytic).
2. Electrolytic (for larger values and which must be connected the correct way round).

ACTIVITIES

If you have a **light emitting diode** and **protection resistor** you can see the effect of charging up a **large capacitor** (about 1000 µF) and then discharge it as shown below.

How long does it take to charge up and discharge?

Drawing A shows how the capacitor is charged up. (The capacitor and LED must be connected the correct way round.)

Drawing B shows how the same capacitor is removed and placed across the LED. It must be the correct way round.

ELECTROLYTIC SYMBOL

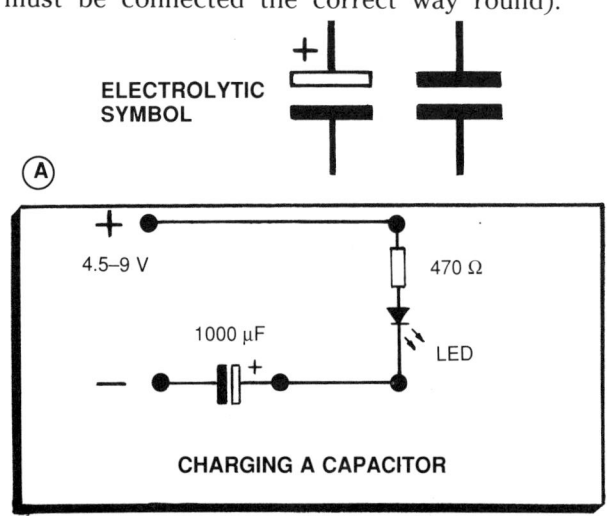

CHARGING A CAPACITOR

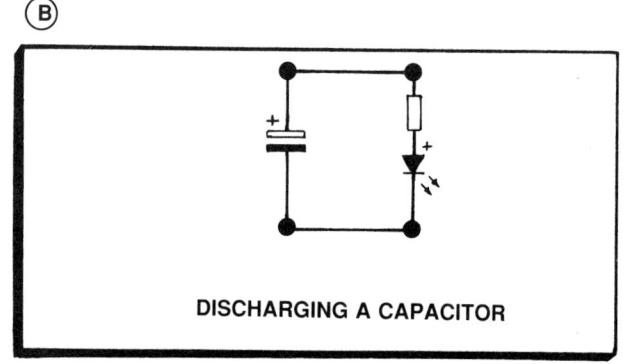

DISCHARGING A CAPACITOR

This page may be copied for use in the classroom (see page ii). Electronic Projects – made easy.

29

SEE SAFETY NOTES BELOW

MEASURING VOLTAGE

The circuits in this book are powered by **low voltage** batteries (or power supplies).. If the wrong voltage is used the circuit may not work or components may **burn out. Here you will find out how to measure voltage across a load, such as a bulb**.

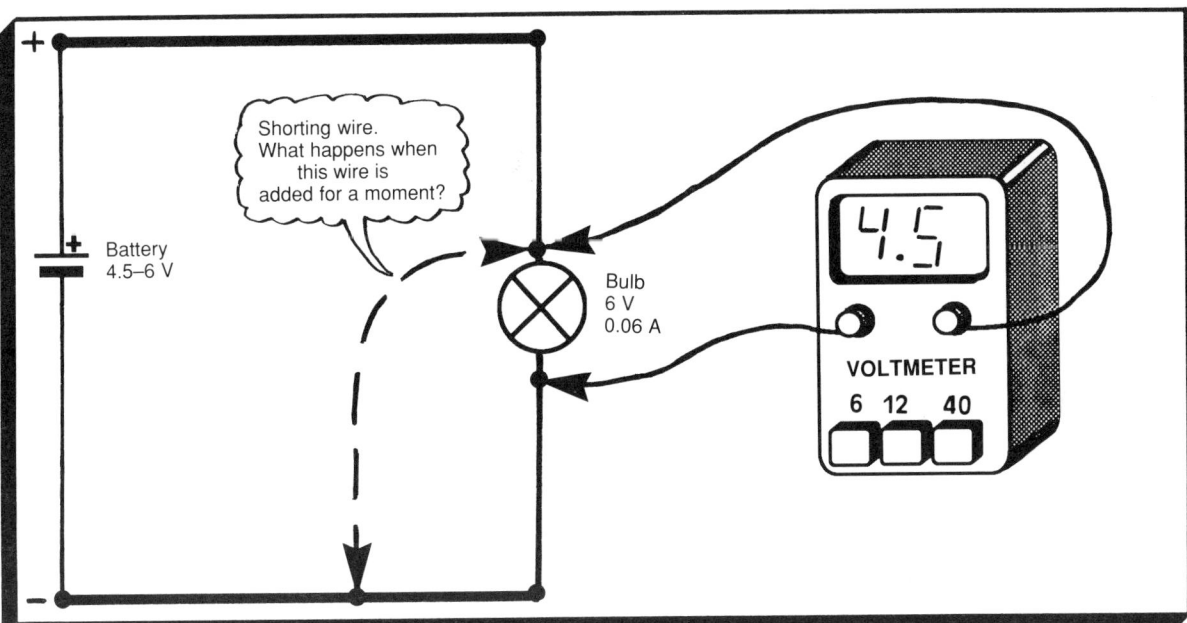

VOLTAGE (measured in volts V)

Voltage can be considered to be the pressure pushing the electricity along. It is rather like the water pressure in a hosepipe which can squirt a long way if the pressure is high. **Voltage** is also referred to as '**potential difference**' (p.d.). Voltage is measured with a **voltmeter** or a multipurpose meter called a **multimeter**.

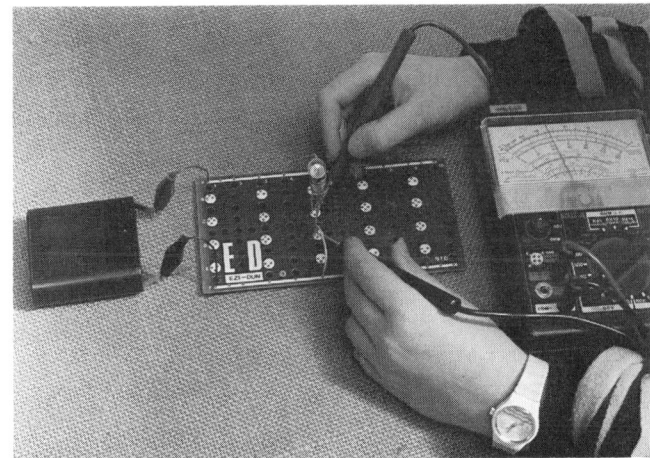

A multimeter set on the voltage scale. Its leads are placed either side of the bulb.

ACTIVITIES

(1) Try connecting up the circuit above and measuring the voltage **across** the bulb as shown. What voltage reading have you got?

Make sure you have the **multimeter** or **voltmeter** connected correctly. Batteries produce **direct current** (d.c.) so it must be set on d.c. voltage.

For example: Set at 12 V d.c. (or higher) when testing a 4.5 V battery.

(2) Replace the bulb with a **buzzer** and measure the voltage across the buzzer. Is the reading the same as for the bulb?

(3) See what happens if a wire is **shorted** across the bulb (as dotted line). **What happened**? This flattens the battery very quickly so **YOU MUST ONLY DO THIS FOR A FEW SECONDS.**

SAFETY

NEVER CONNECT THE CIRCUITS IN THIS BOOK TO THE MAINS ELECTRICITY. IT IS AT 240 V AND CAN KILL YOU. LOW VOLTAGE BATTERIES ARE SAFE TO TOUCH AND USE.

MEASURING CURRENT

Electric **current** is measured in a different way from **voltage** and must not be confused. **Current** is the flow of electricity going round a circuit and is measured with an **ammeter**. The **ammeter is placed in the actual circuit**. It is easy to 'blow' an **ammeter**, so always set the meter high to start with.

MEASURING A CURRENT!

Connect up the circuit shown above without the ammeter in place, and check that the bulb glows by bridging the gap A–B momentarily with a wire.

ACTIVITIES

(1) Place the ammeter across the gap A–B as shown above. The meter setting must always be high first. Set it at 1 A maximum to start with. What reading do you have?
Note: If a needle type of ammeter, or multimeter, is used as shown in the photograph **DO NOT** allow the needle to hit the end of the dial or damage may result.
(2) Connect up **two bulbs in series** as shown below and note the reading. It should be less than the one-bulb reading.

A multimeter set to read amperes. It measures the current flowing through the bulb.

(3) Connect up two bulbs in parallel as shown below and note the reading on the ammeter. How much bigger is it than the one-bulb reading?

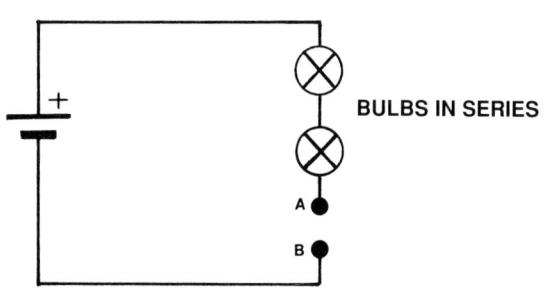

BULBS IN SERIES

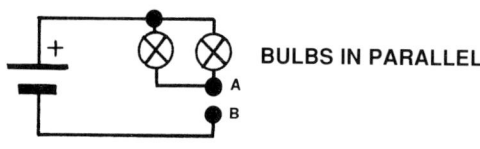

BULBS IN PARALLEL

Now . . .

Record your results neatly and explain how **current can be measured safely.**

BATTERIES IN SERIES

When batteries are connected in **series**, the voltage increases. The **total voltage** is found by adding the voltage of the batteries. **Note**: The batteries **must** be connected up + to - **and not** + to + or - to -.

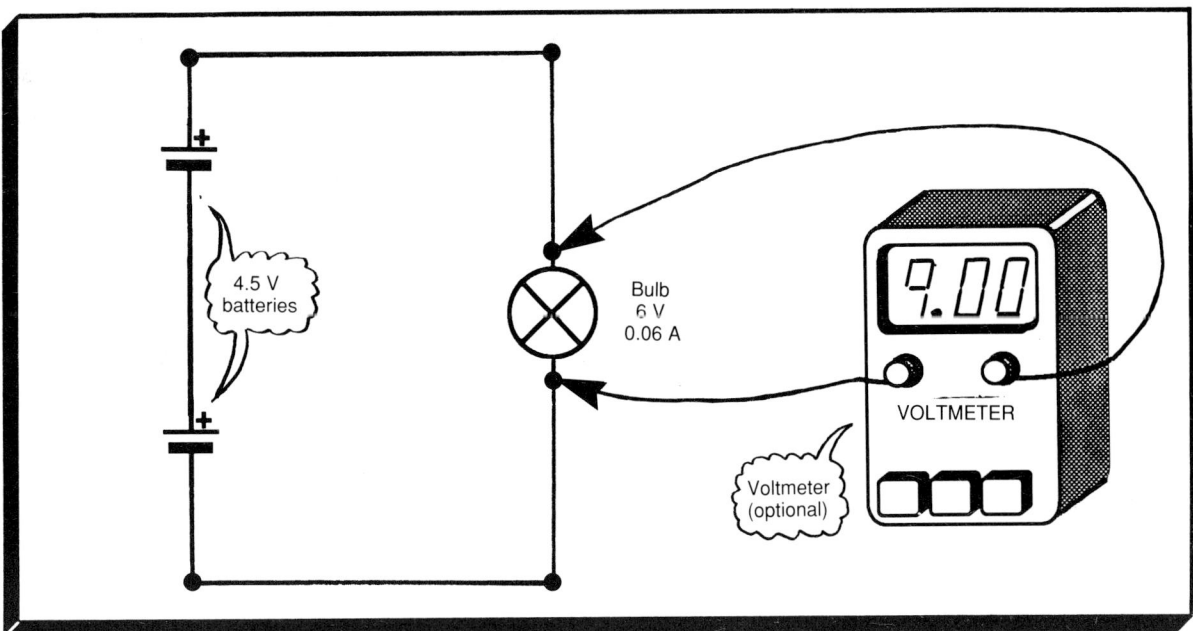

Batteries connected up in SERIES

Series formula
VOLTAGE (total) = VOLTAGE 1 + VOLTAGE 2

Voltage (total) = $V_1 + V_2$

Question
What is the total voltage of two 1.5 V batteries connected in **series**?

Answer
VOLTAGE (total) = 1.5 V + 1.5 V
                = 3 V

ACTIVITIES

(1) Connect up as shown (without voltmeter) and see how bright the bulb is. (Do not leave connected up for long because the bulb is only rated at 6 V and may burn out.)
(2) Remove one battery and connect up the remaining battery to the + and - rail. What is the difference in the bulb's brightness?
(3) Use a **voltmeter** to measure the voltage using one battery, and then two batteries as in activity (1). Is there an obvious relationship between the two voltages recorded? (Make allowances for the condition of the batteries.)
(4) If you have 1.5 V batteries, join three in **series** and observe the brightness of the bulb.
(5) Connect up 1.5 V batteries to produce 6 V. How did you achieve this?

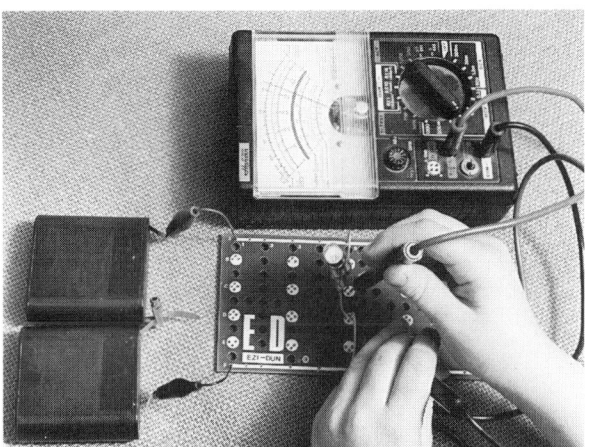

Two 4.5 V batteries connected in series to give an output of 9 V.

Connecting up in parallel

It is important to realise that the other way of connecting up batteries does **not** increase the voltage. Try the following and see for yourself.

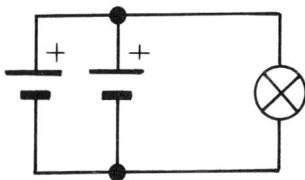

FUN JEWELLERY/BADGE

There are three circuits that could be used to make **electronic jewellery** or **badges** that have **one** (circuit A), **two** (circuit B) or **four** LEDs (circuit C). They could be switched on with a membrane switch (see page 7, 'making switches'). The battery can be separate or part of the product.

FACE WITH LEDs FOR EYES

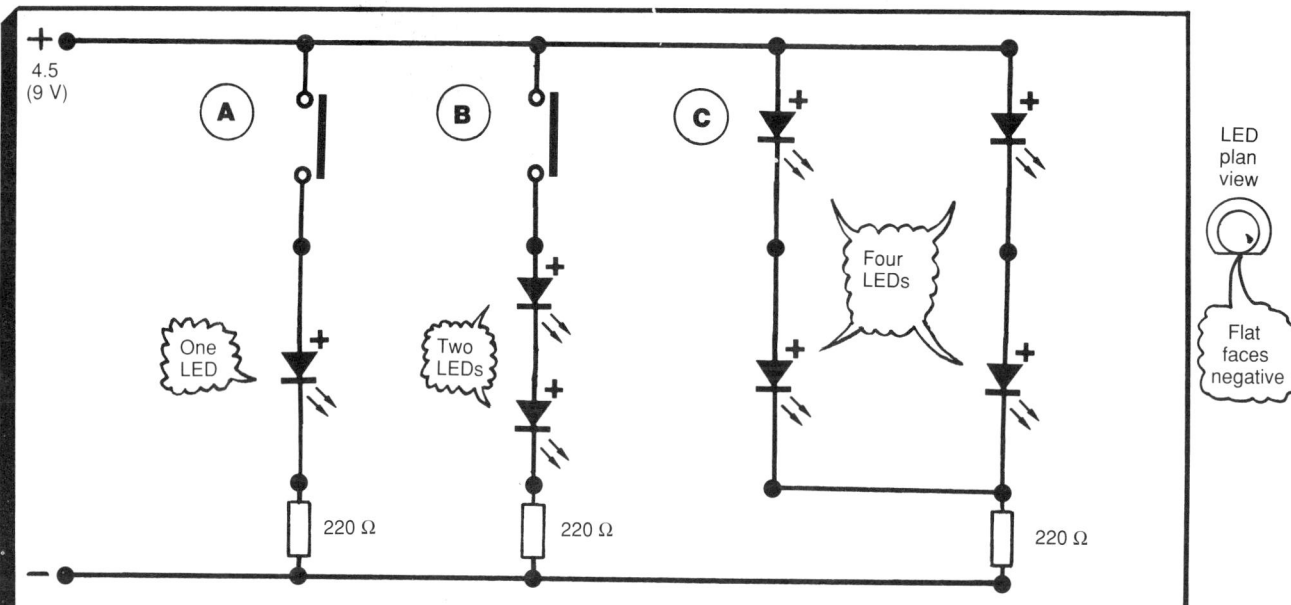

LEDs (LIGHT EMITTING DIODES)

LEDs can be made attractive when mounted in a hole so that only the top part shows.

A protection resistor is needed if more than about 2.5 V is used. LEDs must be connected the correct way round. The wire from the flat part of the LED goes to the negative rail (-).

Note: Use the 220 Ω resistor if a 4–6 V battery is used. Use a 680 Ω resistor if a 9 V battery is used. If only one LED is to be used it can be driven directly by a 1.5 V battery.

Using bulbs instead. If bulbs are used instead of LEDs, the 220 Ω resistor is not needed.

ACTIVITIES

Using either **bulbs** or **LEDs**, connect up the following:

(1) **Circuit A**. What happens if the LED is connected the wrong way round?

(2) **Circuit B**. The two LEDs are connected up in series.

(3) If you have enough LEDs, connect up two in **series** (**as before**), then add two more in **parallel** as shown in circuit C.

(4) Add switch to circuit C.

Now . . .

Use the knowledge gained to design and make fun jewellery of **badges** or **model radios** etc. Battery size is an important consideration – 1.5 V calculator batteries are small but expensive.

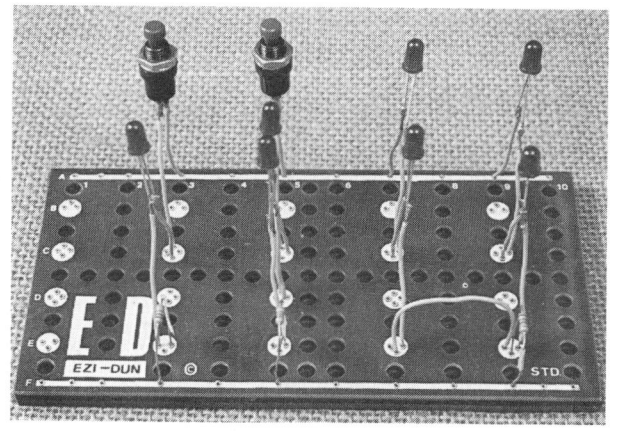

Three different ways of connecting up LEDs.

IDEAS

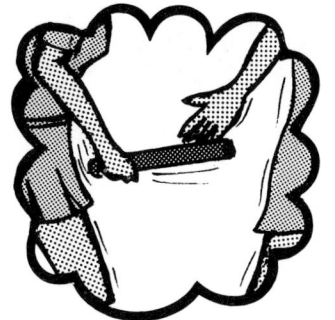

**RELAY 'BATON'
BEING PASSED ON**

RELAYS

THE NEXT FEW PAGES SHOW VARIOUS EXAMPLES OF THE RELAY IN USE

This page shows how a relay can be used to control **output devices**. Real relay applications usually control higher powered **output** devices than the **input** circuit.

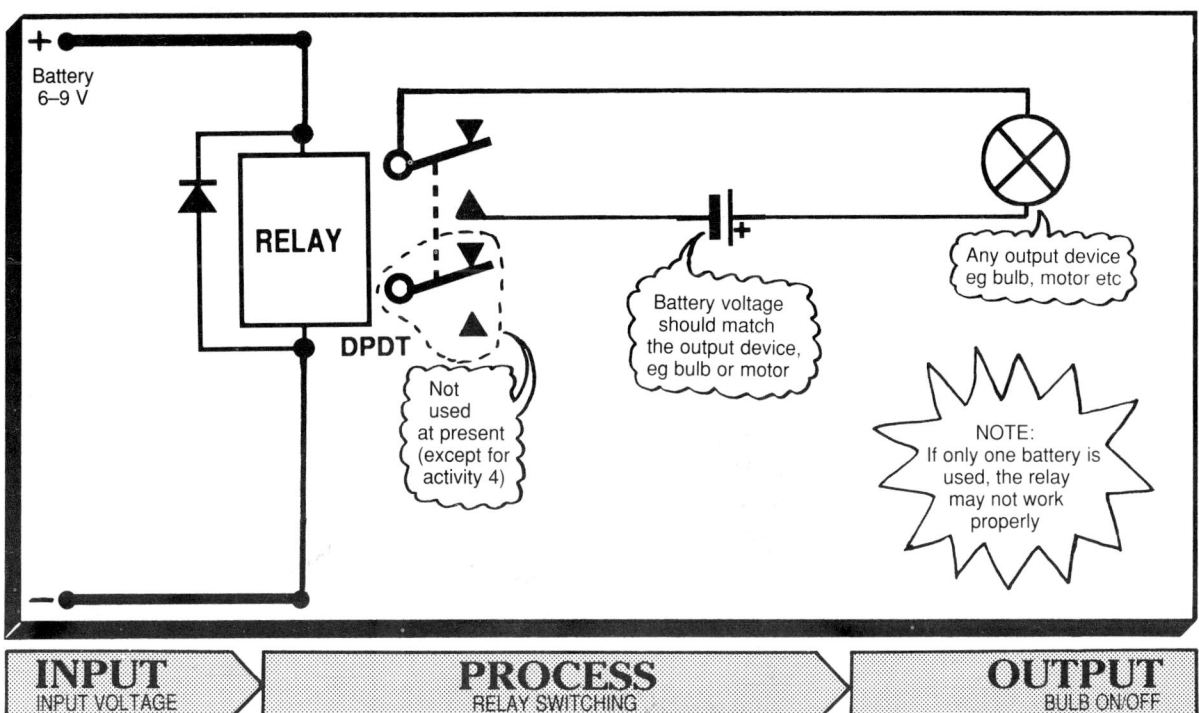

Battery
6–9 V

RELAY

DPDT

Not used at present (except for activity 4)

Battery voltage should match the output device, eg bulb or motor

Any output device eg bulb, motor etc

NOTE:
If only one battery is used, the relay may not work properly

INPUT	PROCESS	OUTPUT
INPUT VOLTAGE	RELAY SWITCHING	BULB ON/OFF

Relays allow small delicate circuits to control more powerful devices such as large motors. On this page you will be using it only to see how it can be used to turn 'ON' and 'OFF' various **output devices**. A **relay** is rather like a **switch** but is controlled by an **input voltage** rather than by a person's hand.

The **diode** connected in parallel with the relay helps protect delicate semiconductors (not actually needed on this page but fitted as standard in most kits).

The relay **output** voltage can be different from the **input** because it is isolated; for example, a relay can be operated by a 4.5 V battery but the output could be a car headlight running off a 12 V car battery.

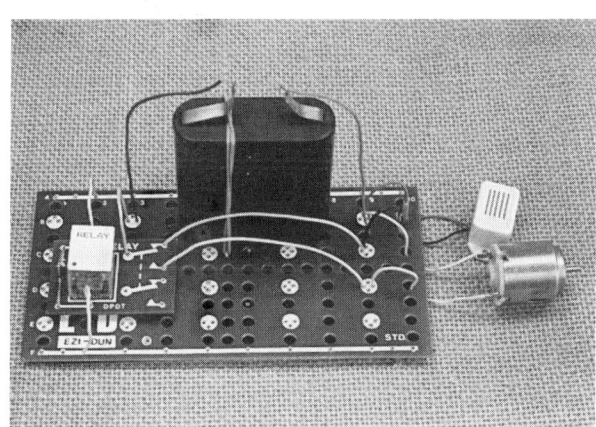

A buzzer is operated when this relay is OFF, and a motor when the relay is ON.

ACTIVITIES

GENERAL COMMENT– Different batteries may be needed to match the output device voltages.

(1) Connect up the circuit as shown above which controls a **bulb**. If a separate battery is not available the output voltage can be shared with the input.

(2) Replace the **bulb** with an **electric motor**.

(3) Replace the **motor** with a **buzzer**. Remember the black negative wire must go to the negative rail.

(4) Connect up a circuit that allows the **motor** to work when the **input is on**, and a **buzzer** to work when the **input is off**. Two batteries are needed and the other contact on the relay used. Draw the circuit you have made.

(5) Try the other output devices you have such as **counters** and **solenoids**.

SOLENOID   BUZZER   COUNTER 12·00

MOTOR REVERSING–1
VEHICLE FORWARD/REVERSING USING A RELAY

A '**double pole double throw**' relay can be connected up to make common **d.c. motors** reverse without needing to change over the wires manually.

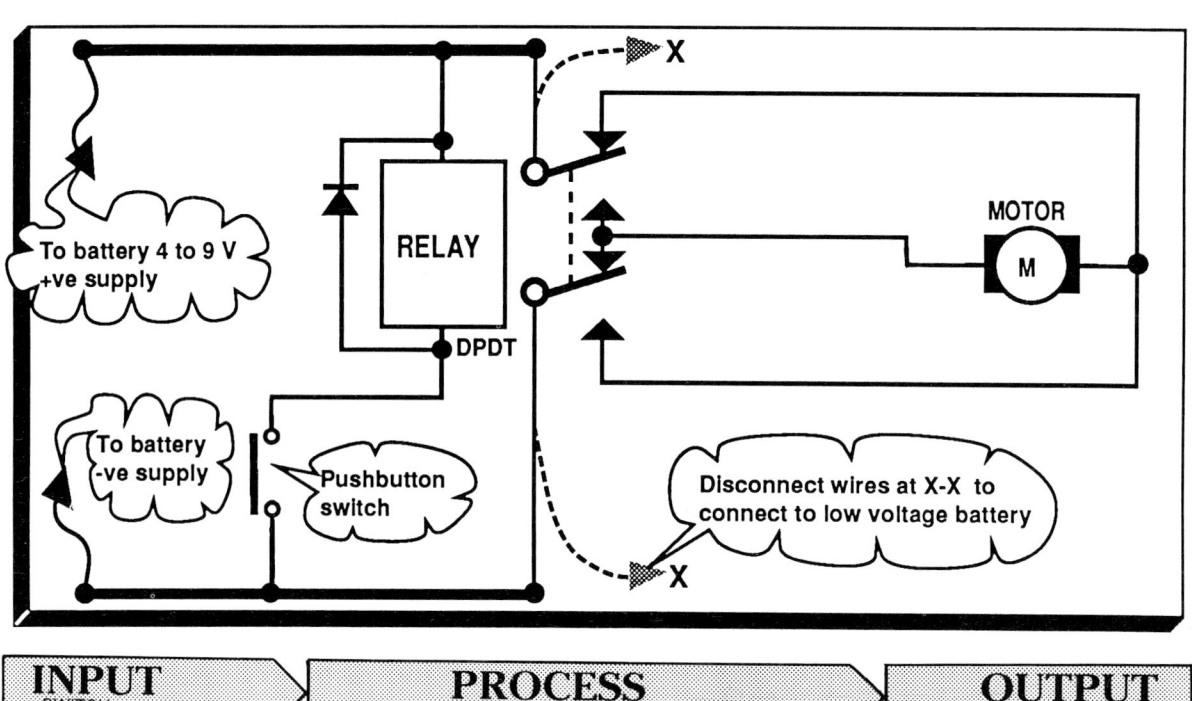

To battery 4 to 9 V +ve supply

RELAY

DPDT

To battery -ve supply

Pushbutton switch

MOTOR

M

Disconnect wires at X-X to connect to low voltage battery

INPUT	PROCESS	OUTPUT
SWITCH	RELAY SWITCHING (DPDT)	MOTOR FORWARD/REVERSE

If the motor is connected to a vehicle it can be made to reverse back and forth as shown in the photograph.

This buggy reverses when the press switch is operated. (A geared-down motor would be more suitable.)

ACTIVITIES

(1) Connect up the circuit shown above. The motor reverses when the switch is pressed.

(2) Add an **extra switch** (slide switch or **reed switch** + magnet) to allow circuit to be **turned off.**

(3) Make a **buggy** vehicle by adding wheels to the EZI–DUN board, as shown in the photograph. See page 14, '**parts for buggy**', for help with construction.

(4) Experiment with the buggy. Try the following:

Use a **reed switch** and **magnet** to control it. Reduce the speed of the buggy by either **gearing down** or using a 1.5 V battery for the motor. This is done by connecting a 1.5 V battery to connections marked X and X. (Disconnect wires that were used to operate the relay coil.)

(5) By adding a reed switch (to replace the push switch) and mounting it at the front of the vehicle, it can be made to follow a magnet in a straight line. Try it and see what happens.

Mouse body made from thin card on simple chassis

Magnet. Disguise it as a piece of cheese

TORCH BEAM

MOTOR REVERSING–2
LIGHT OPERATED MOTOR REVERSING CIRCUIT

This circuit is similar to the last one except that it is controlled by **light**. A **torch** is the easiest way of controlling the relay. A **buggy version** can be built and made to reverse using a torch. (See diagram at bottom of page.)

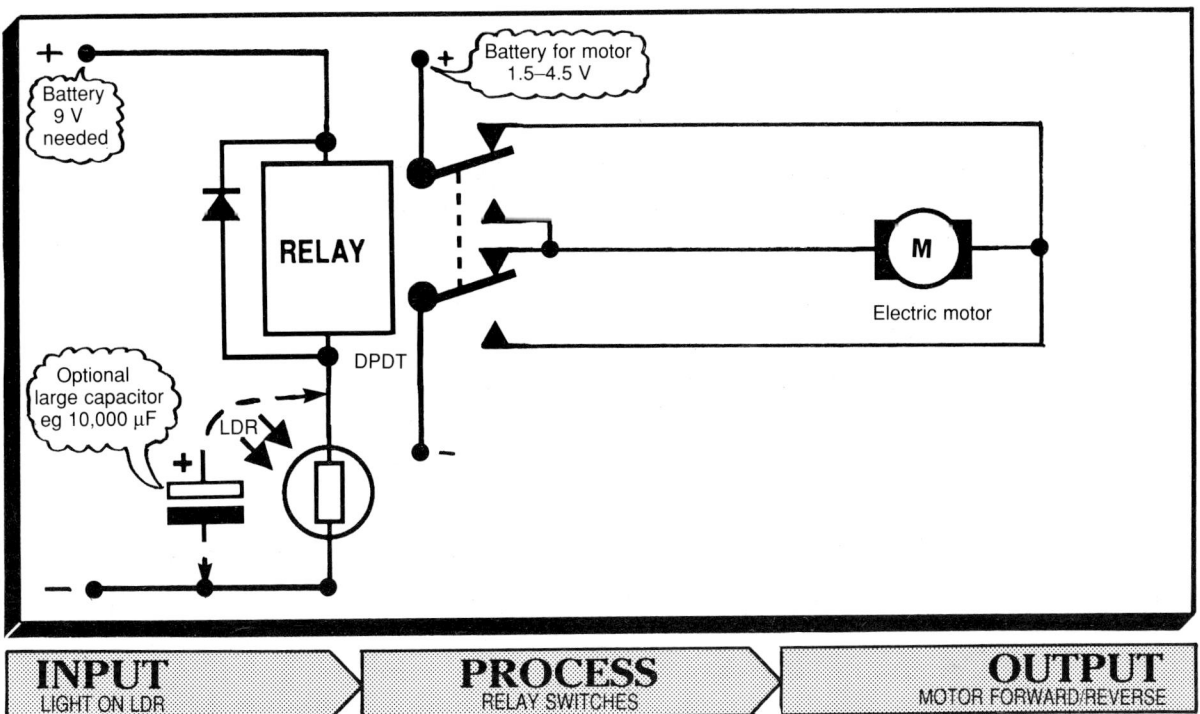

INPUT	PROCESS	OUTPUT
LIGHT ON LDR	RELAY SWITCHES	MOTOR FORWARD/REVERSE

Because there is no amplification the circuit requires quite a bright light to operate it , and it only works if a **9 V battery** is used because of the LDR's resistance. A separate battery is needed for the **motor** and can be 1.5–4.5 V.

If a large **capacitor** of value above 10,000 µF is placed across the LDR, as shown in dotted lines, a small **time delay** can be achieved.

ACTIVITIES

(1) Assemble the circuit as shown above, without the capacitor. **Note**: The circuit needs a 9 V battery to operate the relay and 1.5–4.5 V for the motor. Does the motor change direction when the LDR is placed in a bright light? (Also see photograph.)

(2) Add a large capacitor across the LDR (above 10,000 µF if available) and see if you can obtain a delaying action.

(3) If you have not already made a buggy vehicle, make it now and record your results when the torch is used on the LDR. (The LDR is best mounted on the front end.) The torch can then be pointed towards the buggy. At what distance does the buggy reverse?

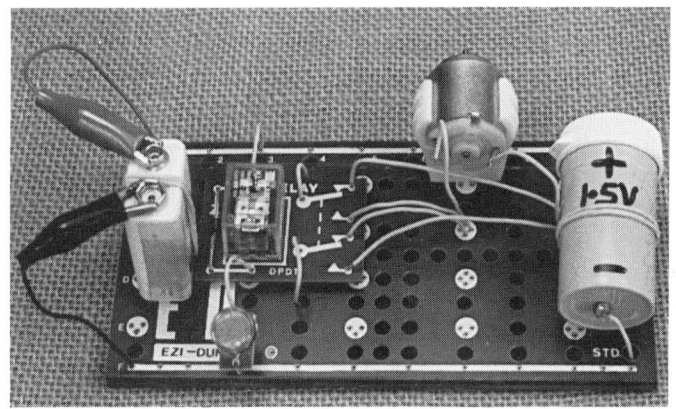

A light–operated motor reversing circuit. The 1.5 V battery (in the container) ensures the motor turns slowly.

HOUSE ALARM

ALARM – LATCHED
ALARM STAYS 'ON' ONCE TRIGGERED

An easy to make alarm, using a **relay**, which **stays 'on' (latches)** once **triggered**. To stop the buzzer sounding, the **battery power** or a **latching wire** has to be removed.

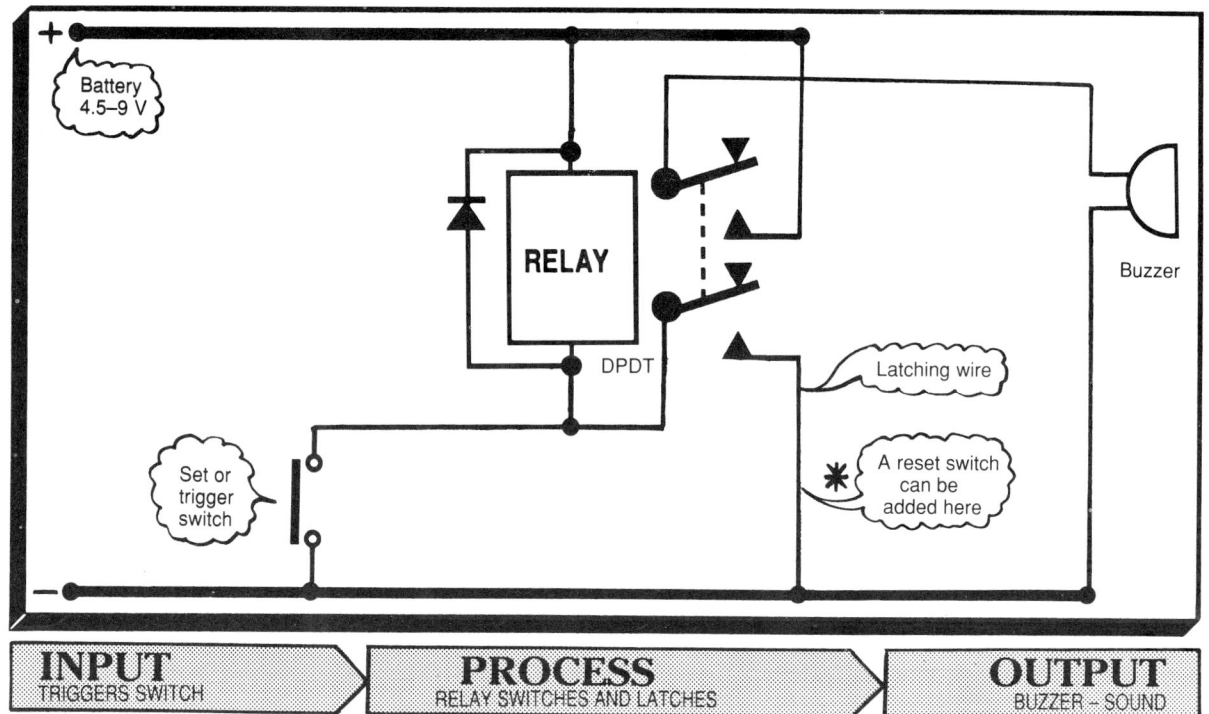

INPUT	PROCESS	OUTPUT
TRIGGERS SWITCH	RELAY SWITCHES AND LATCHES	BUZZER – SOUND

Once **triggered**, the **alarm** cannot be turned **'off'** because the circuit has **latched**, except by disconnecting the battery or **'latching wire'**.

The **buzzer** must be connected the correct way round (ie black wire to negative rail.)

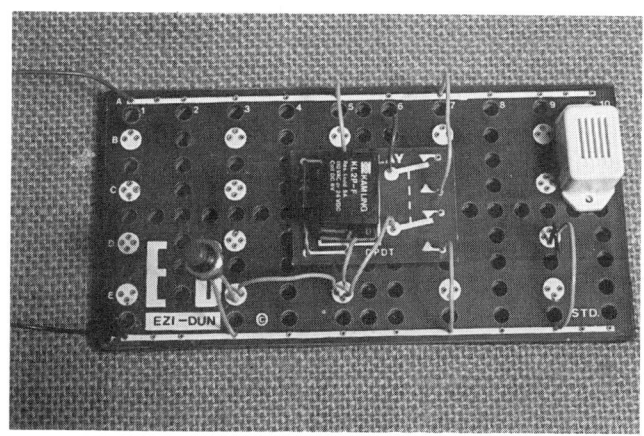

A relay latched alarm circuit. The wires to the buzzer loop through the holes.

ACTIVITIES

(1) Connect up the circuit shown above, but miss out the **'latching wire'** marked. Now what happens when the switch is pressed?

(2) Add the **'latching wire'** marked. Now what happens when the switch is pressed?

(3) Add a **reset switch** in **series** with the **latching wire**. A **push switch** is not suitable but a **reed switch** and **magnet** or a **slide switch** could be used.

(4) Add two **sensing switches** so that either switch could trigger the alarm.

Now . . .

Using the knowledge you have gained, make a **model alarm system** for a **house** with one **door** and one **window** that needs protecting. The **reset switch** must be near the door to allow the user to lock up.

DIVIDE SYMBOL

SENSING CIRCUITS
INVOLVING POTENTIAL DIVIDERS

This page covers potential divider circuit theory needed to help explain how electronic circuits **sense** light, heat, sound, touch etc. Suitable sensors are needed such as an LDR for sensing light and are used within potential divider circuits. A **potential divider** is not a sensor as such but is used to control the effect the sensor has. Make the following circuits and you will get a feel for what a potential divider circuit can do.

The **potential divider** is so called because it is used to split up or divide the voltage as required. The voltage output can be measured using a voltmeter, as shown, or calculated using the following formula:

$$\text{VOLTAGE ACROSS } R_2 = \frac{R_2}{R_1 + R_2} \times \text{SUPPLY VOLTAGE}$$

R_1 = Top resistor
R_2 = Bottom resistor

and

$$\text{VOLTAGE ACROSS } R_1 = \text{SUPPLY VOLTAGE} - \text{VOLTAGE ACROSS } R_2$$

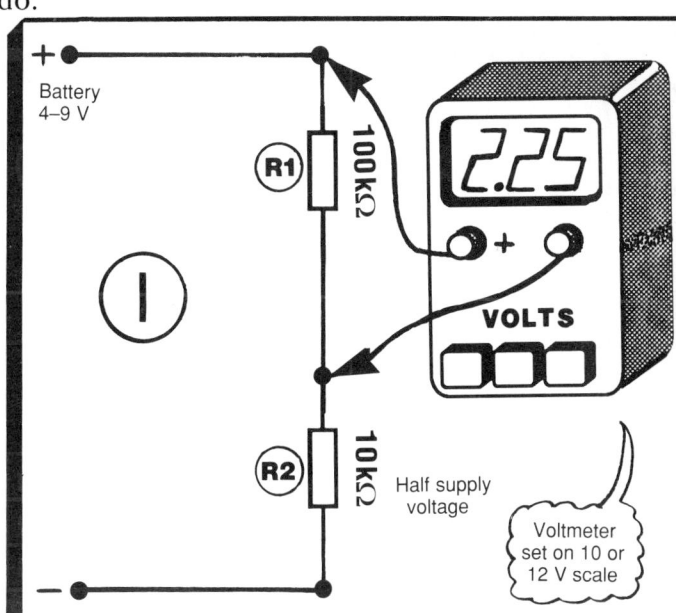

ACTIVITIES

(1) Connect up two 10 KΩ resistors and measure the voltage at the centre as shown in Fig. 1. The voltage reading will be **half** the battery supply voltage. Now replace the top 10 kΩ resistor with a 100 kΩ resistor. How has the voltage been divided up now?

(2) Replace the 100 kΩ resistor just added with a 100 kΩ variable resistor as shown in Fig. 2. Now you can alter the voltage output. What is the maximum and minimum voltage across the variable resistor?

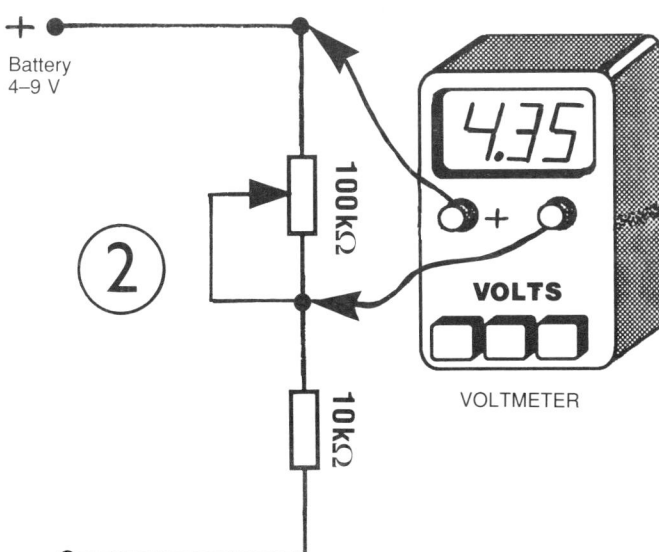

(3) Replace the 100 kΩ resistor with an LDR, as shown in Fig. 3, and notice how the voltage increases as you place your finger over the LDR.

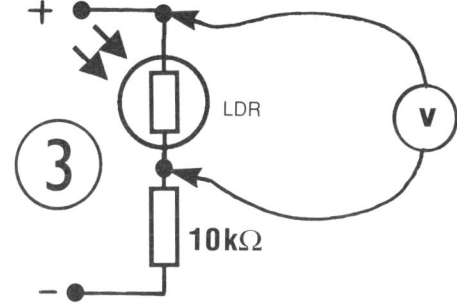

INVERTING

By swopping the resistors, or resistive component, the effect is reversed.
(4) **Invert** the last circuit by swopping over the LDR and the 10 kΩ resistor. Now what happens to the voltage output when your finger is placed over the LDR?
(5) Replace the LDR with a **thermistor**, as shown in Fig. 4, and notice how slowly it changes its voltage when held with two fingers.

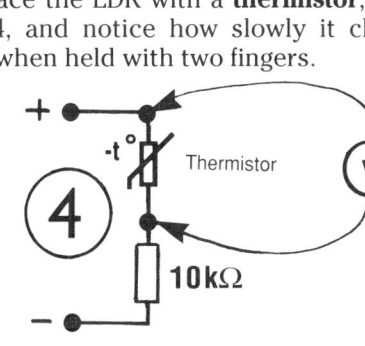

LIGHT/TEMP. SWITCHING

This **one–transistor** amplifier is easy to make but of limited practical use. The **bulb** switches ON when the LDR (light sensor) is covered. If a **thermistor** (heat sensor) is used in place of the LDR the bulb changes in response to **temperature** changes.

It is used to make **automatic street lighting**, **ice alarms** and **heat alarms**.

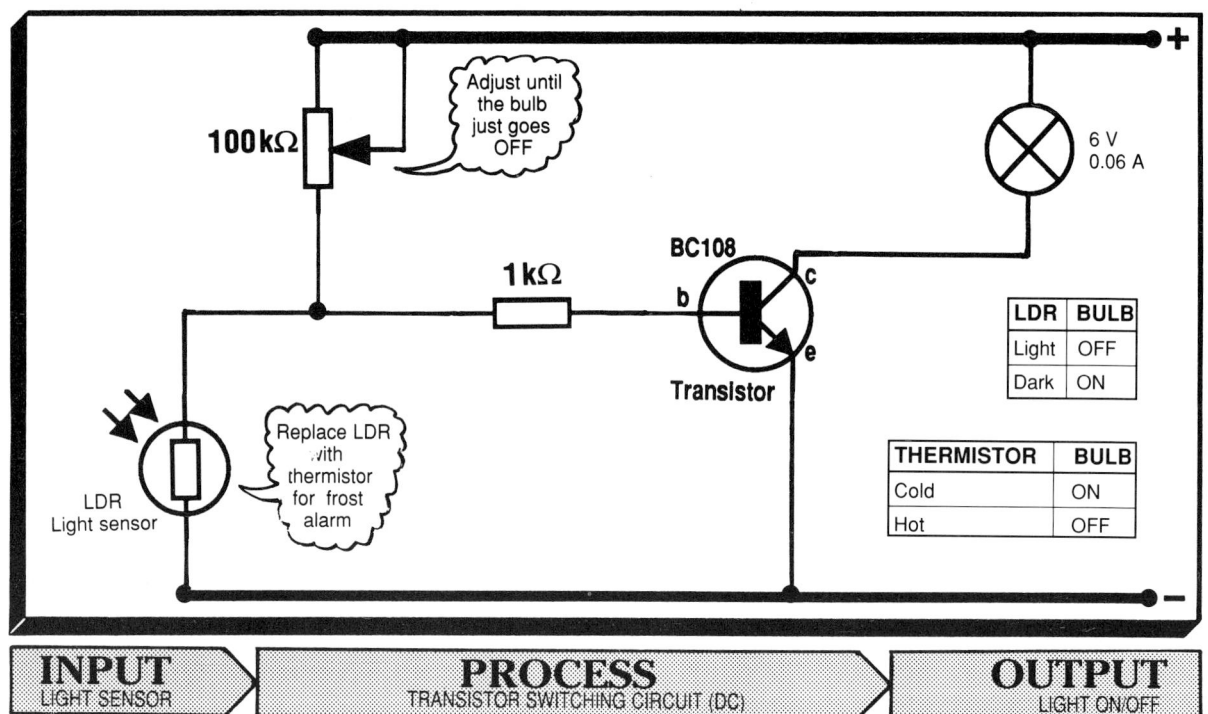

LDR	BULB
Light	OFF
Dark	ON

THERMISTOR	BULB
Cold	ON
Hot	OFF

INPUT	PROCESS	OUTPUT
LIGHT SENSOR	TRANSISTOR SWITCHING CIRCUIT (DC)	LIGHT ON/OFF

The LDR (light sensor) is part of a 'potential divider'. When the light level changes, the LDR's resistance alters which affects the voltage at the base (b) of the transistor. The transistor turns ON when the base voltage is above 0.6 V. The **thermistor** may need heating up with a soldering iron or similar.

ACTIVITIES

(1) Connect up the circuit shown and alter the 100 kΩ **variable resistor** until the bulb just goes OFF. The bulb should go OUT when you place your hand over the LDR. How far away can you make it work?

(2) Replace the **bulb** with a **buzzer**. How far away from the LDR can the circuit be controlled?

(3) **Ice alarm** – Return the **bulb** as in the drawing and connect up a **thermistor** in place of the LDR. Adjust the circuit so the **bulb** is fairly bright, then heat it with your fingers. It will probably not respond very well so heat it up with a soldering iron or similar. **BE CAREFUL.**

(4) Switch the LDR and the 100 kΩ **variable resistor** over as shown at the bottom of the page. Does the bulb now go out when your hand covers the LDR?

(5) Replace the LDR with the **thermistor**. Set the circuit so the bulb is just OFF **then heat the thermistor**.

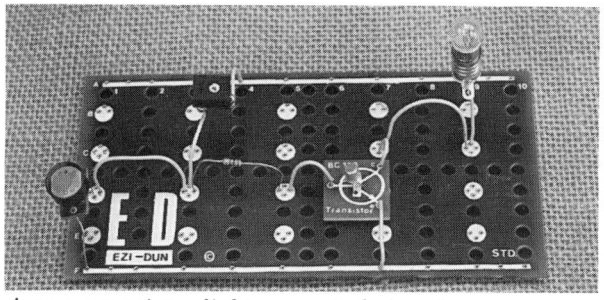

A one–transistor light–operated circuit.

LIGHT (+HEAT) ALARM VARIATION

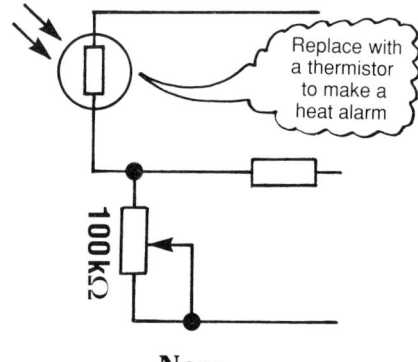

Now . . .

Using the knowledge you have gained, design a game or similar that responds to hand movement.

LIQUID LEVEL INDICATOR

This is a very adaptable circuit that uses two transistors connected up as a **Darlington pair**. It is very sensitive; a finger touching across the sensor plate should make it work. It could be used to make a rain alarm, blind person's 'cup full' indicator, or a bath alarm.

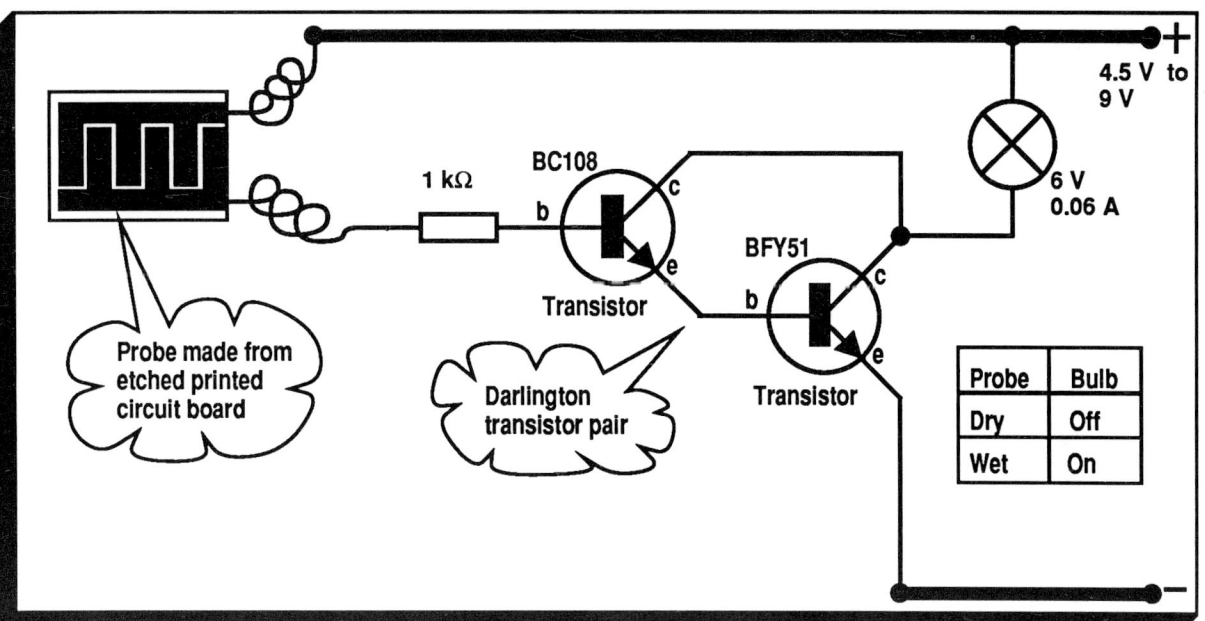

Probe	Bulb
Dry	Off
Wet	On

INPUT	PROCESS	OUTPUT
Water or finger	Darlington pair driver	Light on/off

The input sensor can be as simple as two pieces of bare wire that touch the liquid, or it can be made like the sensor drawn.

ACTIVITIES

(1) Make the circuit as shown using bare wires as sensors if need be. Then test the circuit by touching the sensor with your fingers; the bulb should glow.

(2) Repeat as above but test the circuit by dipping the probes in water.

(3) See if you can imitate rain and make the circuit work – a larger sensor area may be needed.

(4) See if you can adapt the probes to make a 'soil moisture' measuring circuit.

(5) You may now like to try different output devices.

Now . . .

Using the knowledge gained apply it to make something useful of your own choice.

POSSIBLE SITUATIONS

This circuit could be used in:

A hot drink liquid level indicator, suitable for a blind person.

Note: A PCB mask is provided at the end of the book.

Points to consider when designing

Will the choice of materials for the probes be a problem? (Corrosion problems etc.)
Is a different output device needed?
How is a circuit to be turned ON/OFF?
What casing type would be suitable?
What size battery is best to use?
Will it be used in a very wet environment?
How can accidental splashes be prevented?
Will the sensor need to be away from the main circuit?

SENSITIVE SWITCHING
OF BULBS, RELAYS, MOTORS ETC

A sensitive **light-operated circuit** (using a **Darlington pair**), can be used for **alarms**, **countering circuits**, **detection of objects/colours**, a **light searching buggy** (two circuits needed, one for each wheel.

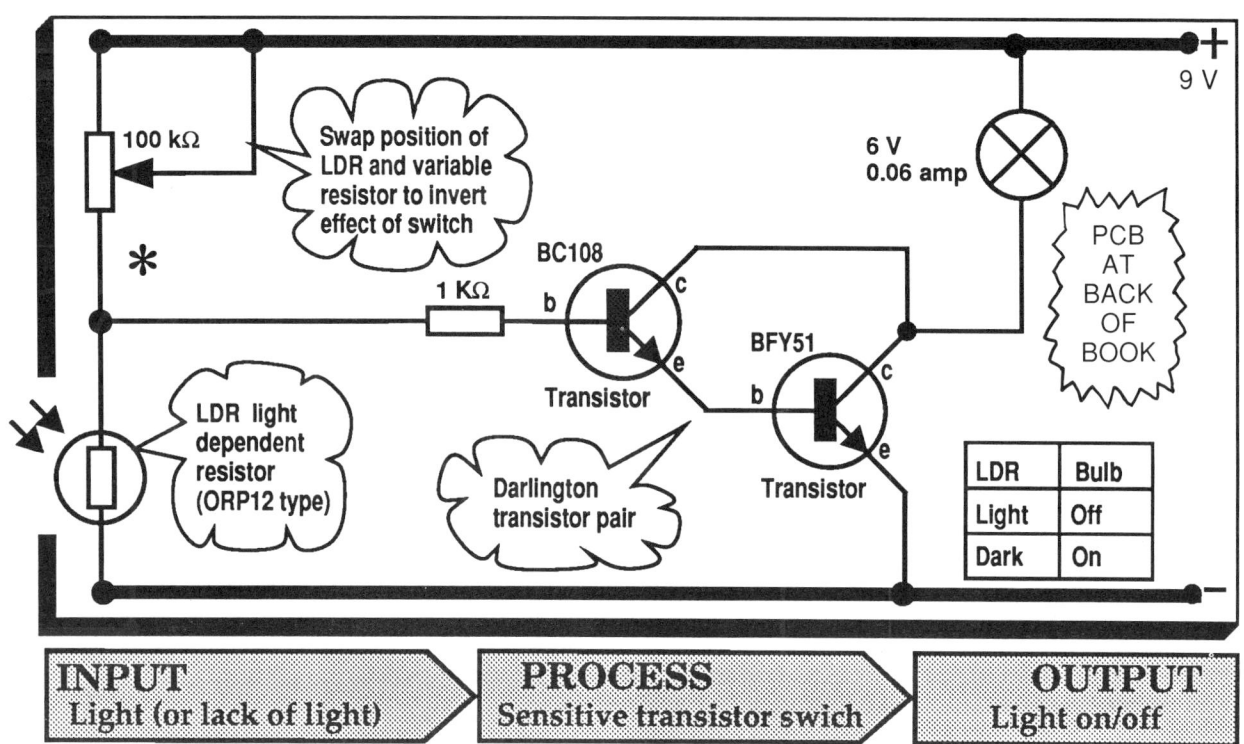

| Swap position of LDR and variable resistor to invert effect of switch |
| 100 kΩ |
| 1 KΩ |
| BC108 — b c e — Transistor |
| BFY51 — b c e — Transistor |
| 6 V 0.06 amp |
| + 9 V |
| PCB AT BACK OF BOOK |
| LDR light dependent resistor (ORP12 type) |
| Darlington transistor pair |

LDR	Bulb
Light	Off
Dark	On

| INPUT Light (or lack of light) | PROCESS Sensitive transistor swich | OUTPUT Light on/off |

The **bulb** in the circuit above comes ON when the LDR is covered. The **100 kΩ variable resistor** will need adjusting until a transistor trigger voltage of about 0.6 V is obtained at ✳.

The bulb can be made to turn OFF by changing the positions of the LDR and the **100 kΩ variable resistor**.

The same basic circuit is being used below to switch a relay. The **relay** can be used to turn ON motors etc. If required, the relay can be made to LATCH ON once triggered (ie it will not turn off even if the light levels change), if the latching wires shown are added.

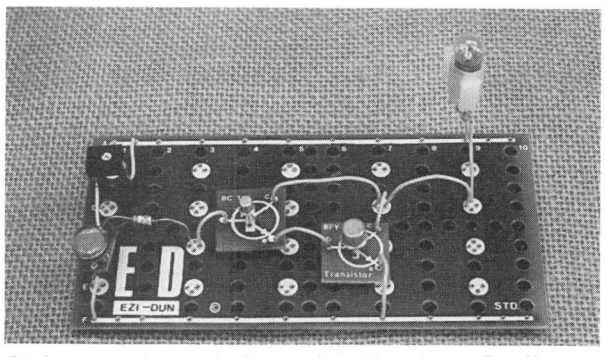

Light–sensitive switching of bulb using a Darlington pair of transistors.

SWITCHING AND LATCHING A RELAY
(IDEAL FOR A BURGLAR ALARM)

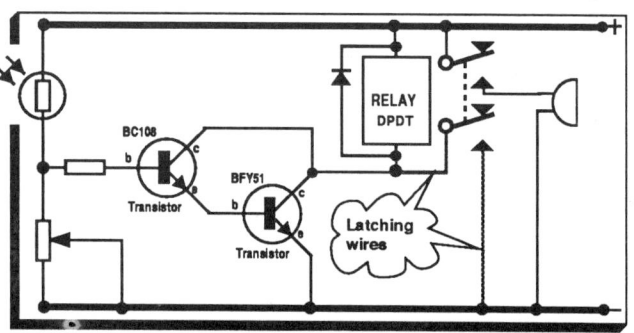

| BC108 — b c e — Transistor |
| BFY51 — b c e — Transistor |
| RELAY DPDT |
| Latching wires |
| + |

ACTIVITIES

(1) Make the circuit above and adjust carefully until it just switches ON. Now place your hand over the LDR and the bulb should go to OFF.

(2) See if you can use this circuit to detect the difference between white and black pieces of paper. A torch could help.

(3) Use a buzzer instead of the bulb.

(4) Switch the LDR and 100 kΩ **variable resistor** positions over. What effect does this have?

(5) Make a burglar alarm that stays ON once triggered (see circuit on right). What situations could it be used in?

TEMPERATURE CONTROLLED HOUSE

VERY SENSITIVE DC AMPLIFIER
LIGHT/TEMPERATURE OPERATED

This useful adaptable **operational amplifier** circuit has a high **gain** of about 10 0000, **two inputs** and **one output**. Its symbol is triangular and it is usually used with two batteries. This circuit only needs one battery.

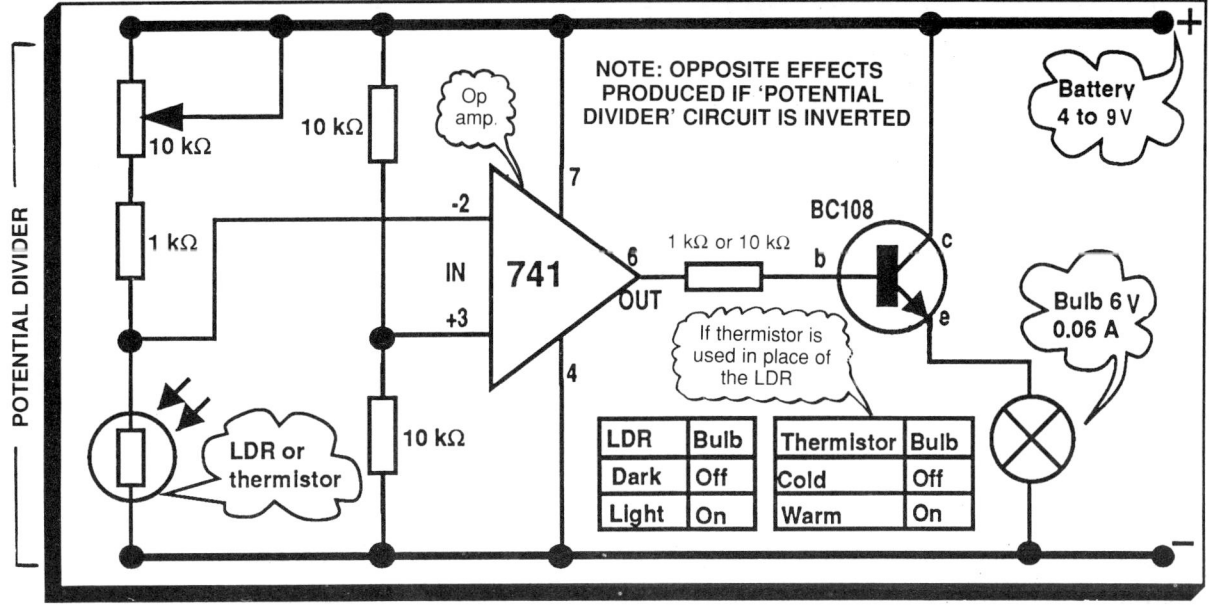

INPUT	PROCESS	OUTPUT
LIGHT/HEAT	VERY SENSITIVE DC SWITCHING AMPLIFIER	BULB ON/OFF

This circuit is very sensitive and can be used in many ways, for example a torch should be able to operate it from quite a distance.

ACTIVITIES

(1) Connect up and adjust the 10 kΩ **variable resistor** so the **bulb** just triggers ON. Place your hand over the LDR and the bulb turns OFF. How far away can you hold your hand and still make it work?

(2) Swop over the positions of the 10kΩ **variable resistor** and the LDR. The **bulb** will now go ON when covered rather than go OFF. This is called **inverting**.

(3) Remove the LDR and replace it with a **thermistor**. Set **bulb** so it just goes OFF. Will it trigger with finger temperature only? **Note: Thermistors** take a little time to cool down.

(4) Replace the bulb with either an **LED** or a **relay**.

A light–sensitive amplifier being used to turn a bulb ON and OFF.

IDEAS

(1) Use the circuit with an LDR to make an **alarm** that can protect a **doorway** or a **display area** by bouncing light back and forth using **mirrors**.

(2) If a relay is used in place of the bulb, a **thermostatically controlled house** can be made. **A car headlight could be used as the heater**.

(3) Design **a garage door opener** operated via the car's headlights.

(4) Make a **colour sorter** to reject dark colours and accept light colours.

PROTECTED DOOR   AUTOMATIC GARAGE   COLOUR SORTER

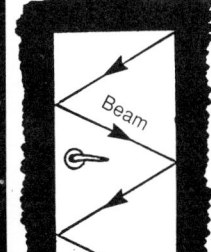
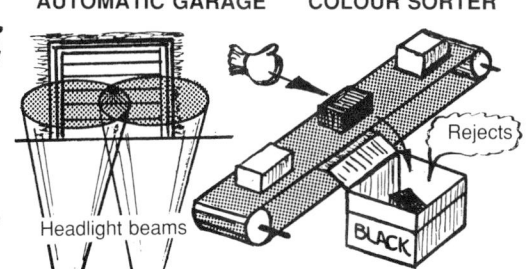

**VOLTMETER CHANGED
TO READ TEMPERATURE**

THERMOMETER
USING AN OPERATIONAL AMPLIFIER

This circuit is very sensitive and can be used either to tell whether the temperature is above or below a **set temperature** or to provide direct **temperature readings** when a 12 V voltmeter is added and converted to read temperature instead.

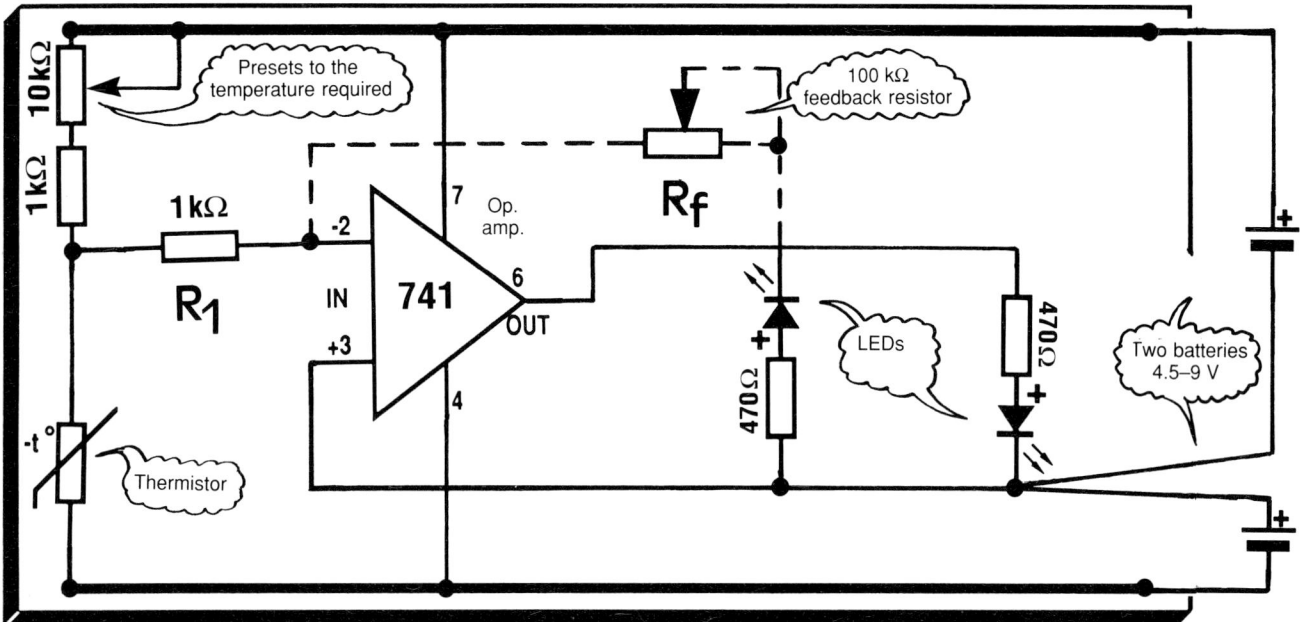

INPUT	PROCESS	OUTPUT
FINGER TEMPERATURE	HIGH GAIN OPERATIONAL AMPLIFIER	LEDs INDICATING HOT OR COLD

The **operational amplifier** measures the difference between **input 3** and **2**. **Input 3** is fixed. **Input 2** can be adjusted above or below input 3's voltage. It is the **difference** between them that is amplified. This means that a **negative** or **positive** voltage can be obtained. This effect can be seen when one LED glows when the voltage is positive and the other glows when the output voltage is negative.

CALIBRATING A HOT AND COLD DETECTOR
Put the **thermistor** and a **thermometer** in a glass of water at the temperature you require it to be set at and adjust the 10 kΩ **variable resistor** so the LEDs are just switching over. **Note**: Protect the thermistor from the water by covering it in a polythene bag before placing in water.

A voltmeter set at 12 V can be calibrated to read the temperature when connected across one of the LEDs.

USING A FEEDBACK RESISTOR
The sensitivity of the circuit is too great for most practical uses, so a negative **feedback resistor** or variable resistor can be added. This can then be adjusted until the reduction in sensitivity you require is obtained. The formula is given below:

$$\text{Voltage Gain} = \frac{R_f}{R_1}$$

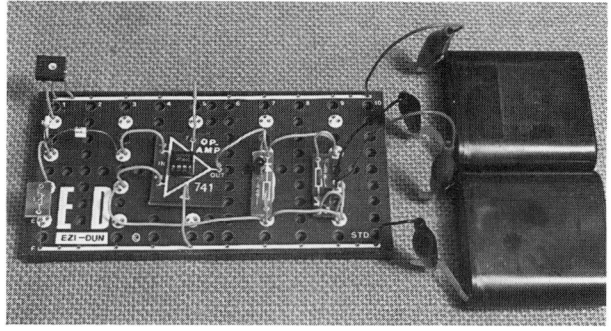

A sensitive thermometer circuit made using a 741 operational amplifier chip. Two batteries are required as shown.

ACTIVITIES

(1) Connect up the circuit as shown above, without the **feedback resistor**, using **two** batteries! Adjust the variable resistor until the LEDs are set at the 'switch over' point. This is difficult due to the circuit gain and sensitivity.

(2) Add a voltmeter across one of the LEDs and observe the effect when the thermistor is touched.

(3) Reduce the circuit's high **gain** by adding the 100 kΩ **feedback resistor** and adjust it so the voltmeter needle moves slowly.

(4) Calibrate the circuit with or without the meter, to indicate 37°C (blood temperature).

LIGHT FOLLOWER

Make a **light-seeking buggy** or adapt it to make a **white line follower**. The two LDRs are its 'eyes'. They sense which way the light is coming from rather like human ears can tell which way sound is coming from.

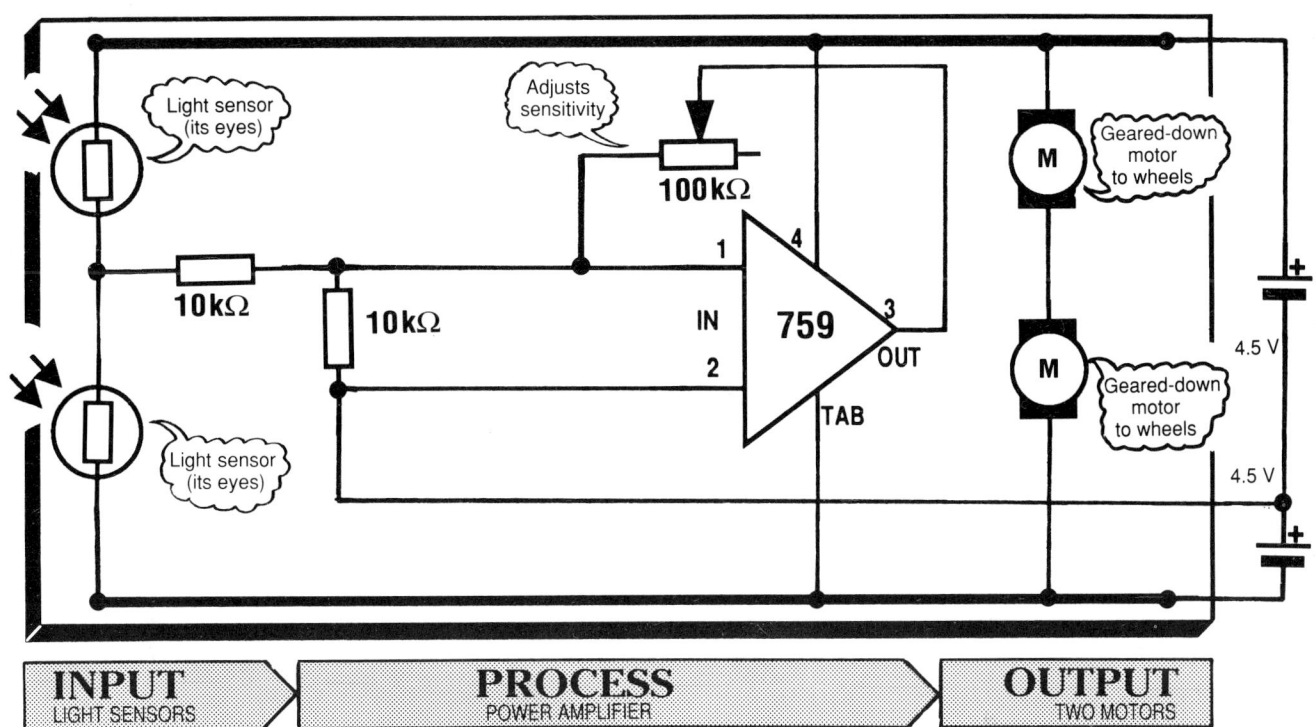

INPUT	PROCESS	OUTPUT
LIGHT SENSORS	POWER AMPLIFIER	TWO MOTORS

The high power **759 operational amplifier** is powerful enough to operate small **DC motors** directly as shown. Two batteries (4.5 V) are needed. The 100 kΩ variable resistor adjusts the circuit's sensitivity.

A light–following buggy. It needs geared–down motors to work effectively.

ACTIVITIES

(1) Assemble the circuit as shown and test it before fixing the wheels underneath the board.
(2) Once the circuit is working properly, make the buggy part by adding an extra piece at the back to place the batteries on and fix the wheels underneath the **ED board** or similar. A caster wheel is also needed at the back under the batteries.
(3) Test it out in a dark place, using a torch, then make alterations to the position of the LDRs and alter the 100 kΩ variable resistor, observing improvements made.

Now . . .

Using the knowledge gained, you could make a **white line follower** by adding a light source and altering the LDR positions.

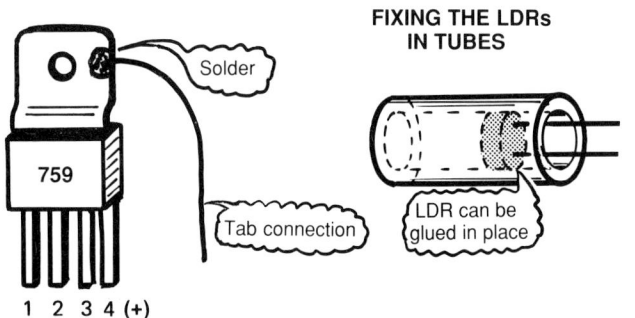

FIXING THE LDRs IN TUBES

LDR can be glued in place

CAR BEING ALARMED

THYRISTOR LATCH
POWERFUL BUT SIMPLE LATCHING CIRCUIT

A simple yet very effective way of making a **latching** circuit that can be used to control large loads. Once triggered, a thyristor stays ON. Operate by a switch or light (second circuit below).

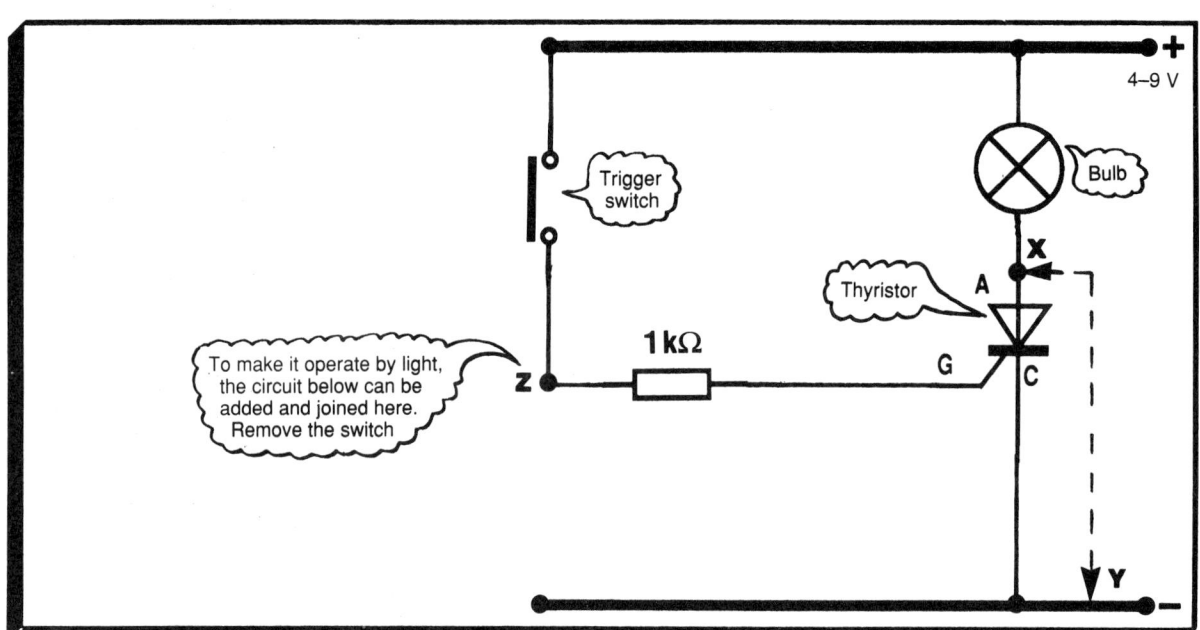

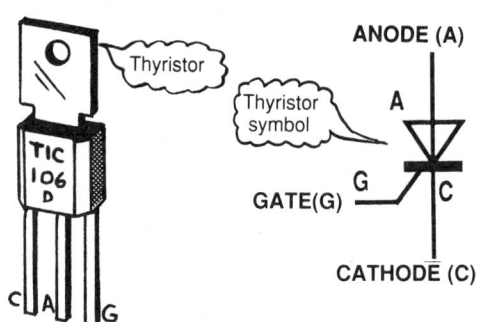

ANODE (A)

Thyristor

Thyristor symbol

GATE(G)

CATHODE (C)

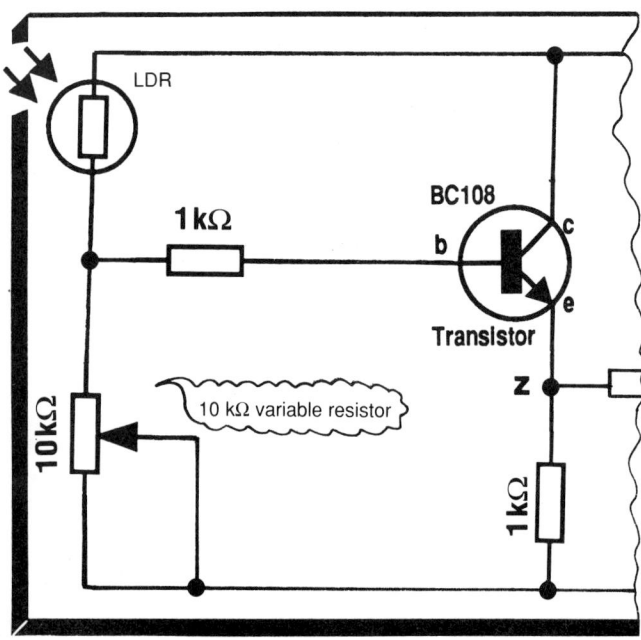

A light–activated thyristor latching circuit controlling a bulb and motor. It is capable of operating quite large loads (up to 4 A).

The **thyristor** used is coded TIC106D (4 A type). Three wires need soldering on the thyristor.

ACTIVITIES

(1) Connect up the circuit shown above. Turn off by removing battery lead or **short across X–Y**. (eg a reset switch).

(2) Add more **outputs** such as two motors across the bulb to show that it can control larger loads.

(3) Remove the switch and replace it with the transistor circuit on the left. It fits on the same board and joins up at junction **Z**. Then set the light level by adjusting the 100 kΩ variable resistor. How sensitive can you make it?

Now . . .

Apply this circuit to make a car alarm.

PLANT WATERER

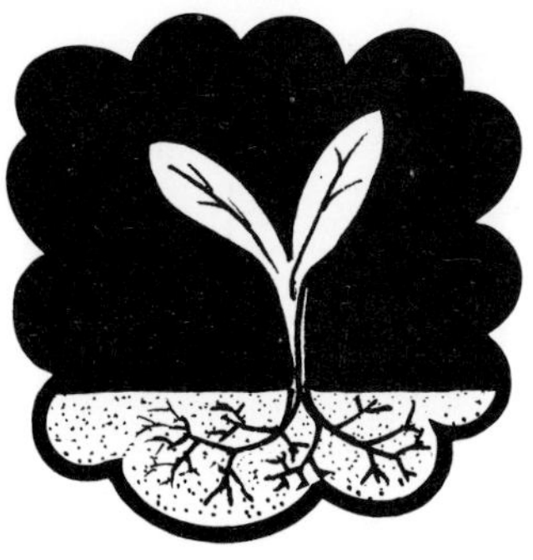

This is a project idea for an automatic plant feeder that senses when the seedlings need more water. It is a practical example of **feedback** in a real situation.

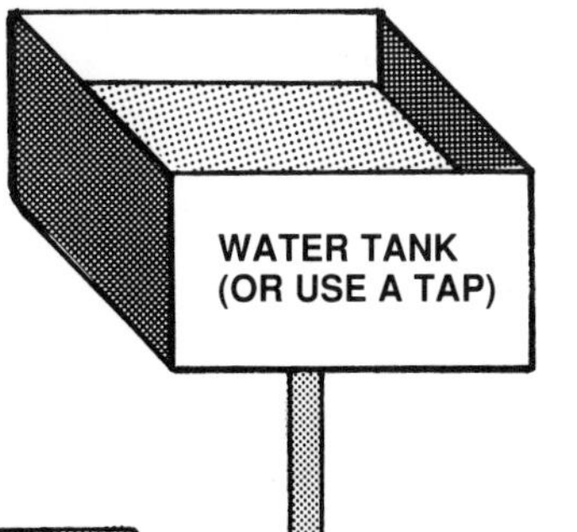

WATER TANK (OR USE A TAP)

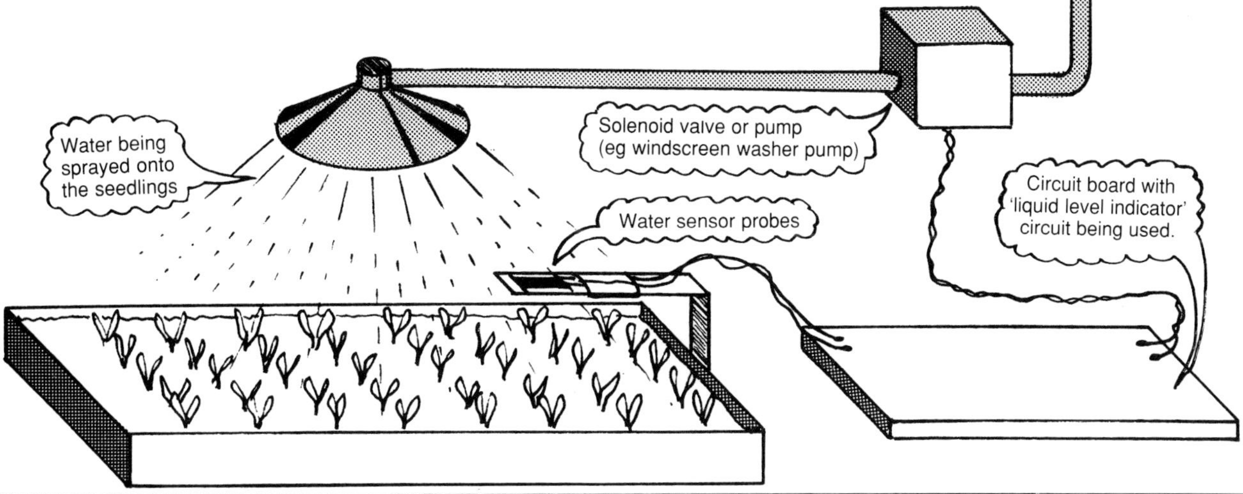

SEEDLING GROWING

Water being sprayed onto the seedlings

Solenoid valve or pump (eg windscreen washer pump)

Water sensor probes

Circuit board with 'liquid level indicator' circuit being used.

AUTOMATIC DOOR/ WINDOW OPENER

Make a door or window open when someone approaches, using a pneumatic cylinder.

Note: The drawing is not to scale and the cylinder's position will need selecting carefully.

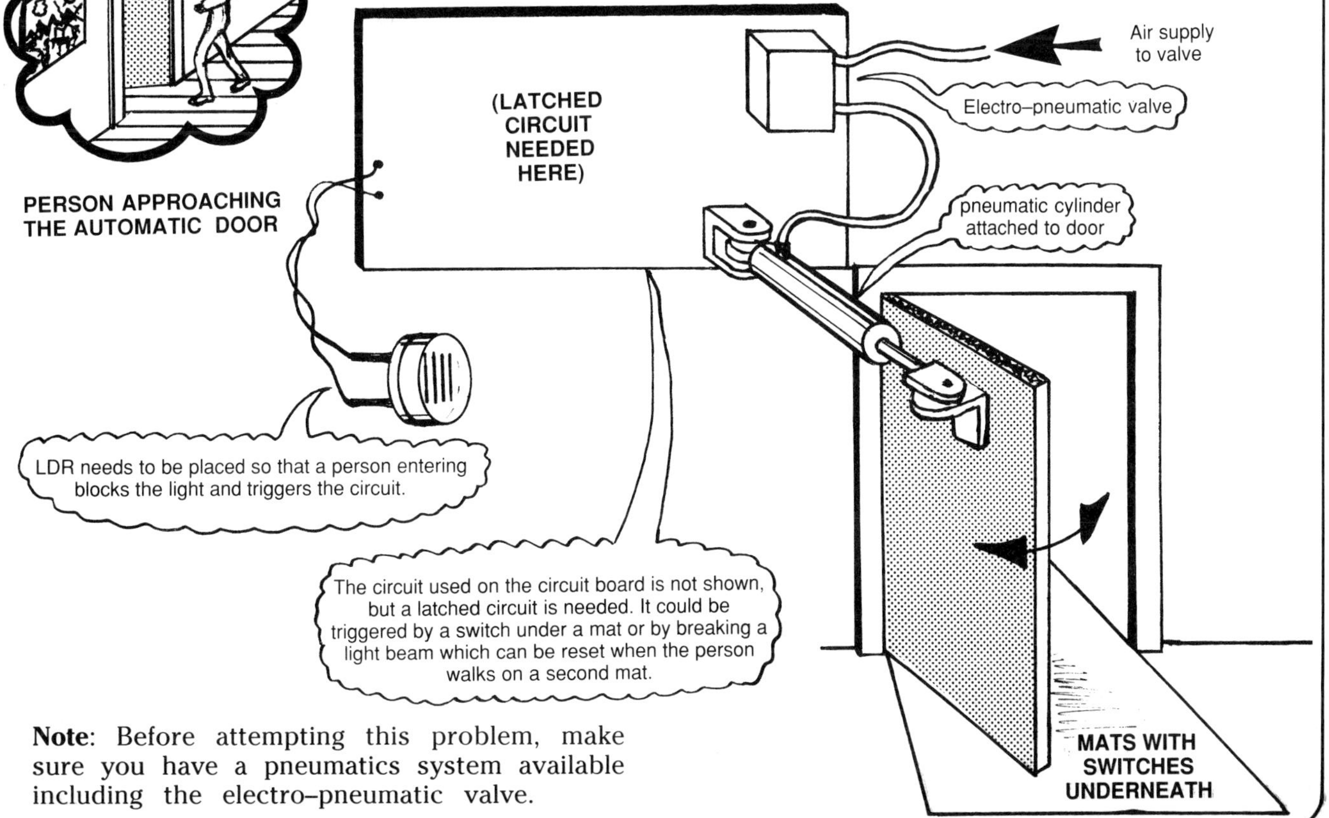

Air supply to valve

Electro–pneumatic valve

(LATCHED CIRCUIT NEEDED HERE)

pneumatic cylinder attached to door

PERSON APPROACHING THE AUTOMATIC DOOR

LDR needs to be placed so that a person entering blocks the light and triggers the circuit.

The circuit used on the circuit board is not shown, but a latched circuit is needed. It could be triggered by a switch under a mat or by breaking a light beam which can be reset when the person walks on a second mat.

Note: Before attempting this problem, make sure you have a pneumatics system available including the electro–pneumatic valve.

MATS WITH SWITCHES UNDERNEATH

THE 'ON' AND
'OFF' POSITIONS

MULTIVIBRATORS
1. ASTABLE (CLOCK PULSE)
2. MONOSTABLE (PULSER)
3. BISTABLE

This page illustrates the **three main types** of **multivibrator circuits** used in electronics. The next few pages provide various examples of practical multivibrator circuits.

1. ASTABLE MULTIVIBRATORS

PRODUCE CLOCK PULSES.

Sometimes called **clock** or **free-running** circuits. Once turned ON, these circuits produce a continuous output of ON/OFF pulses. The ON and OFF time can be altered as required by varying the resistor/capacitor network. They can be used to make music organs and sirens.

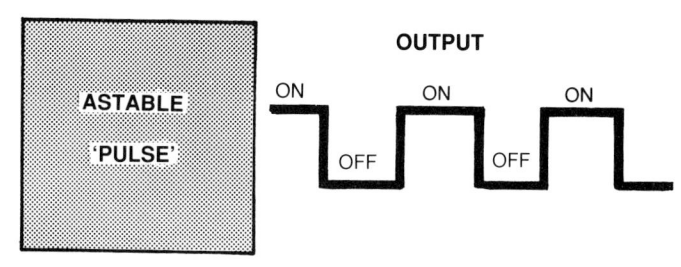

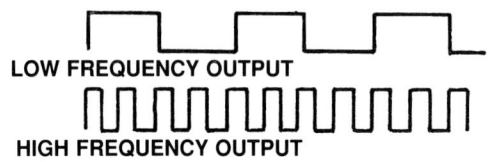

LOW FREQUENCY OUTPUT

HIGH FREQUENCY OUTPUT

2. MONOSTABLE MULTIVIBRATORS

ONE (MONO) PULSE THEN IT STOPS.

Once these circuits are triggered they stay ON for a preset time. They only operate **once** unless **reset**. They can be used to make chess timers, egg timers, photographic timers, museum push button display timers etc.

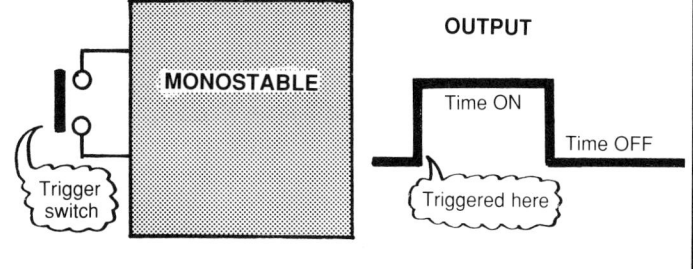

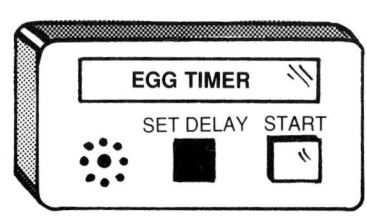

3. BISTABLE MULTIVIBRATORS (OR LATCH)

PROVIDES MEMORY (LOGIC 1 OR 0)

This basic circuit type, sometimes called a **latching** or **flip flop** circuit, provides the basic memory building blocks for **digital electronics** and **computers**. It is called a **bistable** circuit because it has **two** output states, namely **LOGIC 0** (OFF) or **1** (ON). When triggered, the output changes from one logic level to the other. It behaves rather like a table lamp. When turned on it stays ON until it is **reset**. Once turned on, pushing the ON switch again has no effect.

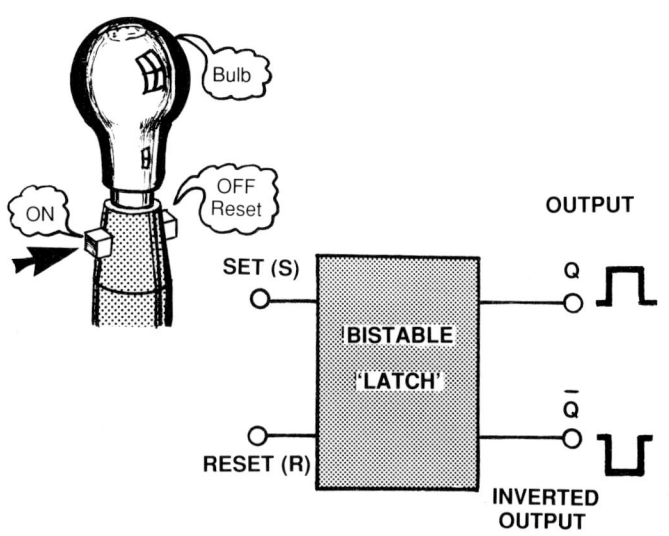

ZEBRA CROSSING

FLASHING LIGHTS
TRANSISTOR–ASTABLE MULTIVIBRATOR

This is a very useful adaptable circuit. The flashing **frequency** and **duration** of the flash can be altered. A **siren** can also be made by replacing one of the bulbs with a speaker, or a buzzer for a weird sound.

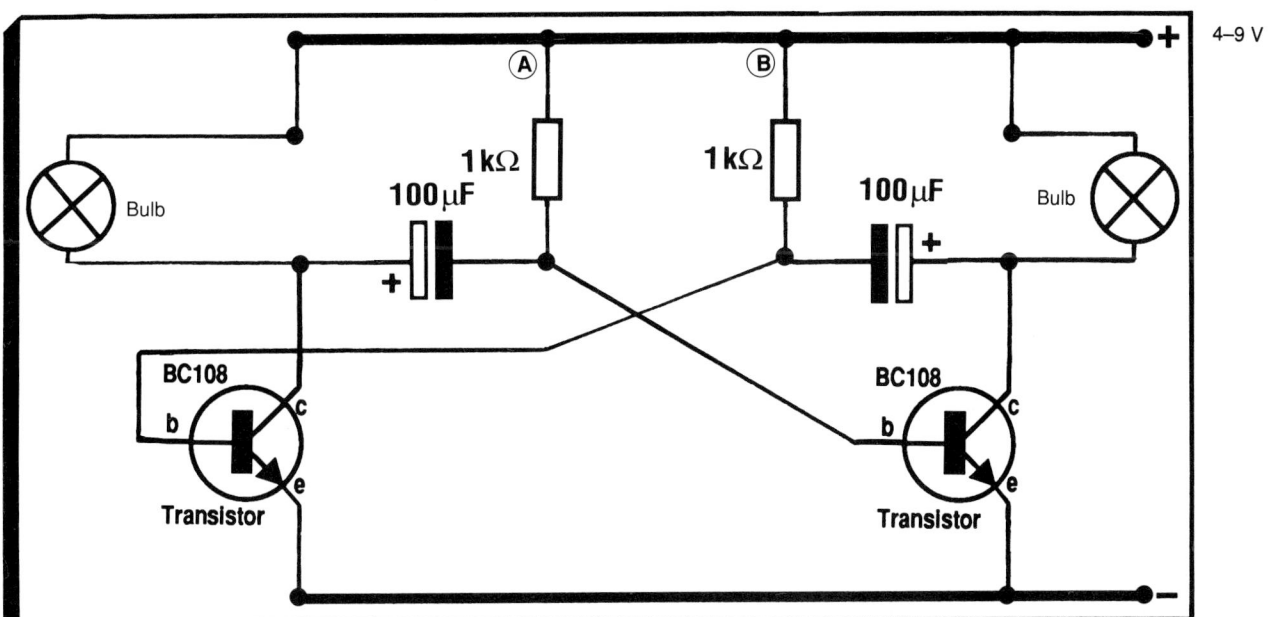

An **astable multivibrator** circuit produces a constant train of ON/OFF electrical pulses. The circuit shown drives two bulbs: when one bulb is ON the other is OFF and vice versa. The circuit shows the effect of altering the resistors and/or the capacitors. A slow flashing rate is produced if two 100 µF capacitors and two 10 kΩ resistors are used. Replace the capacitors with 0.1 µF capacitors and the frequency will be about right to drive a speaker.

It can be used to drive a loudspeaker (60–75 Ω) to make a siren. They are used in place of one of the bulbs.

BE CAREFUL: Connect the capacitors the correct way round.

ACTIVITIES

(1) Connect up the circuit as shown above. The bulbs will flash quickly and evenly.
(2) Now remove resistor (A) and replace it with a 10 kΩ resistor. Do the bulbs flash evenly and at the same speed as before?
(3) Replace resistor (B) with a 10 kΩ resistor. What effect does this have on the flashing rate?
(4a) Place the buzzer across one of the bulbs, in parallel. What sound does it produce?
(4b) If a 60–75 Ω loudspeaker is available it can be used instead of a buzzer.

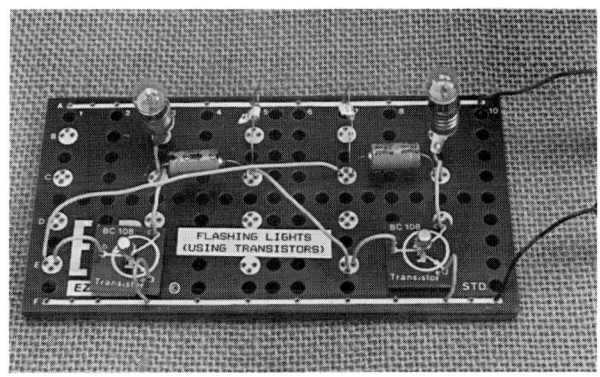

A two–transistor astable – used to flash lights ON and OFF.

Now . . .

From what you have learned you should be able to vary the sound or flashing rate as required by either replacing the resistors with a variable resistor or altering the capacitors.

IDEAS

FLICKERING FIREPLACE

BURGLAR ALARM

A FUN TOY

FLASHER OR SIREN
METRONOME, FISHING HELP OR AS A PULSER

This circuit is very versatile and can be adapted to make all sorts of projects that need either a small flashing light or a circuit that produces a sound. The flashing can easily be altered.

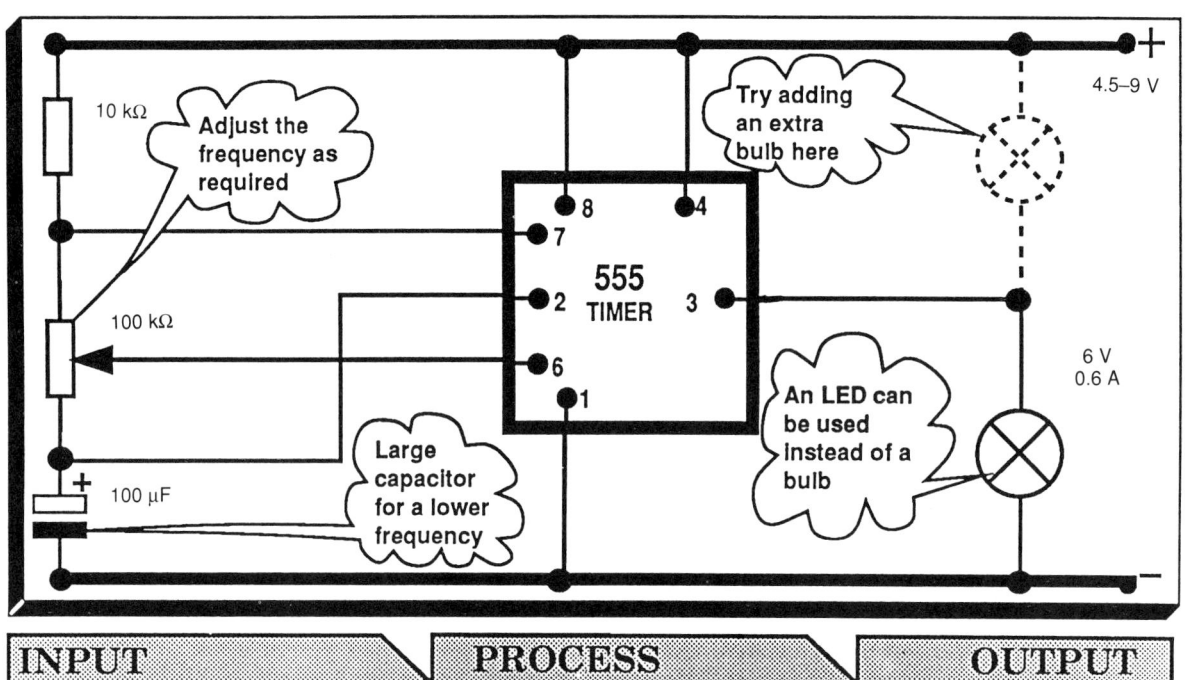

| INPUT Timing components | PROCESS Specialist timer chip | OUTPUT Light on/off |

The 555 timer chip as shown connected up in its **astable**, **free running** or **clock** mode. It is continually switching ON and OFF.

When a large capacitor (eg 100 µF) is used, the bulb will flash slowly. A small capacitor (eg a 1 or 0.1 µF) will make the bulb flash so fast it will appear to be on all the time. This effect can be heard rather than seen if the bulb is replaced with a 10 µF capacitor and a speaker (as shown on the next page). The frequency of oscillation can also be varied by adjusting the 100 kΩ variable resistor.

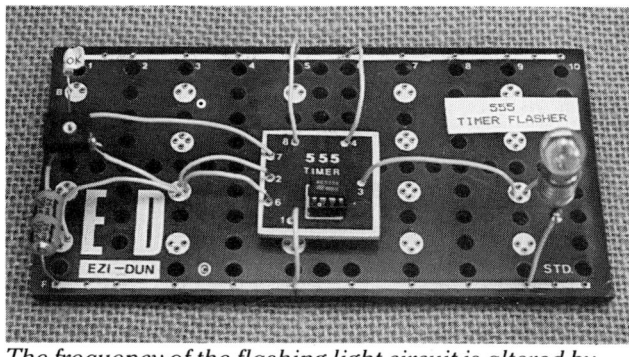

The frequency of the flashing light circuit is altered by adjusting the variable resistor.

ACTIVITIES

(1) Connect up as shown and alter the variable resistor. What happens?

(2) Change the 100 µF capacitor for a smaller one. What happens to the bulb?

(3) Add a second bulb (or LED) as indicated by the dotted line. What happens?

(4) If you have a 30–80 Ω speaker and a 10 µF capacitor, convert the circuit to make a sound (see next page for connections). What sort of sounds can be made?

Now . . .

Using the knowledge gained above to design and make one of the following.

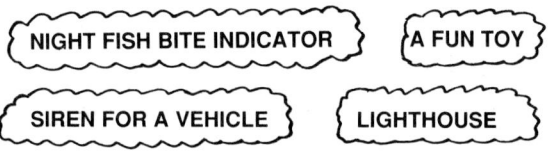

Note: This circuit can also be used as a **pulser** to drive logic circuits etc.

MUSIC ORGAN
HAVE FUN PLAYING YOUR OWN MUSIC

A simple **electronic organ** that can easily be made using a 555 timer chip. More keys can be added if required. The 100 kΩ preset resistors are used to tune the four organ keys.

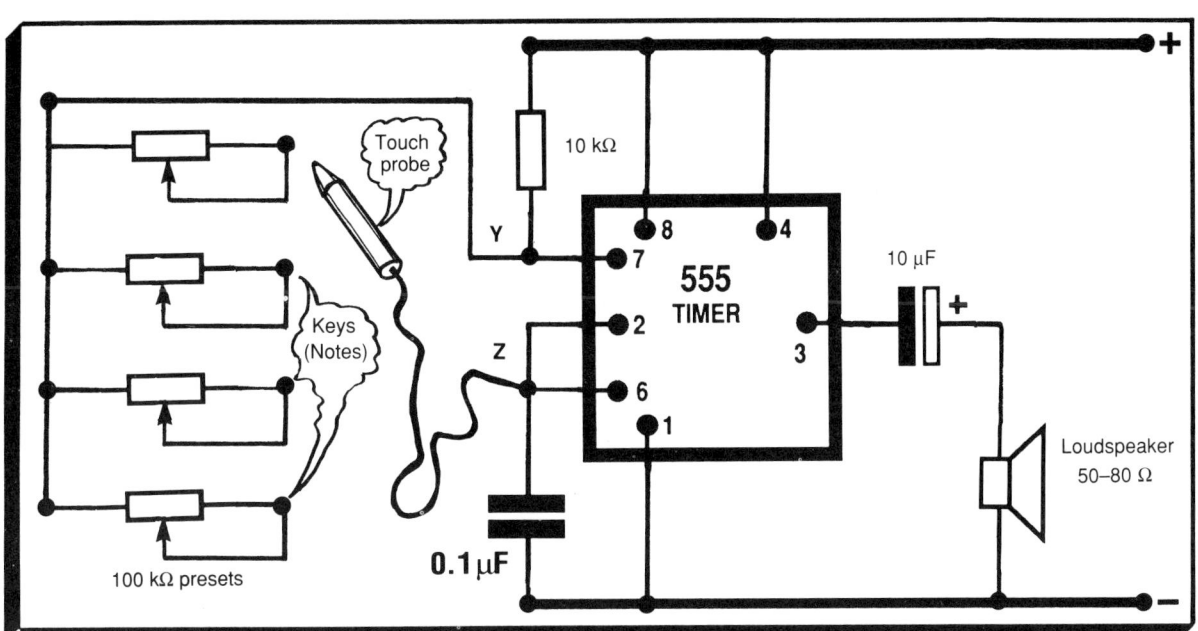

Touch probe

Keys (Notes)

10 kΩ

555 TIMER

10 µF

Loudspeaker 50–80 Ω

100 kΩ presets

0.1 µF

INPUT	PROCESS	OUTPUT
KEYS TO TOUCH	CLOCK CIRCUIT PRODUCING PULSES	SOUND

ACTIVITIES

(1) Assemble the circuit as shown. Use the probe to touch the keys then tune it to get four musical notes.

(2) Replace the 0.1µF capacitor with a 0.01 µF capacitor and observe the difference.

(3) Get a nursery rhyme music book or similar and play a tune.

Now . . .

Make a separate **keyboard** that could replace the four keys on the EZI–DUN board. It will need to join the rest of the circuit at points Y and Z. It is best to have an **octave** of notes, the eight notes being C, D, E, F, G, A, B and C as shown below. It can be tuned by ear or use an **oscilloscope** as shown to measure the frequency using a **microphone**.

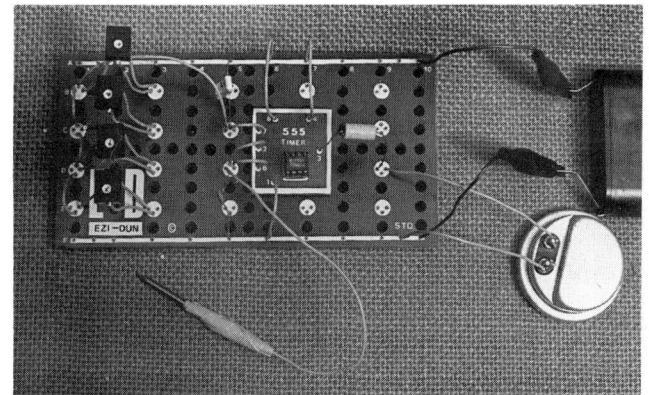

A model of an electronic organ. A more useful organ would have at least eight 100 kΩ presets (to make an octave).

ONE OCTAVE ON THE KEYBOARD

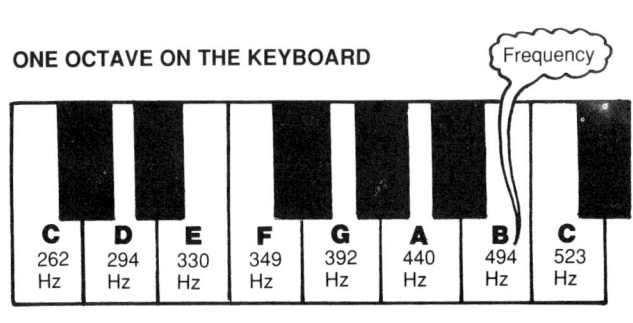

C	D	E	F	G	A	B	C
262 Hz	294 Hz	330 Hz	349 Hz	392 Hz	440 Hz	494 Hz	523 Hz

Frequency

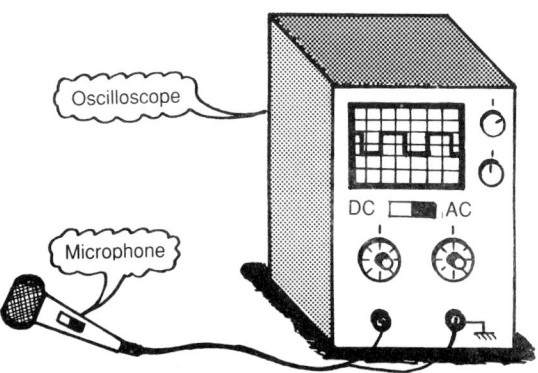

Oscilloscope

DC   AC

Microphone

HORN RECORD PLAYER

GOOD MOTOR CONTROL

Good motor control is obtained by **pulsing** an ordinary **DC motor**. The motor can be made to turn very slowly so that it can imitate a clock **second hand** or at faster speeds to drive **model electric trains**, **cars** etc. It is also useful when fine adjustment is needed, under load, such as a **record player**.

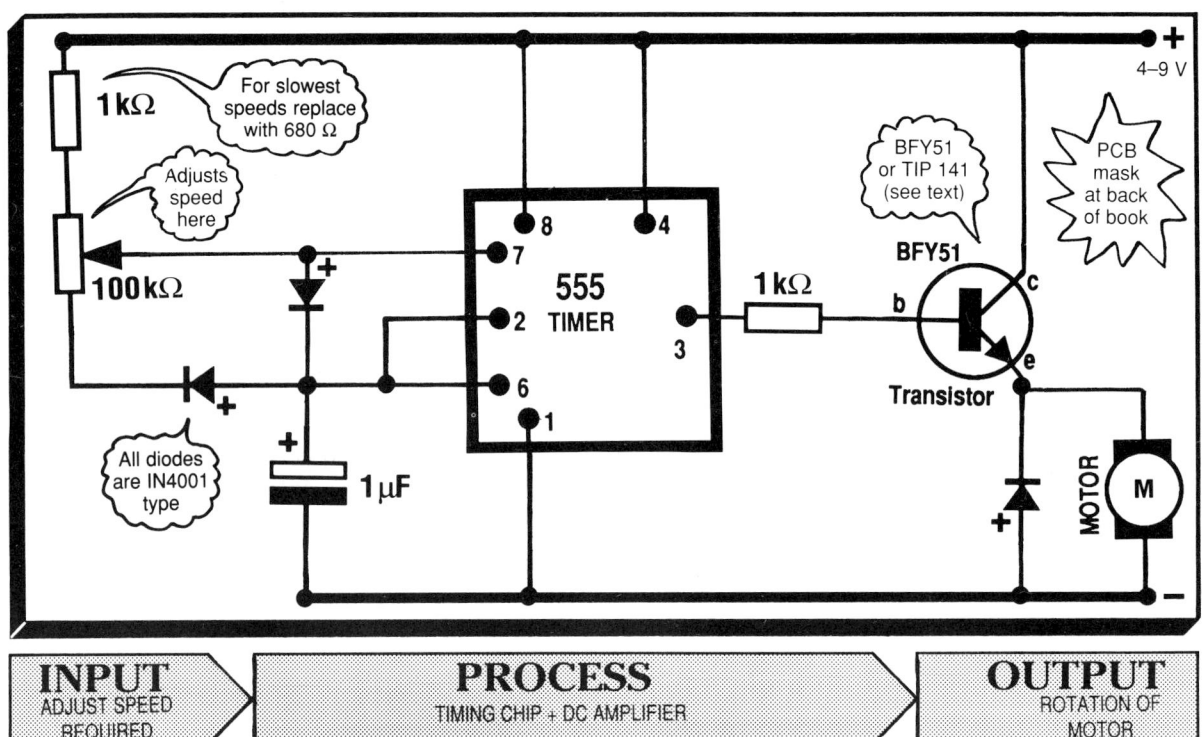

INPUT	PROCESS	OUTPUT
ADJUST SPEED REQUIRED	TIMING CHIP + DC AMPLIFIER	ROTATION OF MOTOR

This circuit can control small motors if a BFY51 transistor is used, as shown, and the speed is slow. **Larger motors** can be controlled using **larger transistors** or a TIP 141 **Darlington pair** which can handle up to 8 A. (**Details at back of book**.)

The speed is controlled by **pulsing** ON and OFF as shown.

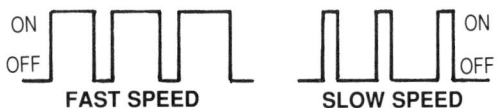

FAST SPEED   SLOW SPEED

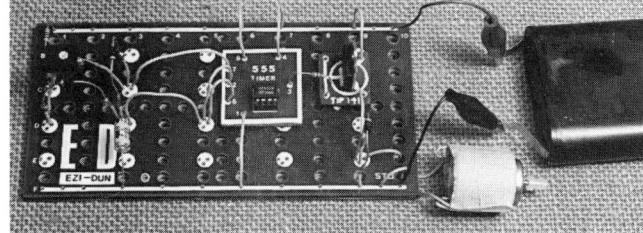

DC motor control is possible using pulses provided by the 555 timer chip. A TIP 141 transistor is used to enable large motors to be driven if required.

Now . . .

Using the knowledge gained, apply it to a problem of your own choice.

ACTIVITIES

(1) Connect up the circuit as shown making sure the diodes are connected the correct way round (the marked end facing the same way as the arrow on the diode symbol). Adjust the 100 kΩ variable resistor and observe the speed changes. What is the slowest it can go? Time it for one revolution.

(2) Change the 1kΩ resistor on the input side of the circuit for a 680 Ω resistor. Does the motor now go faster or slower?

(3) Connect a disc (or gearwheel or pulley) to the motor spindle and then experiment with it to see how much weight the motor can spin around when the disc is held horizontally.

POSSIBLE IDEAS

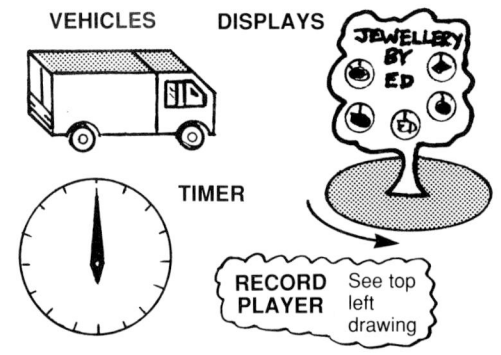

VEHICLES   DISPLAYS

TIMER

RECORD PLAYER   See top left drawing

TIMER
PUSH THE SWITCH TO START DELAY

A very useful **general purpose timer** that switches an LED ON when the **input switch** is momentarily pressed. The LED stays on for a time, set by the 100 kΩ variable resistor. It could be used as an egg timer.

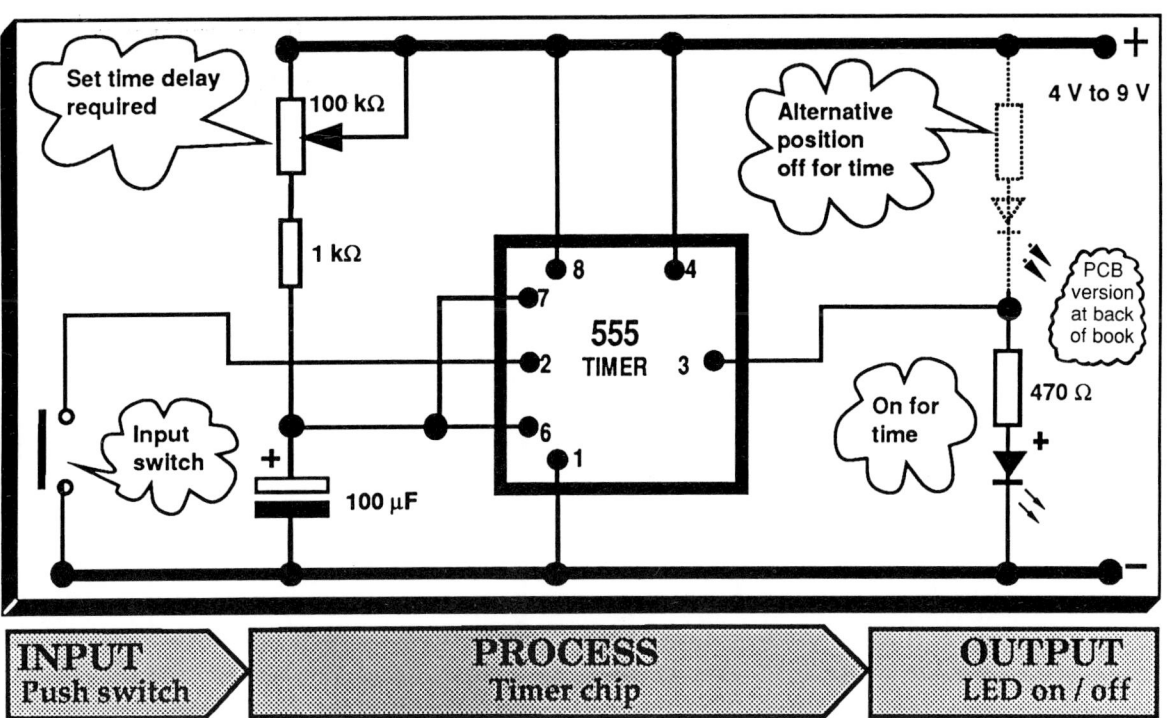

Set time delay required

100 kΩ

1 kΩ

Input switch

100 μF

8   4
555
TIMER
7
2   3
6
1

Alternative position off for time

4 V to 9 V

PCB version at back of book

On for time

470 Ω

INPUT	PROCESS	OUTPUT
Push switch	Timer chip	LED on / off

ACTIVITIES

(1) Assemble the circuit above and then momentarily press the **start switch**. The LED will light for a time and then turn OFF. If the LED stays on for too long adjust the 100 kΩ variable resistor.

(2) Place the LED in the top position, the **correct** way round, and then press the start switch. What happens to the LED this time?

(3) Add a second switch to the circuit.

Now ...
Use the timer in a situation of your choice such as:

KITCHEN   GAMES

TELEPHONE

COMPETITIONS

PHOTOGRAPHY

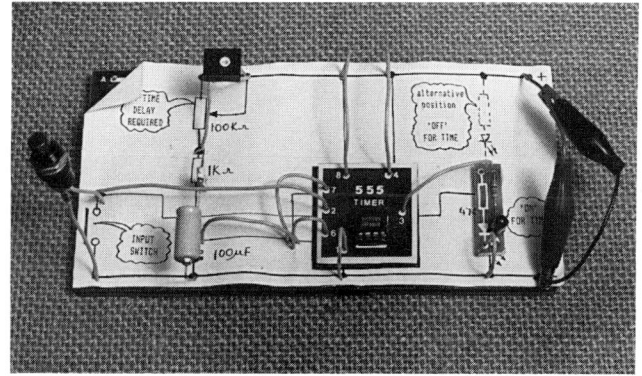

A general purpose timer circuit assembled on a photocopy of the above circuit.

Note: To control larger loads, like motors, a **relay** is needed, see next page.

ALTERING THE TIME DELAY
To extend the time delay , a larger capacitor is required. A delay of up to an hour is possible.

TOUCHING THE
'TOUCH PLATE'
DISPLAY

TIME DELAY
TOUCH OPERATED RELAY UNIT

This circuit is basically the same as the last one except that it is operated by a **finger** touching the **touch sensor**. The touch sensor can be any shape or just two bare wires. The relay output allows large loads, such as motors, to be controlled.

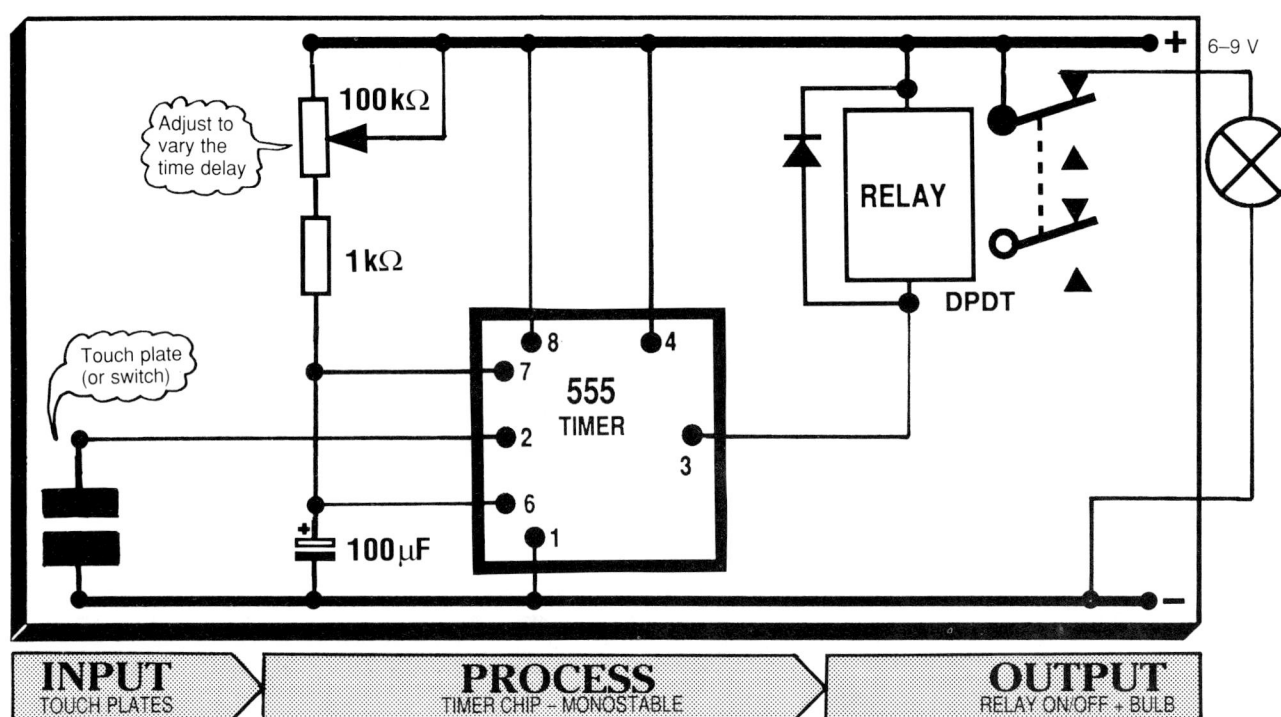

INPUT	PROCESS	OUTPUT
TOUCH PLATES	TIMER CHIP - MONOSTABLE	RELAY ON/OFF + BULB

This circuit is very sensitive but needs at least 6 V to operate the 6 V relay.

ACTIVITIES

(1) Assemble the circuit as shown with an output bulb connected. Touch, using your finger, the **touch sensor**. The bulb will then turn OFF for the time set.
(2) Replace the bulb with a different output such as a motor.
(3) Obtain a time delay of 5 seconds by adjusting the 100 kΩ variable resistor.
(4) Obtain a time delay of 10 seconds by adjusting the 100 kΩ variable resistor and by using a 1000 µF capacitor (not in standard ED kits).
(5) Make a circuit that operates one bulb, which turns ON, and another bulb that goes OFF when the sensor is touched.

Now . . .

Using the knowledge gained from this page, use the circuit to control a mechanical display or a fan which must stay on for at least 5 seconds. (See next page for more ideas).

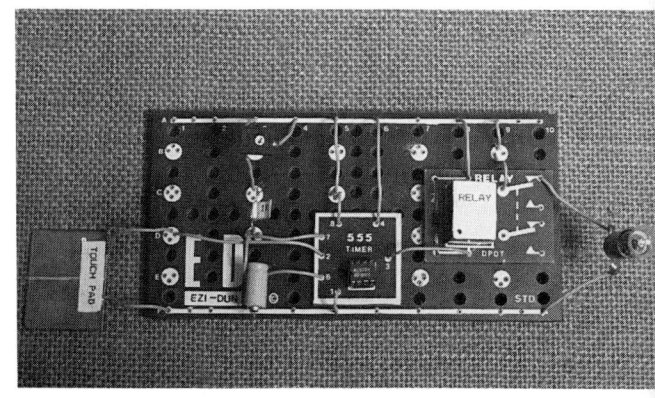

Touch–operated time delay circuit with a relay–controlled output.

DISPLAY IDEAS

Make a **display** similar to the ideas given here using one of the **flashing light circuits** shown on the last few pages.

EYES FLASH

BOAT CABIN LIGHTS TWINKLE

DESTECH

TEXT MADE TO FLASH

? PRESS

LOTS OF FLASHING LIGHTS

SKYSCRAPER LIGHTS FLASH

FLASHING TRANSPORT

Make a **transport model** come to life by adding one of the **flashing light circuits** shown on the last few pages.

FLASHING LIGHTS

FLASHING LIGHTS

FLASHING LIGHTS

A van made from card with a flashing LED on top. A flashing light circuit makes the LED flash.

CAR ALARM OR DISCO

A **car alarm** or **disco effect** can be made using this circuit. It is basically an **astable multivibrator** ('clock' pulses) circuit that turns a relay ON and OFF. The relay then operates the 12 V car battery circuit which can have bulbs and buzzers connected as shown.

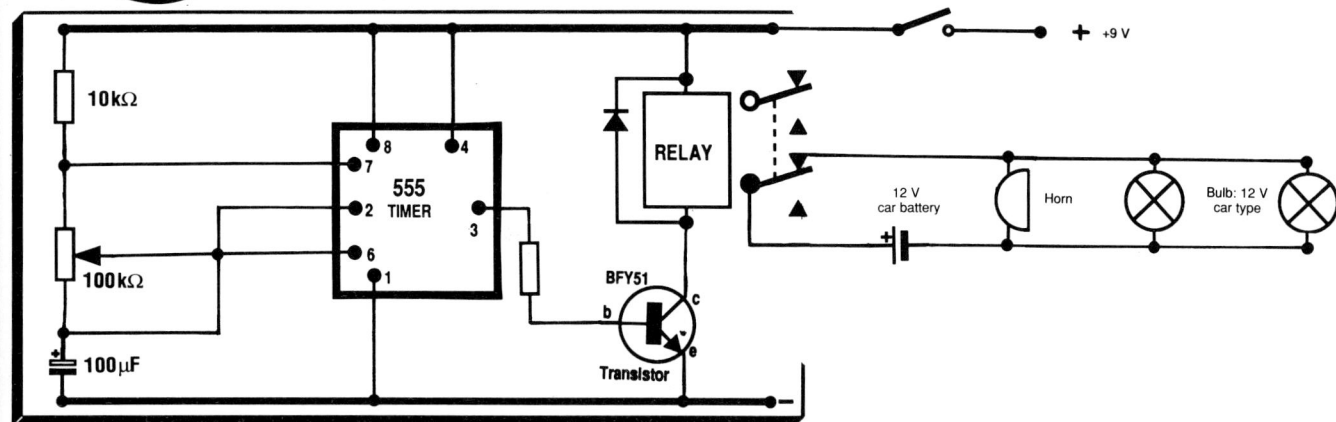

The circuit above turns two 12 V car bulbs and buzzers ON and OFF together. To make it more dramatic, the other relay switch output can be connected to make bulbs flash ON and OFF alternately. Before going to the trouble of getting a 12 V car battery and bulbs, you can try out the ideas using other bulbs and batteries. The flashing rate is controlled by **adjusting the 100 kΩ variable resistor.**

A QUIZ INDICATOR

The **bulb** indicates which team presses the answer button first. It can also be used to find who has the quickest **reaction time**.

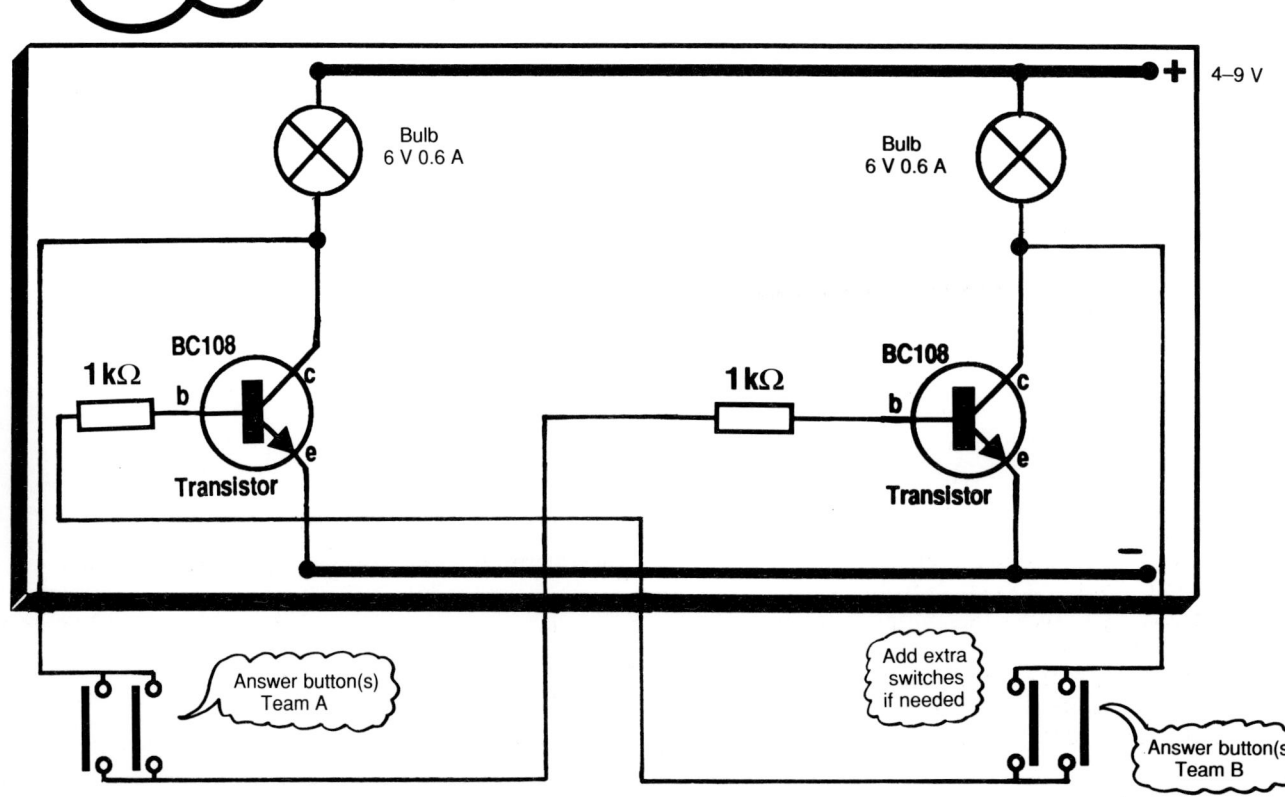

A.C. SIGNAL

AC AMPLIFICATION
INTERCOMS, RADIOS ETC – ANALOGUE SIGNALS

Alternating current is different from the types of current used so far. The diagrams below show the difference between the three main types of current you need to become familiar with.
1. **Direct current** (d.c.)
2. **Alternating current** (a.c.)
3. **Digital**

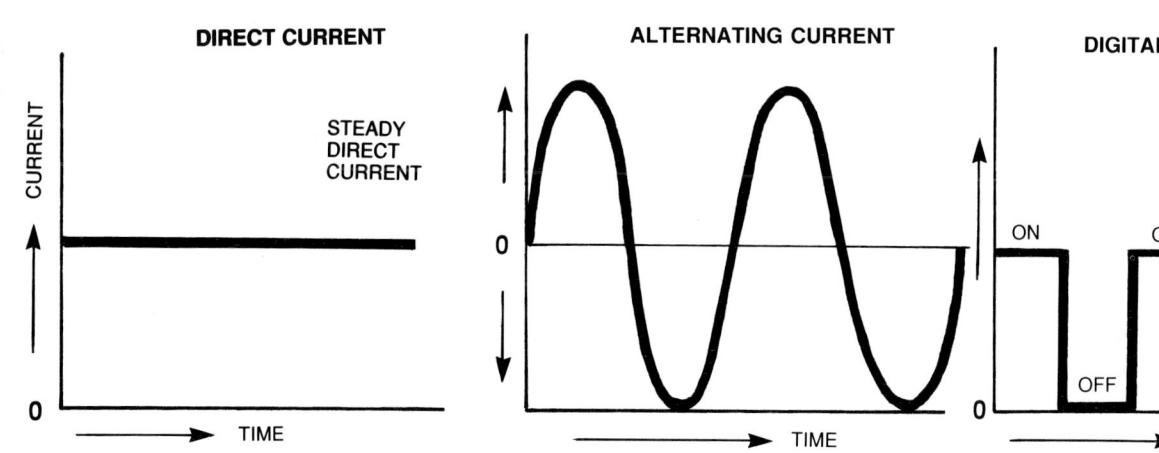

Radios, record players and intercoms need an amplifier to increase the weak **alternating current** (a.c.) signals so that they can be heard when fed into a loudspeaker.

The **block diagram** illustrates how an a.c. signal is amplified. It should be noticed that the wavelength stays the same. The voltage is amplified but it cannot go above the battery supply voltage.

Note: If you have an **oscilloscope**, the waveforms discussed above can be seen on a screen.

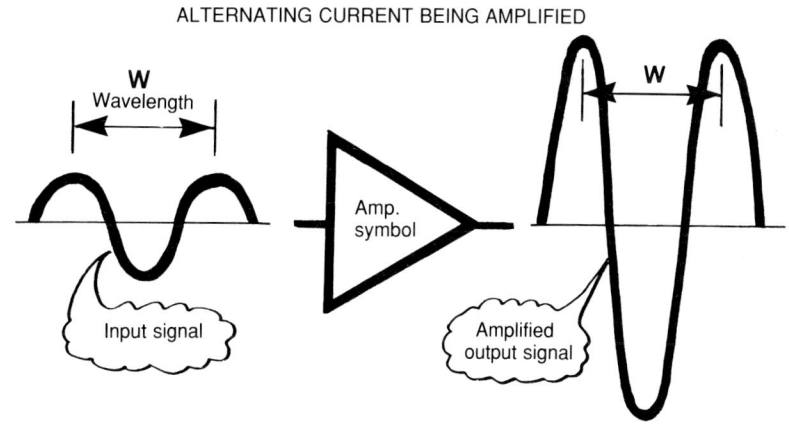

ALTERNATING CURRENT BEING AMPLIFIED

ONE–TRANSISTOR A.C.AMPLIFIER

The **one-transistor amplifier** shown is not very practical because it cannot amplify very much. Practical amplifiers are given on the next few pages.

The circuit uses a battery (direct current) but actually amplifies the **alternating current** (a.c.) input signal. In order to keep the a.c. and d.c. voltages separate, capacitors are used at the input and output stages. The path of the a.c. signal is shown as a thick line.

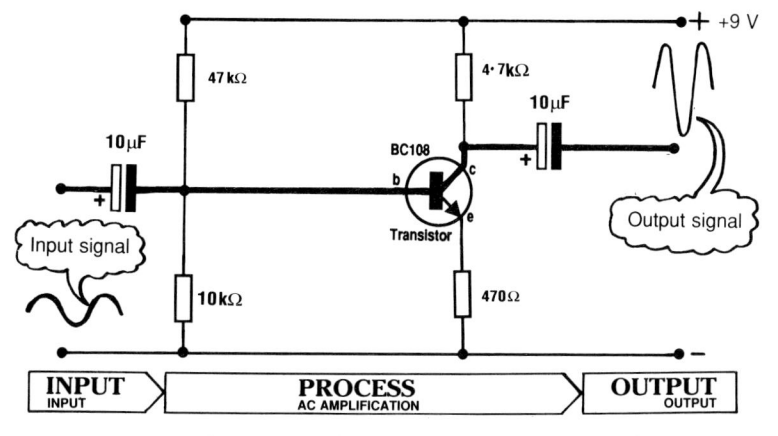

SOUND AMPLIFIER

This is an easy-to-make **sound amplifier** which could be used to make an **intercom**. It uses an **operational amplifier** which can produce sound equivalent to that of a cheap radio. A loudspeaker and microphone are needed. The circuit requires **two batteries** connected up as shown.

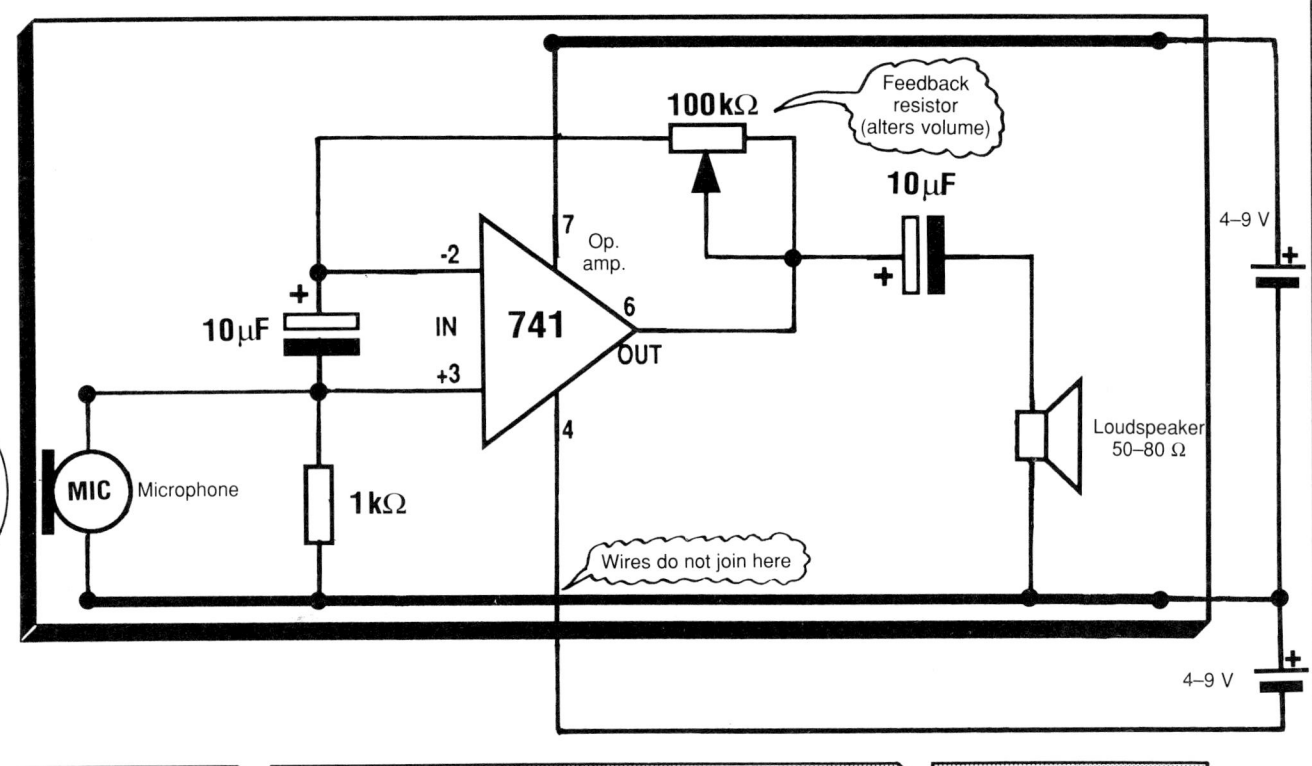

INPUT	PROCESS	OUTPUT
SOUND	OP. AMP. AMPLIFIES SOUND	AMPLIFIED SOUND

This circuit is fun and fairly quick to make but two batteries, a loudspeaker and microphone are needed. Some loudspeakers can be used as microphones. The 100 kΩ variable resistor acts as a volume control by altering the amount of feedbaack the amplifier receives. Use two 9 V batteries for best results. For a **two-way intercom**, use the switching circuit shown on the next page.

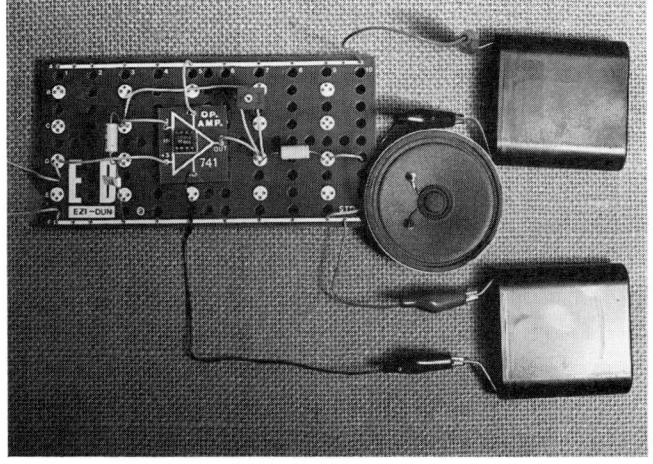

A 741 sound (audio) amplifier.

ACTIVITIES

(1) Assemble the circuit as shown, then tap or speak into the microphone. This is best done with two people because the microphone needs to be quite a long way from the loudspeaker. If not very loud adjust the 100 kΩ volume control. **Important**: Check the two batteries are connected the correct way round.
(2) Place the loudspeaker in different enclosures to improve sound.
(3) Remove the microphone and place your fingers where the microphone was connected (both connections). What strange sound do you get?

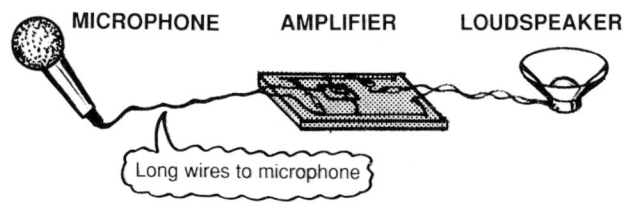

2–WATT AUDIO AMP.

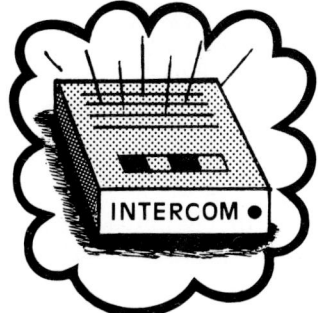

A very useful amplifier can be made by using a specialist LM380 **audio amplifier chip**. It is best to mount it on a piece of PCB.

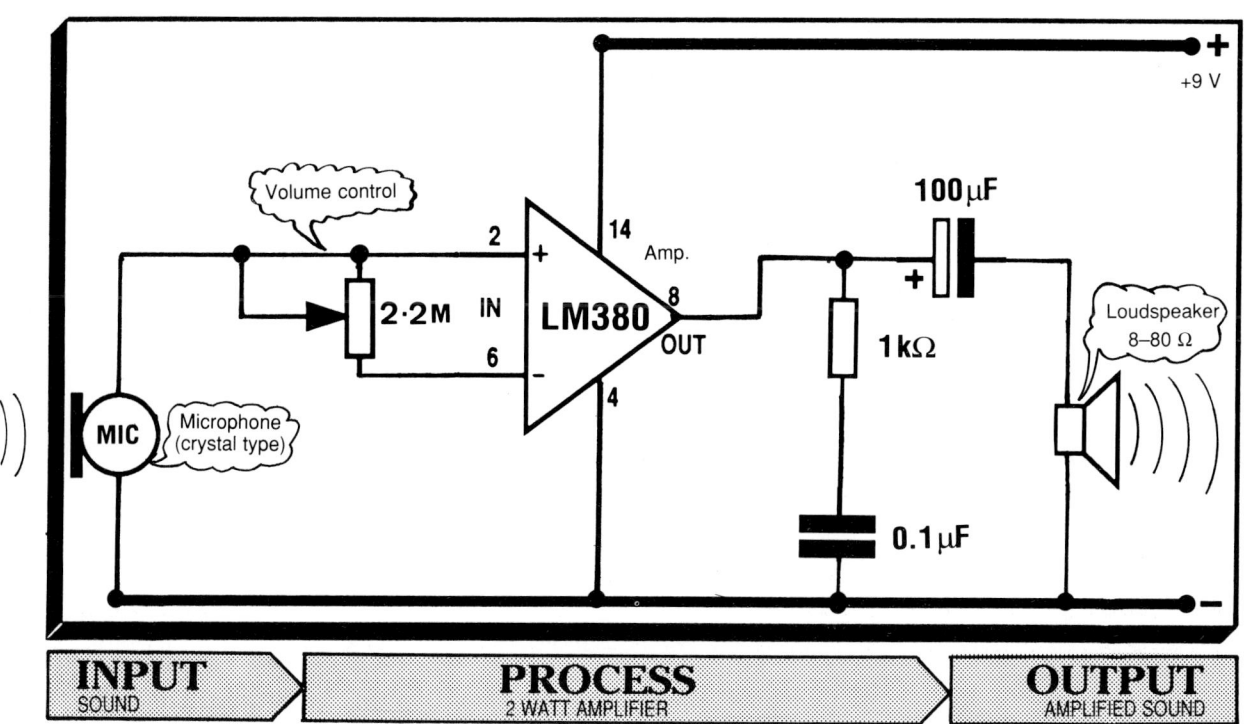

INPUT	PROCESS	OUTPUT
SOUND	2 WATT AMPLIFIER	AMPLIFIED SOUND

The LM380 chip is best mounted on a piece of printed circuit board, details on page called **'using other components'**. The microphone works best if it is the crystal type. (For a two-way intercom use two 8–35 Ω speakers.

ACTIVITIES

(1) Make and test the circuit above. If it whistles, you need to reduce the volume or move the microphone further away. How loud can you make it work?

(2) If available, connect it to a radio earphone socket. Does it sound as good as a bought amplifier?

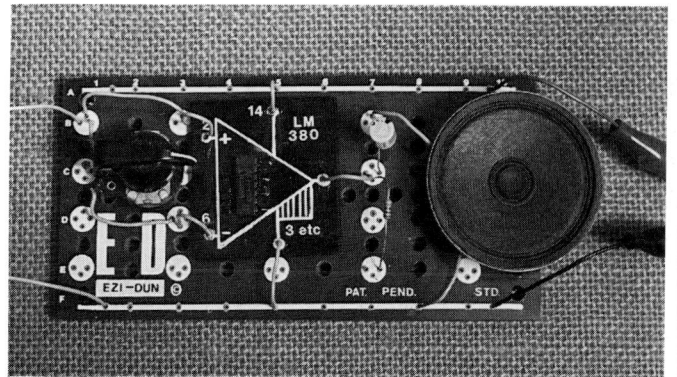

A useful two watt sound (audio) amplifier.

TWO–WAY INTERCOM

The circuit above can be converted into a **two-way intercom** by connecting it up with a **double–pole double–throw switch** as shown below.   35 Ω loudspeakers work as microphones and loudspeakers.

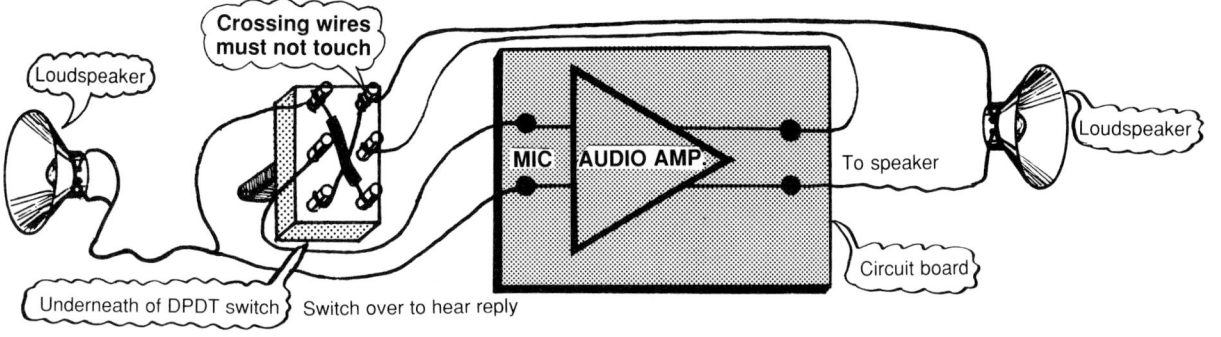

DISCO DISPLAY

DISCO – SOUND OPERATED

This **disco lighting system** responds in time with the music. The input wires need to be connected across a loudspeaker that is producing sound such as a cassette player or radio. An easy way to do this is to connect up to the earphone socket.

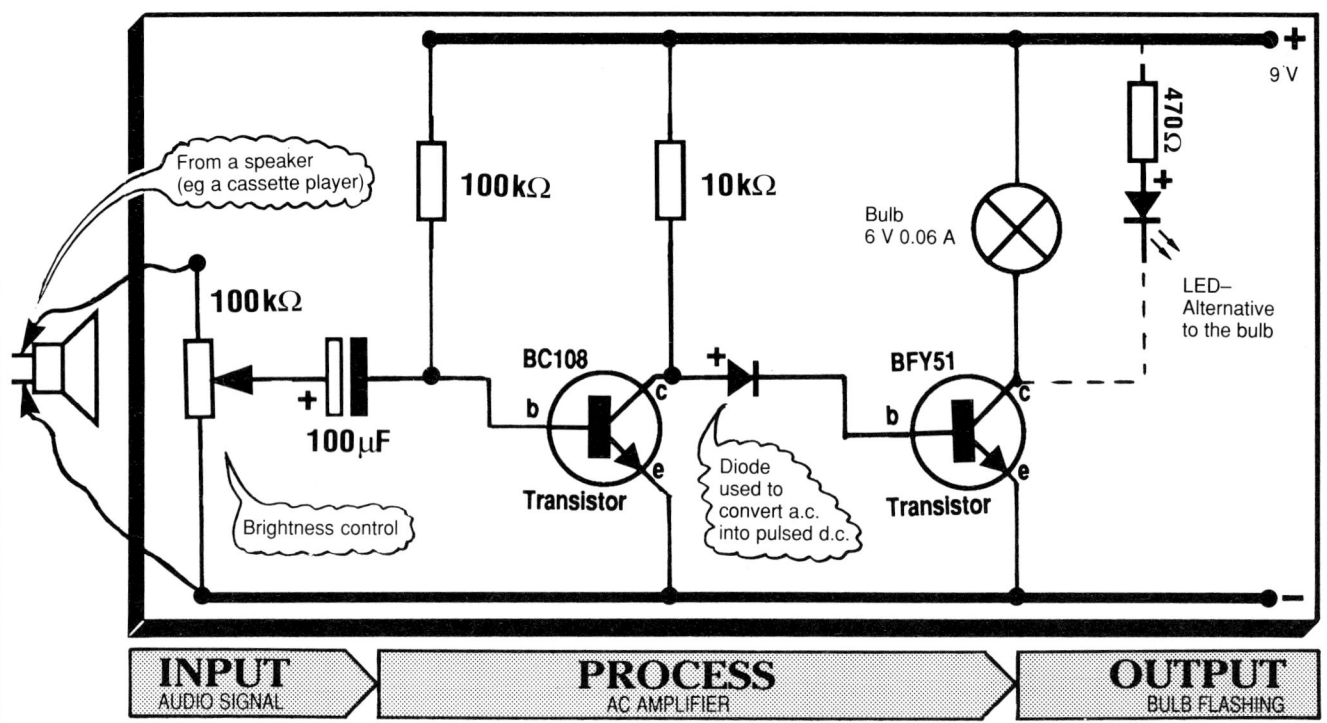

INPUT	PROCESS	OUTPUT
AUDIO SIGNAL	AC AMPLIFIER	BULB FLASHING

The circuit responds to an a.c. signal. This circuit uses only a very small proportion used by the source loudspeaker; it amplifies it and converts it into a pulsating d.c. signal which drives the bulb. LEDs can be used instead of the bulb.

MORE CHANNELS
Two or more channels can be built. Each one should be able to respond to a different frequency by altering the capacitor's value. For higher frequencies, try a 0.01 µF capacitor or similar instead of the 100 µF.

ACTIVITIES
(1) Connect up the circuit as shown above. Nothing will happen until the sound source such as a cassette is playing and the input wires are placed across the cassette loudspeaker. Switch the diode round if it does not work.
   Also adjust the variable resistor until the bulb brightness and volume are as you require.
(2) Connect another bulb across the present one. What happens?
(3) Remove the 100 µF capacitor and replace it with a 0.01 µF capacitor. It will now respond to different frequencies.
(4) Connect up two LEDs in place of the 6 V bulbs.

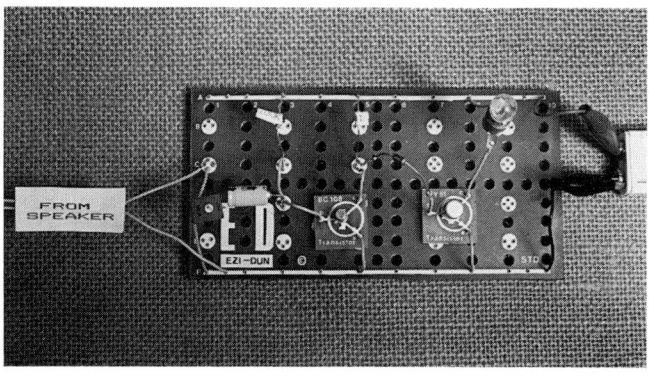

The disco–sound operated circuit. The input is from a speaker, the output is a flashing LED.

Now . . .
Make a display for the bulb(s) so that the **light show** is attractive using reflective materials (that do not conduct electricity).

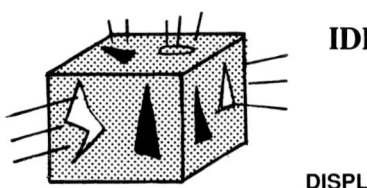 **IDEAS**

DISPLAY CONTAINERS

RADIO
A GOOD, SIMPLE–TO–MAKE PORTABLE MW RADIO

Make a quality fun radio using a ZN4142 radio chip which drives an earphone as shown, or if more amplification is added, a loudspeaker can be driven (eg The '**2 watt audio amp.**').

Note: Extra parts are needed in addition to those provided in the EZI–DUN kits.

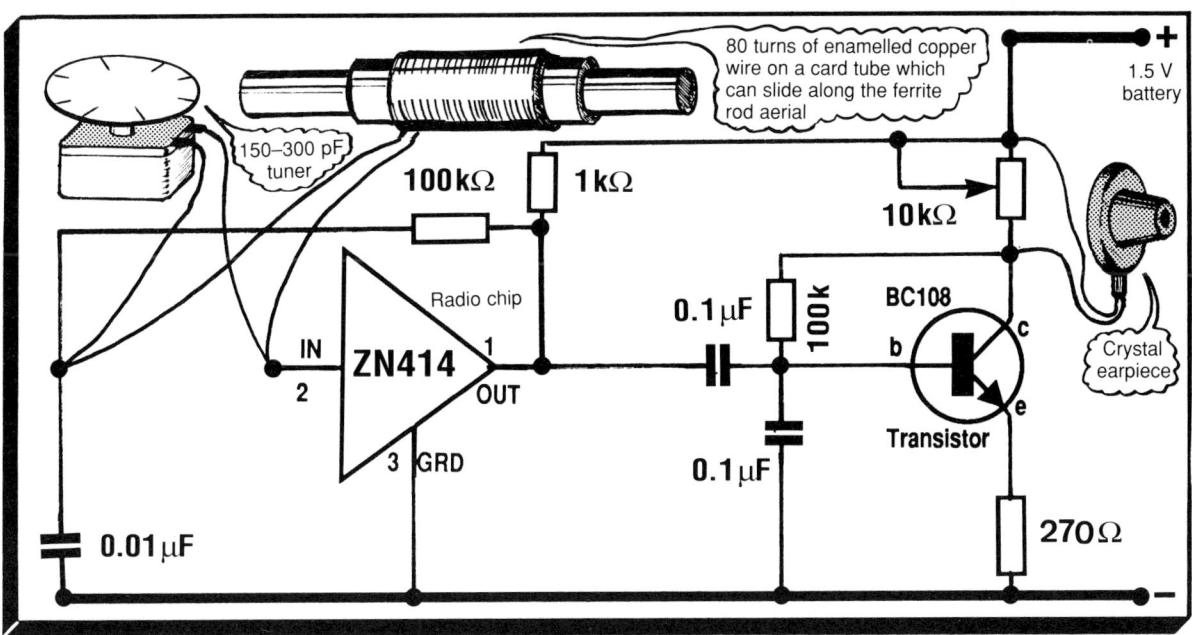

INPUT	PROCESS	OUTPUT
AUDIO AND CARRIER WAVE RECEIVED	CARRIER WAVE REMOVED AND AUDIO SIGNAL AMPLIFIED	AMPLIFIED SOUND

AM (Amplitude Modulated) radios tune into the broadcast **modulated signal** transmitted through the air, using the **coil** and tuning **variable capacitor**. The signal is then **demodulated**, the **carrier wave** being separated from the **audio signal**. The **audio signal** is then **amplified**.

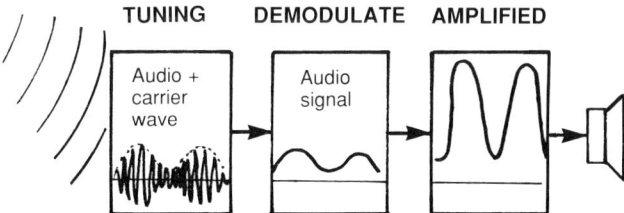

No separate aerial or earth connections are needed. The **coil** on a ferrite rod and **tuner** are quite expensive but can be reclaimed from old portable radios. The ZN4142 chip and crystal earpiece may need to be bought. Only a small 1.5 V battery is needed.

ACTIVITIES

(1) Make the circuit as shown above.

To select a station, move either the **tuning variable capacitor** or move the **coil** along the **ferrite rod**. Is the best station dependent on the radio facing a particular way? **Note**: Some buildings block the audio signals.

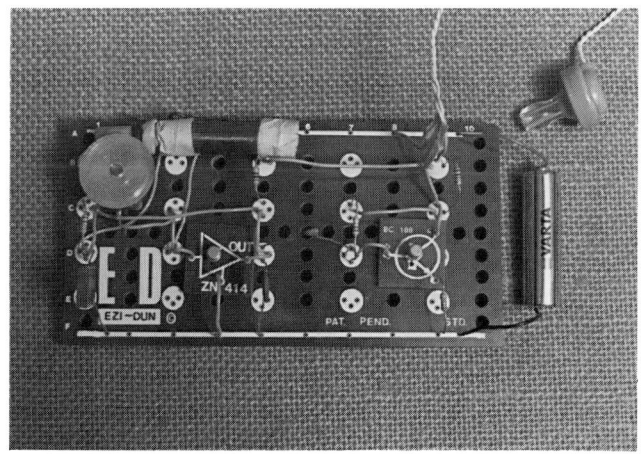

The AM (or MW) radio with earphone output.

(2) Experiment with the position of the coil and tuner for best results.

Now . . .

(A) Make an attractive container so the radio can be used on the move, **or** (B) Connect up to a more powerful amplifier. You could use the microphone socket of a cassette player or use the '**2 WATT AUDIO AMPLIFIER**' circuit in this book.

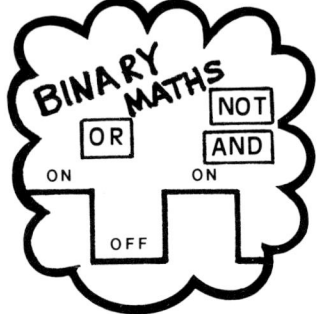

DIGITAL ELECTRONICS
AN INTRODUCTION TO DIGITAL ELECTRONICS

Digital electronics is very important. It is the most common way of transmitting information in computers and between associated machines such as robots etc. Digital electronic 'chips' are relatively cheap, reliable, efficient, use very little power and can carry out complex calculations very fast. The **information technology** revolution has been made possible because of digital electronics.

WHAT IS DIGITAL ELECTRONICS?

Digital electronics is concerned with switching circuits. The switches can be either ON or OFF, their output voltages being either **high** (logic 1) or **low** (logic 0).

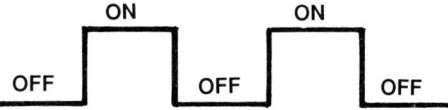

Digital circuits are now being used to replace some traditional **analogue circuits** such as in televisions and radios. They do this by simulating the analogue signals as shown below. Digital electronics reproduce sound and pictures more reliably.

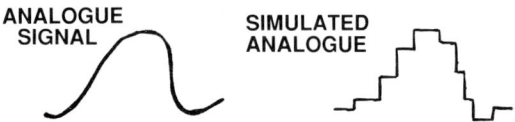

There are only **three basic building blocks** used in digital electronics, the three logic gates being AND OR and NOT .

If an AND and a NOT are combined, a NAND gate is produced.

If an OR and a NOT are combined, a NOR gate is produced.

A **truth table** shows what each logic gate type does. The most common logic symbols used are the American ones and are used in this book.

THE AND GATE

If inputs 'A' AND 'B' are high (ON), the output is ON. The electrical equivalent circuit is also shown.

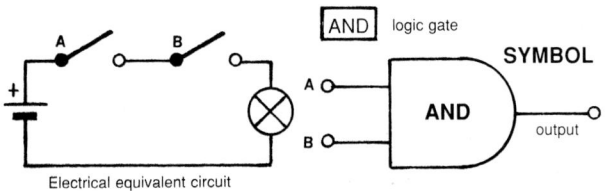

Electrical equivalent circuit

TRUTH TABLE		
A	B	OUTPUT
0	0	0
0	1	0
1	0	0
1	1	1

Practical circuit

THE OR GATE

If inputs 'A' OR 'B' are high (ON), the output is ON. The electrical equivalent circuit is also shown.

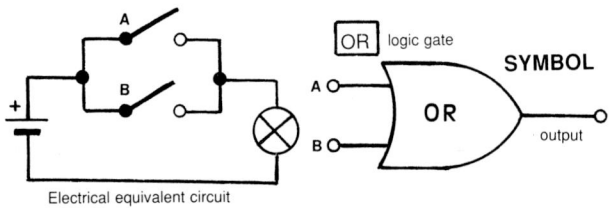

Electrical equivalent circuit

TRUTH TABLE		
A	B	OUTPUT
0	0	0
0	1	1
1	0	1
1	1	1

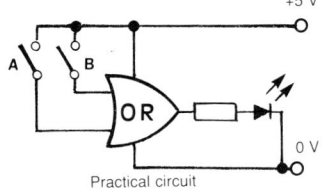

Practical circuit

THE NOT GATE

The **inverter** gate. If the input is high (ON), the output in OFF. If the input is low (OFF), the output is ON.

TRUTH TABLE		
IN	OUT	
0	1	Output is opposite the input
1	0	

THE NAND GATE

If inputs 'A' AND 'B' are high (ON), the output is NOT ON.

TRUTH TABLE		
A	B	OUTPUT
0	0	1
0	1	1
1	0	1
1	1	0

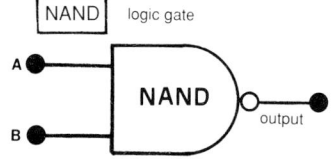

THE NOR GATE

If inputs 'A' OR 'B' are high (ON), the output is NOT ON.

TRUTH TABLE		
A	B	OUTPUT
0	0	1
0	1	0
1	0	0
1	1	0

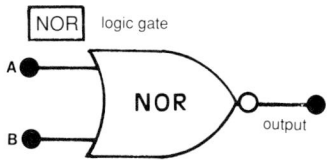

'CHIP TYPES'

There are two main types:
(a) The CMOS (Complementary Metal Oxide Semiconductors) type. It is used in this book because it can work on 5–15 V, but care needs to be taken with static electricity which can destroy the chips.
(b) The TTL (Transistor Transistor Logic) type needs to work off a 5 V supply.

The circuits given on the next few pages all use NAND gates but are connected up to produce NOT gates by linking the NAND gates together. This may seem illogical but is standard practice to avoid stocking lots of different chip types.

USING ORDINARY SWITCHES
Ordinary manual switches can be used with digital circuits but they usually require a **debouncing circuit** to ensure reliable results.

MELTING ICE CREAM

LIGHT/TEMP SENSING
USING 'NAND' LOGIC GATES

This is a sensitive circuit that responds to small changes in **light** level (or **temperature** when substituting a **thermistor** for the **LDR**). The output of a CMOS chip is limited.

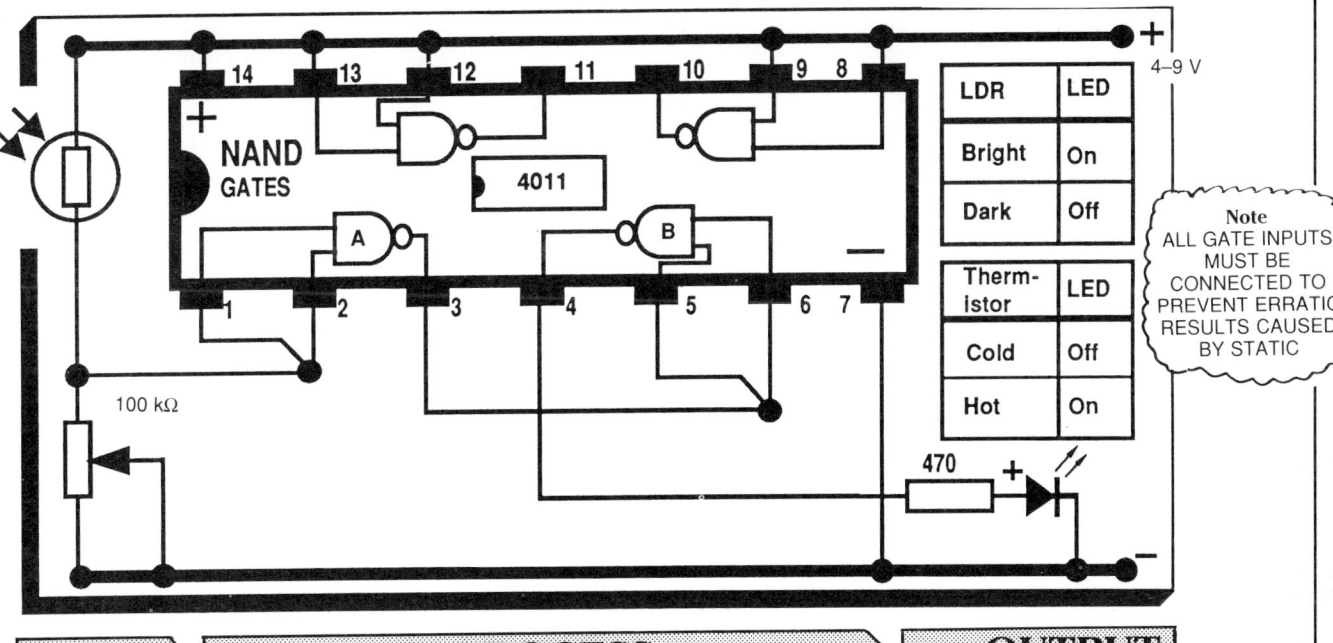

LDR	LED
Bright	On
Dark	Off

Therm-istor	LED
Cold	Off
Hot	On

Note ALL GATE INPUTS MUST BE CONNECTED TO PREVENT ERRATIC RESULTS CAUSED BY STATIC

INPUT LIGHT/TEMP	PROCESS LOGIC GATES SWITCHING	OUTPUT LED ON/OFF

The **LDR** is part of a **potential divider**. When the potential divider is above or below half the supply voltage the logic gates switch over.

The circuit's output is inverted (changed over) if the **LDR** and 100 kΩ **resistor** are changed over.

Driving **larger loads** than an LED requires a **driver circuit** which could be a **Darlington pair** (eg TIP141). The two inputs of the **NAND gates** (A and B) are connected up to produce logic NOT gates. The theoretical circuit is given below.

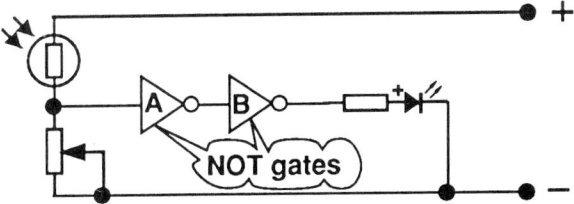

ACTIVITIES

(1) Connect up as shown above using a **CMOS 4011** chip in the **NAND PCB** holder. Adjust the 100 kΩ variable resistor until the light just comes on. The circuit should now turn ON when the LDR is covered.
(2) Replace the LDR with a **thermistor** and carefully set the 100 kΩ variable resistor so it responds to a change in heat. Use a soldering iron or similar as a source of heat if need be.
(3) Make the circuit produce the opposite to that found so far (ie invert the output).

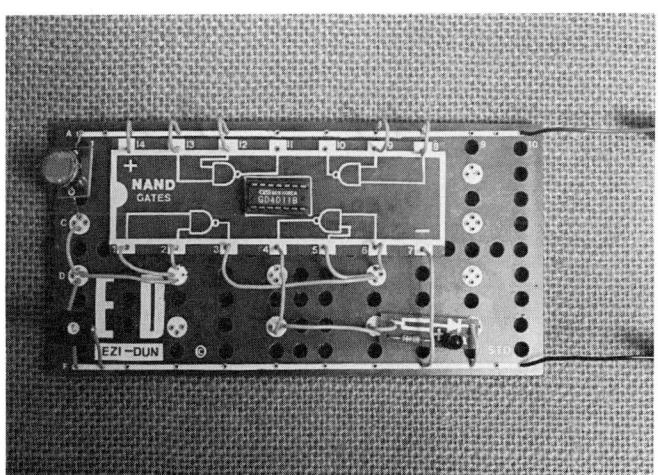

Using digital electronics to respond to light. The LED glows when light falls on the LDR.

Now . . .

Using the knowledge gained, design a game or similar that could make use of this circuit's features; or design a device that tells an ice cream salesman if the temperature has risen above a predetermined level.

TOUCH LATCHING SWITCH

FINGER TOUCH

This **touch–sensitive latching circuit** can be turned ON and OFF by touching the contacts with a finger. Useful for displays, alarms etc. A **transistor output stage** is required to enable it to control larger loads such as bulbs and motors etc as shown in the small drawing below.

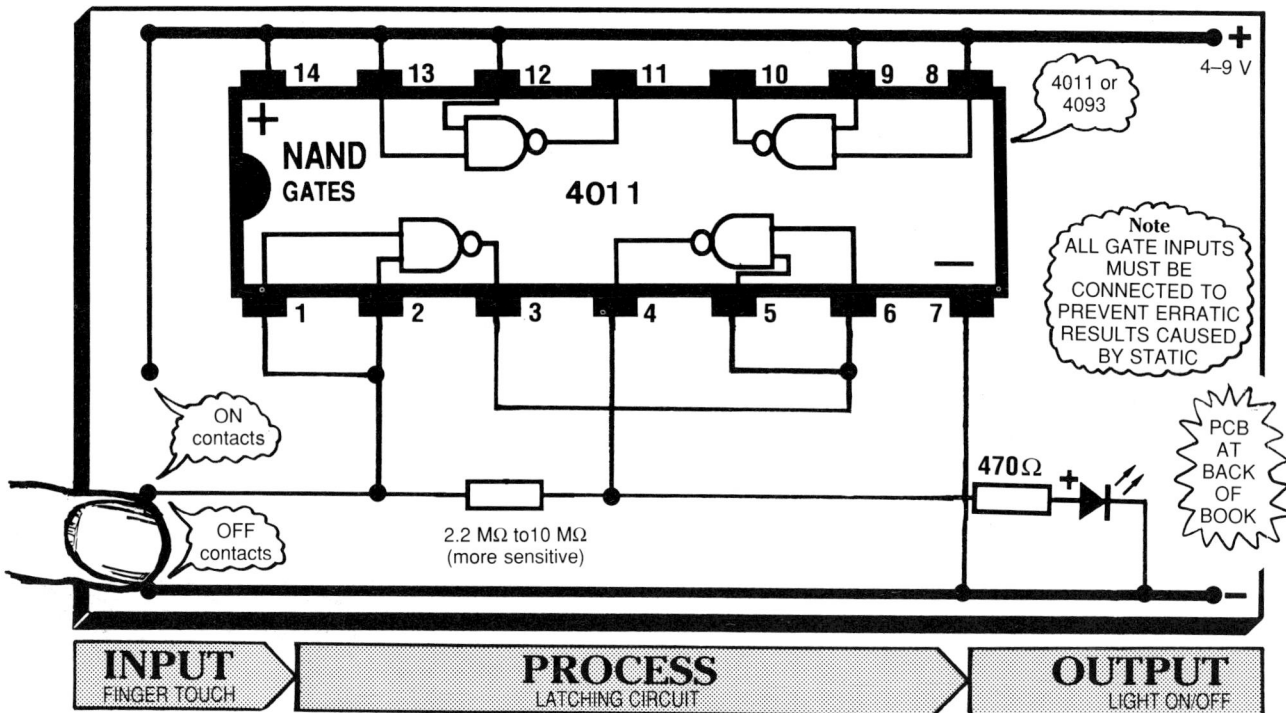

| INPUT FINGER TOUCH | PROCESS LATCHING CIRCUIT | OUTPUT LIGHT ON/OFF |

The circuit uses **two** of the **four** NAND gates marked **A** and **B**. (The other two NAND gates are not needed.)

The inputs of NAND gates **A** and **B** are actually joined together to convert them into NOT gates. The theoretical circuit is given below.

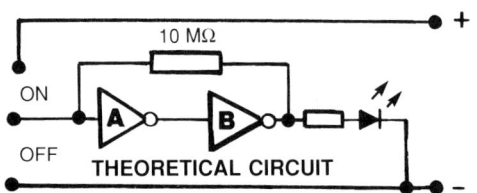

ACTIVITIES

(1) Connect up the circuit shown above using a **CMOS 4011** or a **4093 chip**. Touch the ON contacts then the OFF contacts with a damp finger. The LED should turn ON and OFF.
(2) Connect another LED from the output of **A** gate to the – rail. What happens now?
(3) **ONLY IF A 4093 CHIP IS USED**: Replace the LED with a resistor and transistor, as shown in the small drawing. A bulb can now be controlled or a motor if a suitable transistor is used.
(4) List two ways in which a circuit like this could be applied to particular problems.

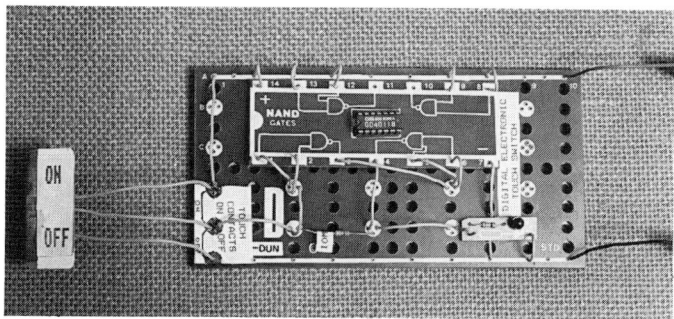

The touch sensitive ON and OFF latching control.

Now . . .

Using the knowledge gained, use this as part of a product of your own choice.

Controlling larger loads

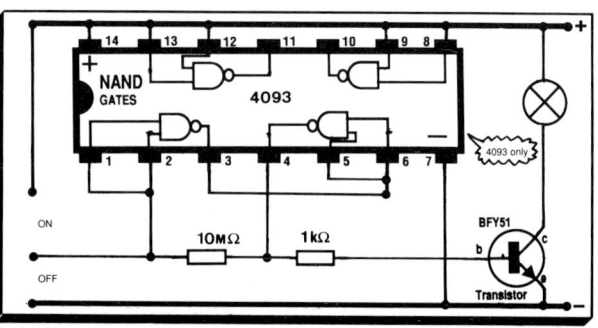

SQUARE WAVE CLOCK PULSES

MULTIVIBRATOR 'CLOCK'

Here is a **versatile circuit** that can be used as an **LED pulser**, **LED flasher** or **clock**. It cannot power much (eg an LED). If a **piezo sounder** is available, it can make sounds. The **frequency** can be easily altered. It can be used to pulse other circuits such as a **seven segment** counting display.

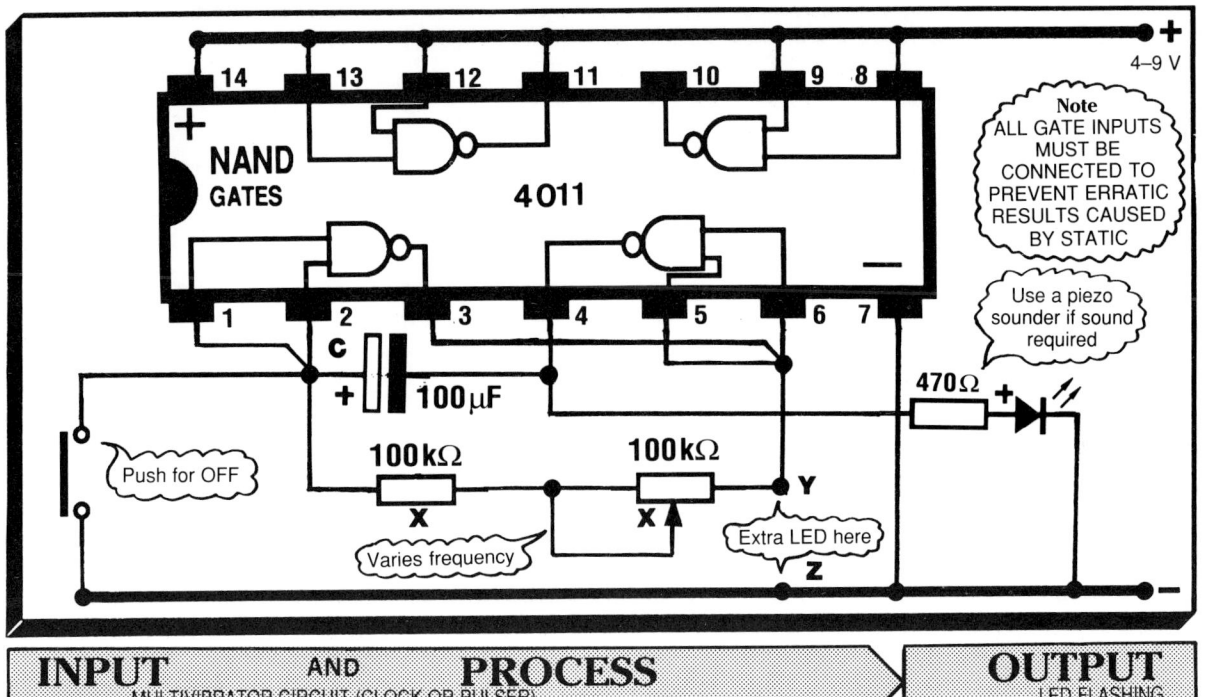

INPUT	AND	PROCESS		OUTPUT
		MULTIVIBRATOR CIRCUIT (CLOCK OR PULSER)		LED FLASHING

Two NAND gates are connected up to produce NOT gates. It behaves in a similar way to other flashing light circuits in this book but uses only one standard NAND logic chip.

The theoretical circuit is shown below.

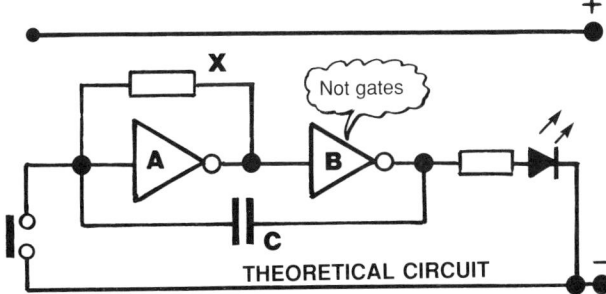

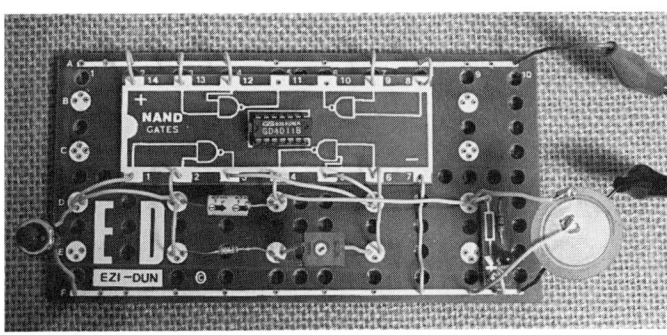

A flashing LED (or clock) circuit. A piezo sounder is also being used with the LED.

ACTIVITIES

(1) Connect up the circuit as shown above missing out the **push switch**. The LED should then flash about once per second (1 Hz).

(2) Try other **capacitors** and **resistors** and note the results. Does a larger capacitor make it slower? See **Altering the Frequency** opposite.

(3) Add the **switch**. Does it turn the LED 'ON' or 'OFF' when pushed?

(4) Add a **piezo sounder** instead of the LED to produce sound (**if you have one**) and reduce the size of the capacitor to 0.01 μF.

(5) Add another LED to the circuit from point **Y** to **Z**. Do they flash alternately or together?

Now...

Using the knowledge gained, **design** and **make** either:

Jewellery, a turntable speed checker (stroboscope principle) or a sound generator with scaled frequency dial.

ALTERING THE FREQUENCY

This is controlled by the resistance at X and the capacitor C.

100 kΩ and 1 μF capacitor – range **slow** (1 Hz).

2 MΩ resistor and 1 μF capacitor – **slower**.

100 kΩ resistor and 0.01 μF – **fast** (Suitable for producing sound when a piezo sounder is used.)

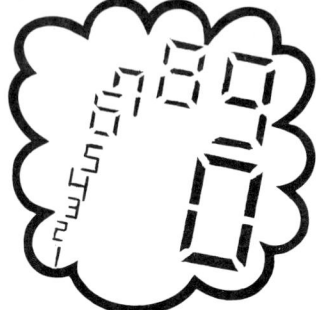

A COUNTING CIRCUIT

This is a **seven–segment counting circuit** that can count up to 9. Using the circuit without extra circuitry produces interesting results which can be used to make dice (0 to 9) or a random number generator. Stable counting circuits are on the next few pages.

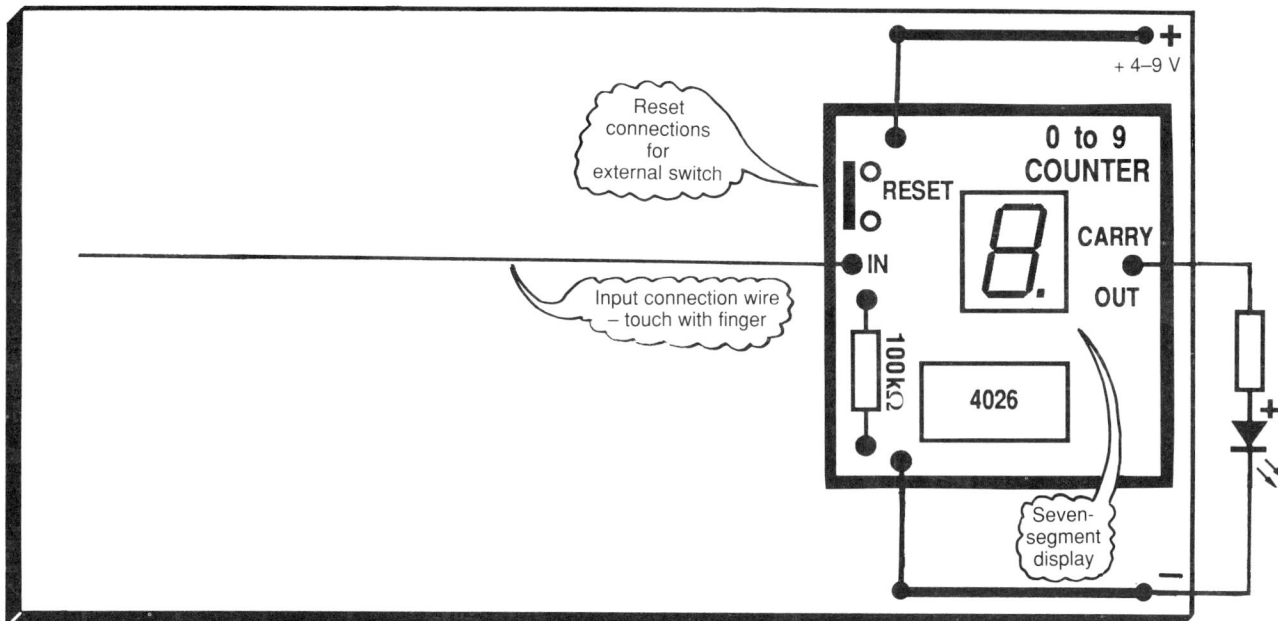

This circuit uses a ready–made counting circuit. If two of these circuits are linked together they can be made to count to 99. The circuit can be made using the PCB **mask** below.

ACTIVITIES

(1) Connect up the circuit as shown using the ready made counting circuit, but omitting the LED. When the battery is connected, the circuit starts at 0.

    Touch the **long input connection** with your finger. Do the numbers change fast or slow?

(2) Try to count one digit at a time. Can you do it?

(3) Reset the number to 0 by linking a wire across the RESET connections.

(4) Add an LED as shown and make a note of it indicating when it turns 'ON'. It is the divide-by-10 output which can also be connected to another display board, allowing the circuit to count up to 99.

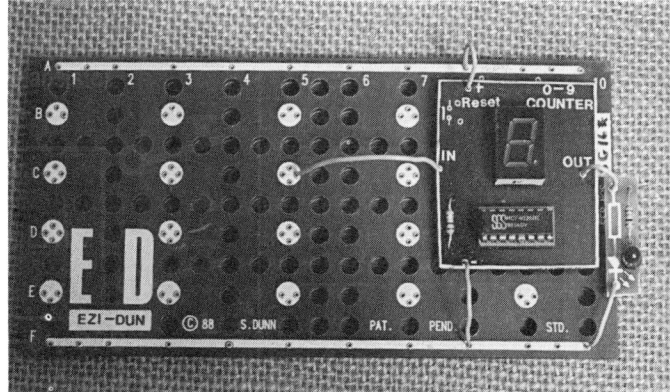

Using a seven–segment counting circuit.

Now . . .

Either (A) Make it into an attractive dice game, or (B) Go to the next page.

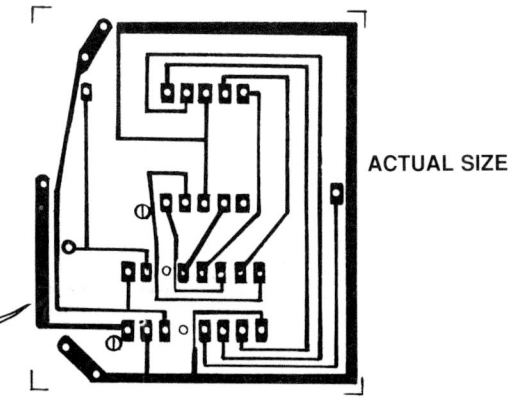

ACTUAL SIZE

PCB mask for the counting circuit (see also PCB circuits)

LAP COUNTER

This circuit is ideal for **counting the laps** a vehicle or person makes. It is basically the same as the 0–9 **counter circuit**, on the last page, but it has been adapted so it can be operated by breaking a light beam or a mechanical switch.

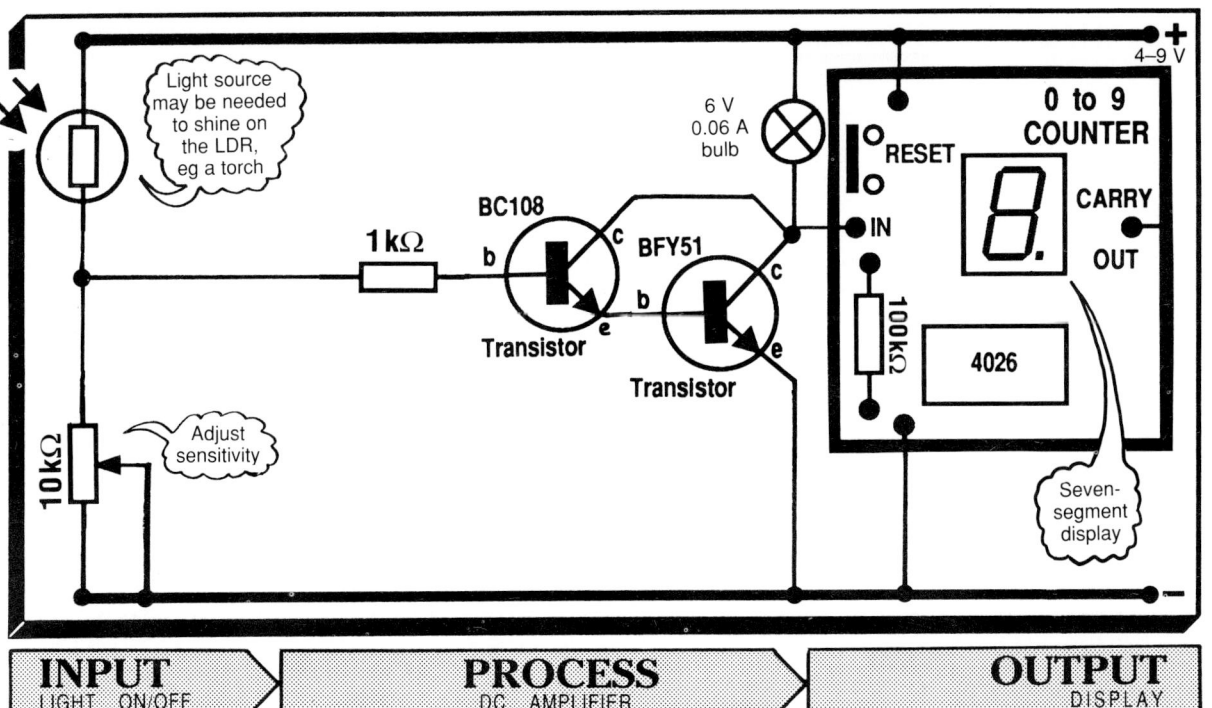

Light source may be needed to shine on the LDR, eg a torch

1 kΩ

BC108

b   c

e

Transistor

BFY51

b   c

e

Transistor

10 kΩ

Adjust sensitivity

6 V 0.06 A bulb

RESET

IN

100 kΩ

4026

0 to 9 COUNTER

CARRY

OUT

Seven-segment display

+ 4–9 V

−

INPUT	PROCESS	OUTPUT
LIGHT ON/OFF	DC AMPLIFIER	DISPLAY

The setting of the variable resistor is critical when setting up this circuit. The display changes when the light reaching the LDR is broken. Switches can also be used. An LDR hood and bright light source may improve sensitivity if using the LDR to respond over a distance.

ACTIVITIES

(1) Assemble the circuit as shown (or alter the last circuit) then adjust the 100 kΩ variable resistor so that the circuit responds when the LDR is covered.
(2) Replace the LDR with a **reed switch**. Very reliable results can be obtained.
(3) Remove the **reed switch** and see if you can get a **push switch** to work as well as the reed switch did.
(4) Add a 1 μF capacitor across the **push switch**. Does it work more reliably now? (The 10 kΩ variable resistor may need adjusting again.)
(5) Replace the **bulb** with a 100 kΩ **resistor**. Does the circuit still work?
(6) Add a **push switch** to the **reset** connections. Is this facility useful when restarting a race?
(7) Connect another **counter circuit board** to the **output** connection if you want to count up to 99.

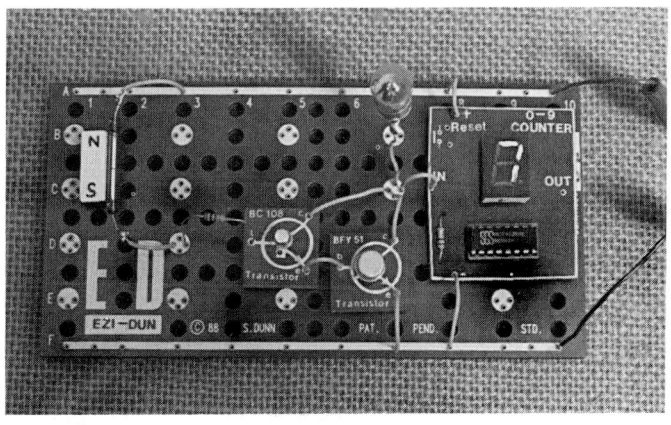

A 0 to 9 number counter operated via a reed switch using a magnet.

Now . . .

Use the circuit to count the number of laps a vehicle makes or the number ot times a pendulum swings.

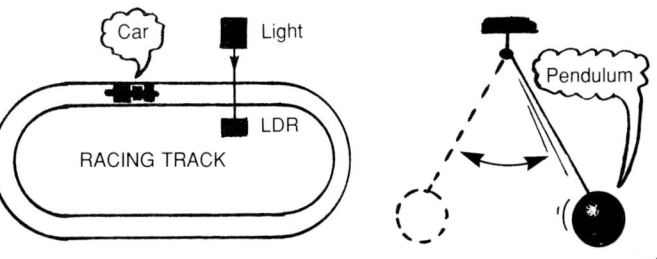

Car   Light

LDR

RACING TRACK

Pendulum

0 TO 9 COUNTER
CAN BE TOUCH OR MAGNET OPERATED

Touch the **probes** and the **counter adds one** digit. It counts to 9 then starts again at 0. If another seven–segment display board is added it can count to 99. It can be operated by touch or by a magnet.

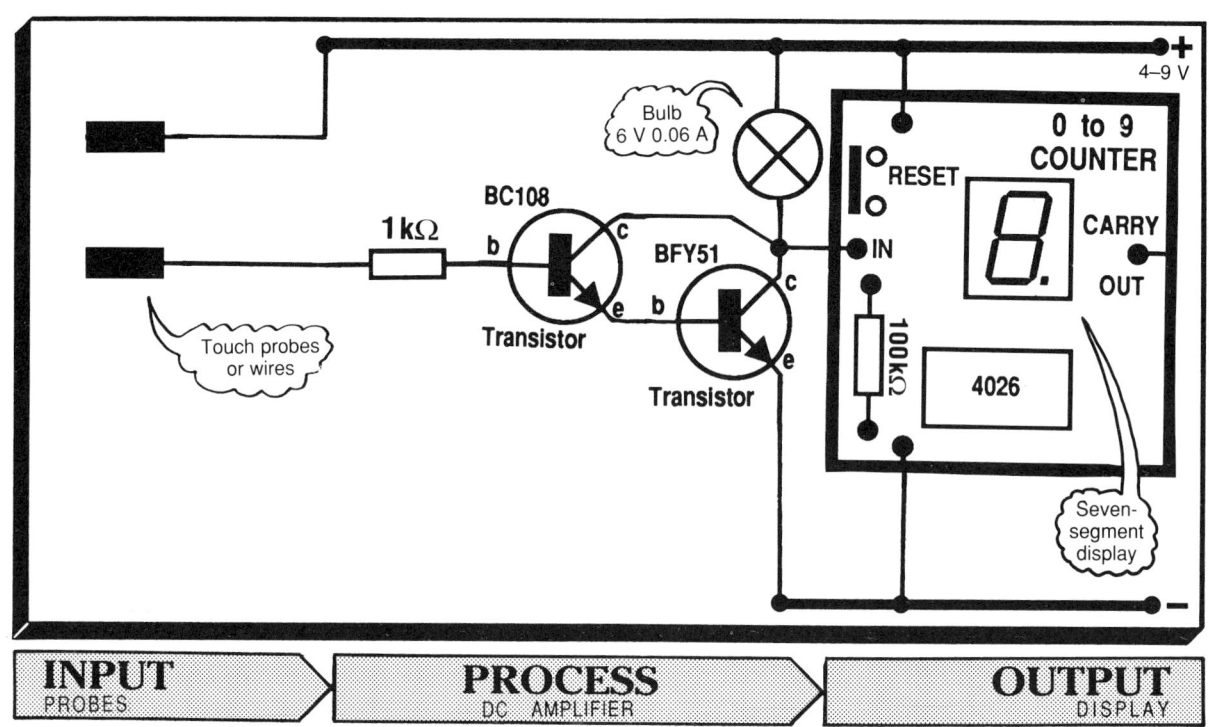

INPUT	PROCESS	OUTPUT
PROBES	DC AMPLIFIER	DISPLAY

The circuit works when a finger touches the probes. Dampen your fingers if it does not work very well. The bulb turns on every time the probes are touched.

ACTIVITIES

(1) Assemble the circuit as shown. Touch the probes and watch the seven–segment counter change.
(2) See if you can make the circuit miss a number as it adds up. Did you succeed?
(3) Remove the bulb. Does it work now?
(4) Use a **reed switch** instead of the touch probes. Connect up across the touch probes, as shown in photograph.
(5) Add a push–button mechanical switch in place of the probes and operate it. You may be surprised to find that the counter behaves rather erratically. This is caused by the mechanical switch producing contact bounce. It can be prevented by adding a **debouncing** circuit. In practice this is done using a Schmitt trigger (not shown here).

Now . . .
Make a circuit that indicates when the circuit has counted up to 10 using an LED.

Using the reed switch as input to the counter circuit.

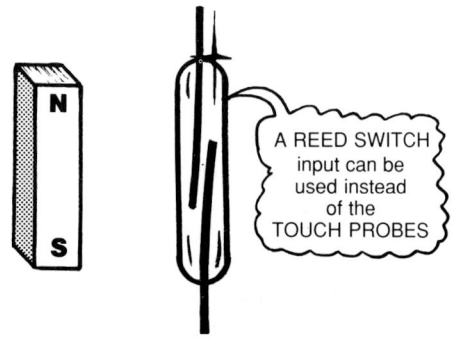

A REED SWITCH input can be used instead of the TOUCH PROBES

STOP–WATCH

Make a **stop–watch** that records the number of seconds an action takes, up to 9 seconds. 99 seconds can be recorded if another 0 to 9 counter is connected to the output.
It could also be used to make a **lap timer** for a racing track, or used to make a **reaction timer**.

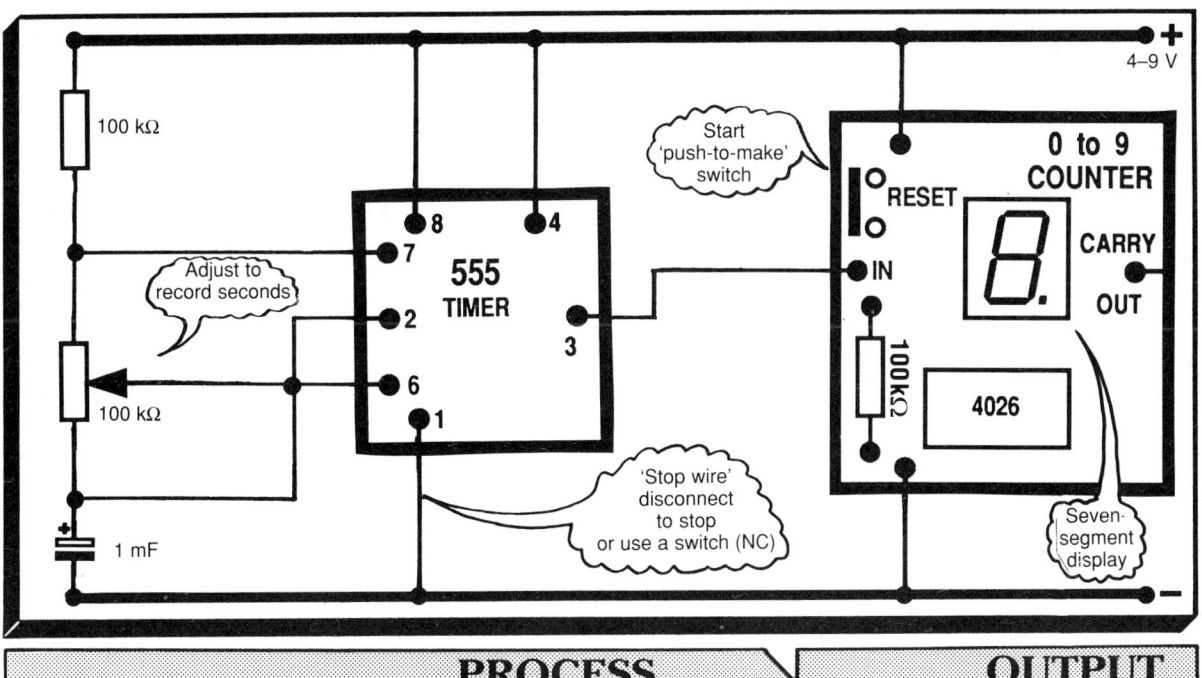

PROCESS	OUTPUT
PULSING CIRCUIT ON/OFF/ON/OFF...	DISPLAY 0–9 SECONDS

Stopping and starting this stop–watch is achieved as follows:

The start switch uses a '**push-to-make**' switch and is connected to the **reset** connectors on the 0 to 9 **counter board**. To **stop** the circuit the 555 timer is disconnected by removing **wire 1**, or a normally closed (NC) switch could be used in its place.

The 'clock' can be made to pulse slower or faster. The 1 μF capacitor, the 100 kΩ variable resistor and 100 kΩ fixed resistor can be altered to vary the pulse speed to the display.

ACTIVITIES

(1) Assemble the circuit as shown above. It will start to work when the battery is connected.
(2) Add a **push–to–make** switch to the **reset** connections on the 0 to 9 counter. What happens when the switch is pressed?
(3) When the **stop–watch** is working, disconnect **wire 1** on the 555 timer and the circuit will stop.
(4) Calibrate the **stop–watch** so that it reads seconds.
(5) Time how long it takes a partner to write their name.
(6) Remove the 1 μF capacitor and replace it with a 10 μF capacitor. Vary the 100 kΩ variable resistor. What happens? Could it now be used as a timer that measures in quarter minutes?

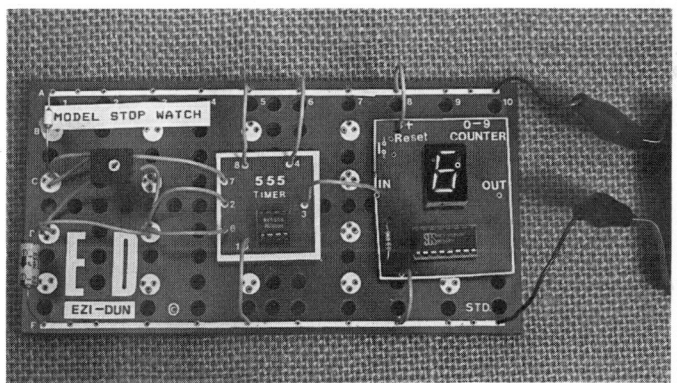

A simple stop–watch that can count up to nine. The counting speed can be altered.

Now . . .

(a) Use the stop–watch to time something of your own choice. For example: tying a shoe lace, putting an apron on.
(b) Using a partner make a **reaction timer**. Your partner can start the display using a **start switch** which is hidden from you. Long wires will be needed for the start switch so that the switch can be hidden.

ELECTRONIC SYMBOLS

To enable **electronic engineers** throughout the world to understand each others' drawings, standard **international symbols** are used. Try covering the symbols column and then naming the drawings.

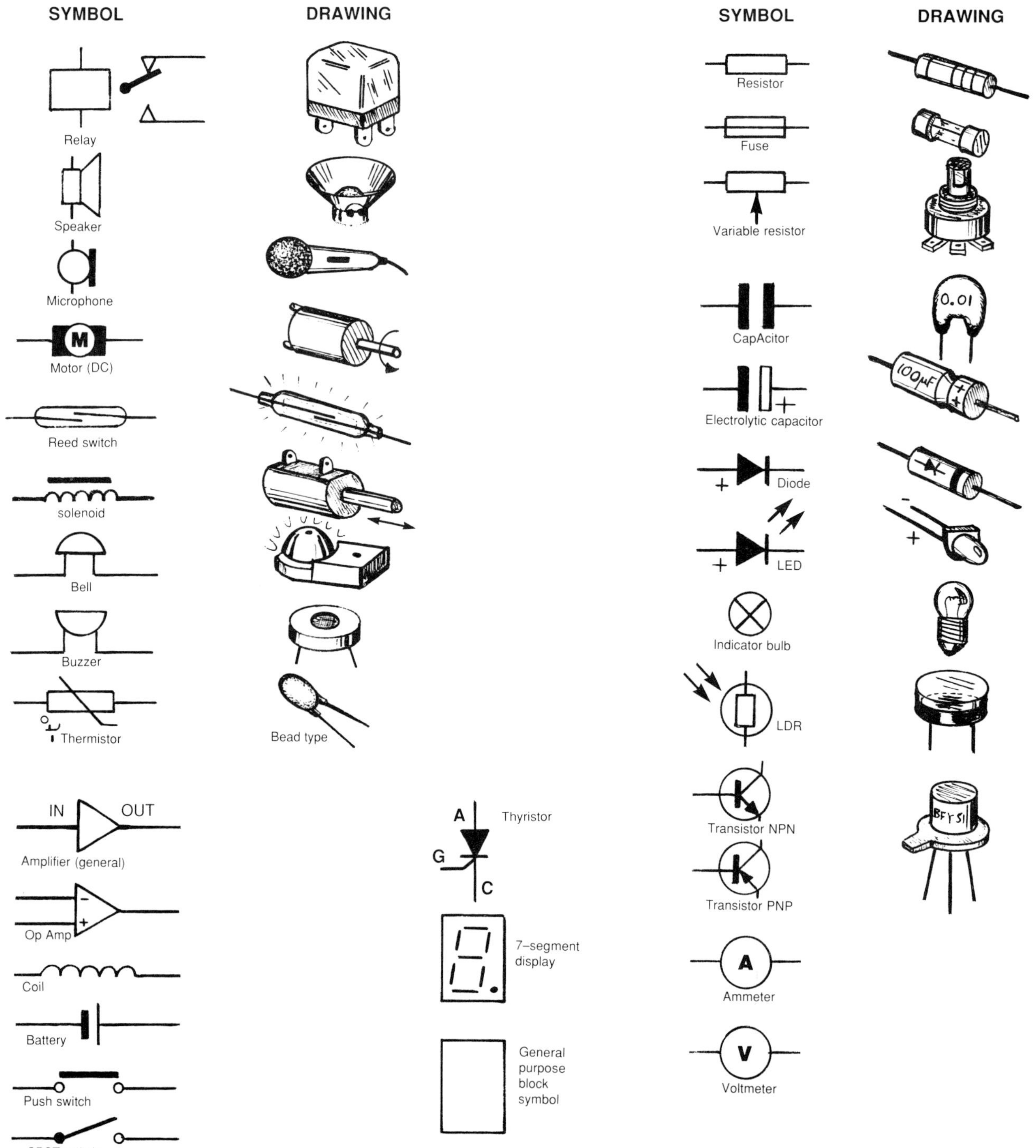

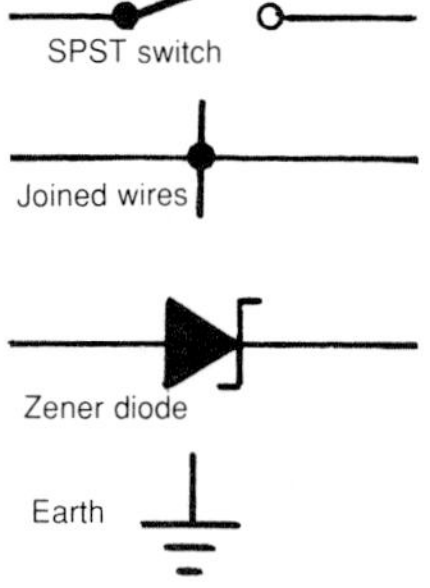

SYMBOL	DRAWING
Relay	
Speaker	
Microphone	
Motor (DC)	
Reed switch	
solenoid	
Bell	
Buzzer	
Thermistor	Bead type

Amplifier (general) — IN / OUT

Op Amp

Coil

Battery

Push switch

SPST switch

Joined wires

Zener diode

Earth

A — Thyristor — G — C

7–segment display

General purpose block symbol

SYMBOL	DRAWING
Resistor	
Fuse	
Variable resistor	
CapAcitor	0.01
Electrolytic capacitor	100µF
Diode	
LED	
Indicator bulb	
LDR	
Transistor NPN	BFY51
Transistor PNP	
Ammeter	A
Voltmeter	V

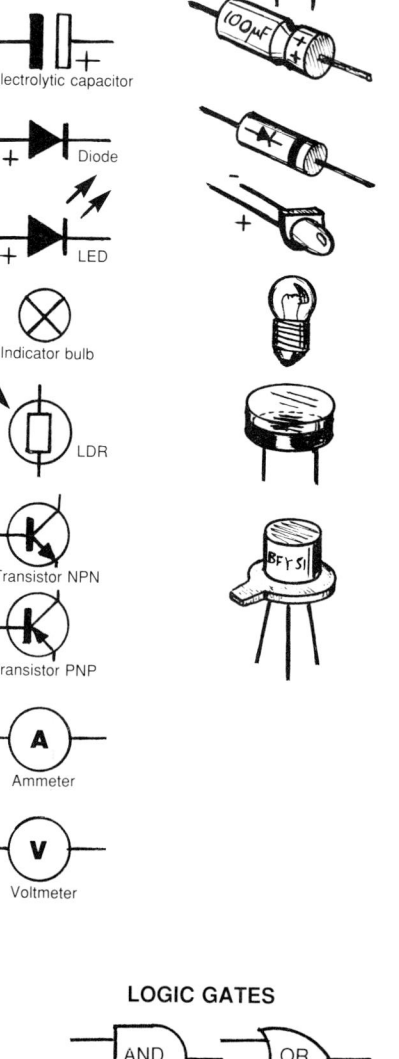

CIRCUIT DIAGRAM CONVENTIONS

• The negative (–) or 0 V rail is placed at the bottom of circuit diagrams.

• It is best to read the diagrams from left to right.

• Lines should be vertical or horizontal.

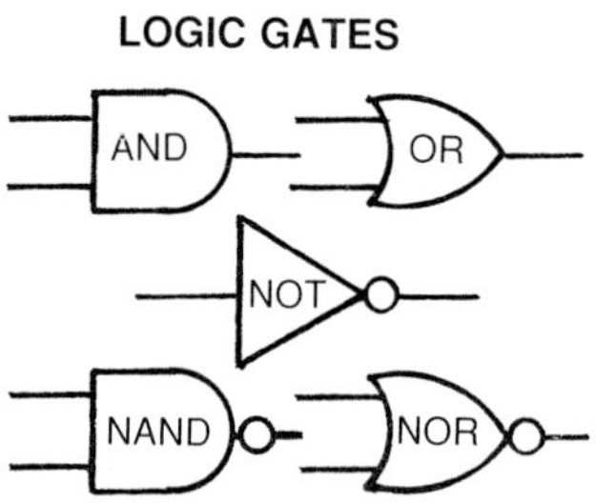

LOGIC GATES

AND   OR
NOT
NAND   NOR

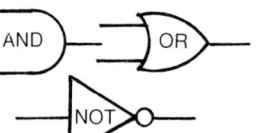

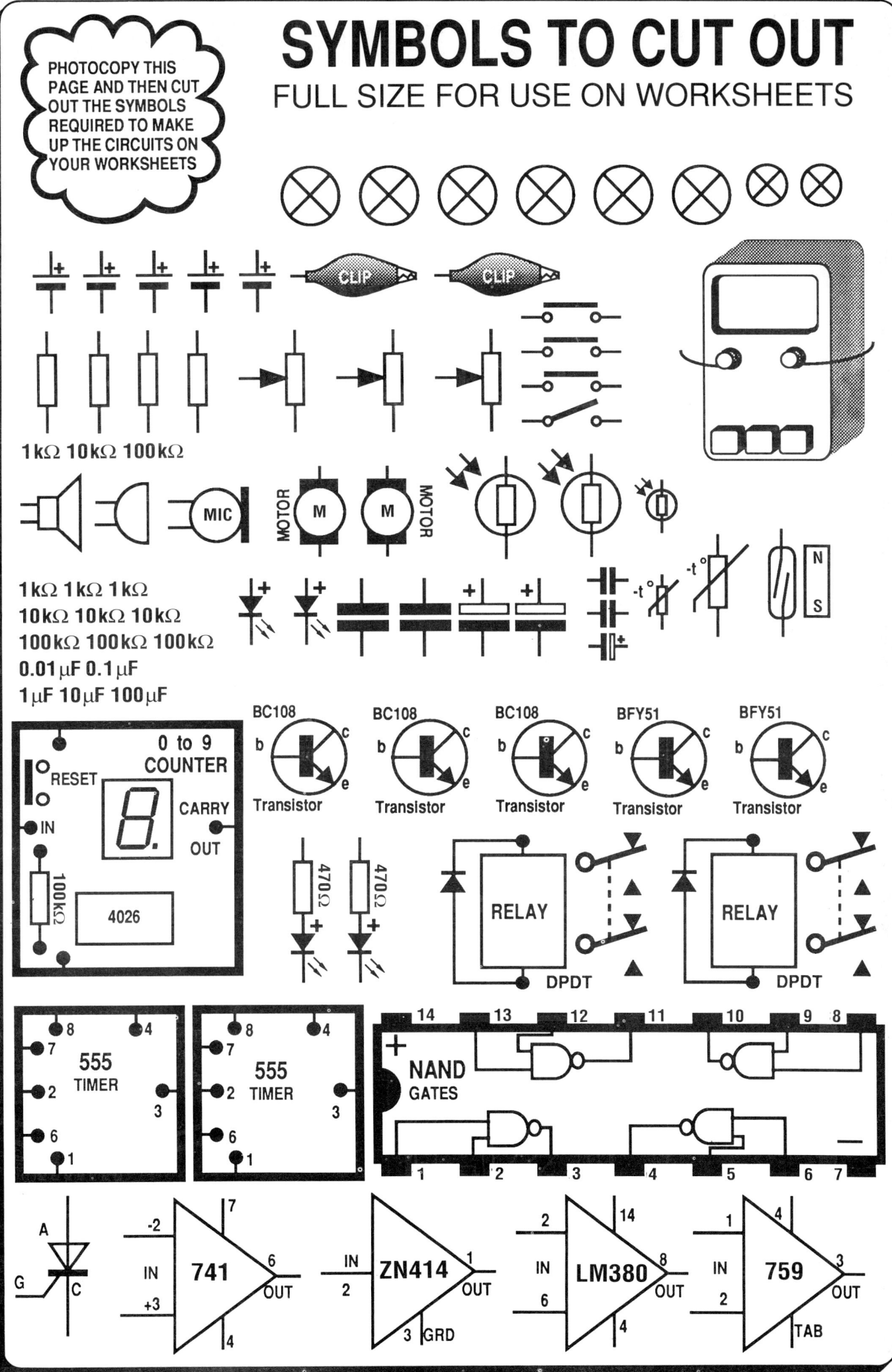

SYMBOLS TO CUT OUT
FULL SIZE FOR USE ON WORKSHEETS

PHOTOCOPY THIS PAGE AND THEN CUT OUT THE SYMBOLS REQUIRED TO MAKE UP THE CIRCUITS ON YOUR WORKSHEETS

1kΩ 10kΩ 100kΩ

1kΩ 1kΩ 1kΩ
10kΩ 10kΩ 10kΩ
100kΩ 100kΩ 100kΩ
0.01μF 0.1μF
1μF 10μF 100μF

MIC

MOTOR M　M MOTOR

0 to 9 COUNTER
RESET
IN
CARRY
OUT
100kΩ
4026

BC108 Transistor
BC108 Transistor
BC108 Transistor
BFY51 Transistor
BFY51 Transistor

470Ω
470Ω

RELAY
DPDT

RELAY
DPDT

555 TIMER

555 TIMER

NAND GATES

741
IN
OUT

ZN414
IN
OUT
GRD

LM380
IN
OUT

759
IN
OUT
TAB

SOLDERED WIRE GIRL

SOLDERING SHAPES

The fun shapes on this page, made from bare wire, can be bent easily by hand then soldered. Practise your soldering skills by making a fun shape like those below so that any alterations or repairs can be carried out quickly.

YOU NEED THE FOLLOWING

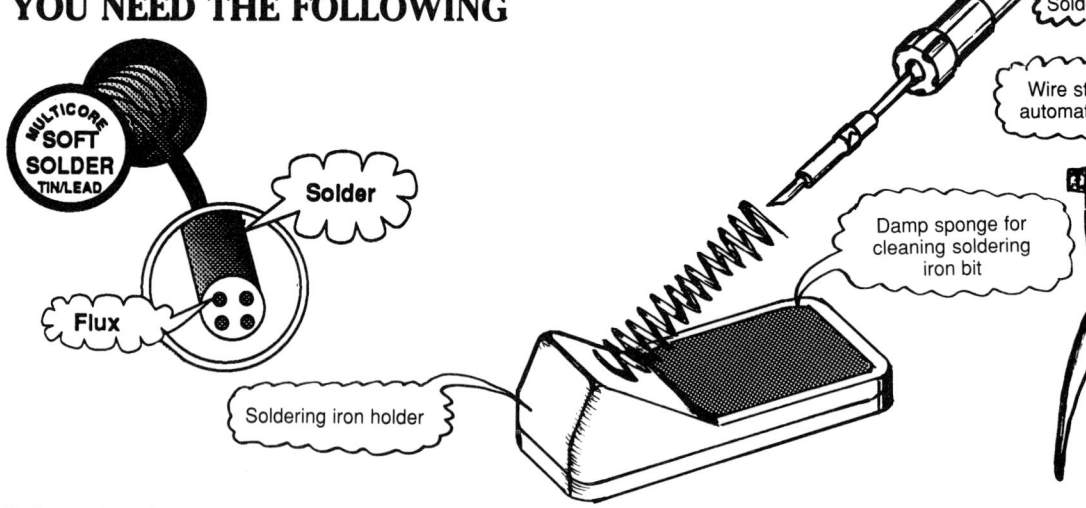

Soft soldering is a hot method (200°C) of joining wires to electrical components. **Soft solder** is made from an alloy of **tin** and **lead**. Good clean joints and flux must be used. Electricians' soft solder has flux built into the solder as shown in the diagram above.

TO SOLDER

(1) Apply soldering iron to the joint for a few seconds.
(2) **Apply the soft solder to the joint**, but **NOT** directly on the soldering iron.
(3) **Remove** soldering iron and allow joint to **cool**.
(4) Check soldered joint is **shiny**. If not, repeat again.

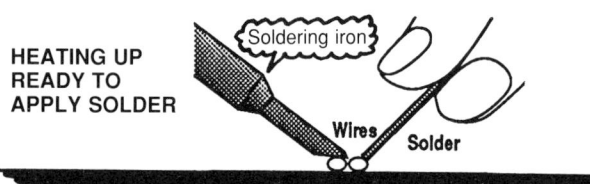

HEATING UP READY TO APPLY SOLDER

BAD JOINTS ARE USUALLY THE RESULT OF:

(a) Not heating the joint for long enough to allow the solder to **alloy** with the joint. 3 to 5 seconds are needed.
(b) Not getting enough heat due to poor soldering iron contact. If a big joint is being attempted a larger soldering iron is needed.
(c) Not cleaning the joint beforehand, (eg with emery).
(d) Moving the joint parts before the solder has 'set'.

EXAMPLES

Footballer

Daisy

NOTE
All made from bare pieces of bent tin plated copper wire then soldered

Glasses. Stick coloured cellophane in for lenses

Dinghy. Hull is made from copper clad board

NOTE:

(A) The soldering iron must be wiped clean now and again on the damp sponge.
(B) Sometimes it is easier to solder parts separately, then place them together and heat up again. This is called a 'sweated joint'.

MAKING A PCB

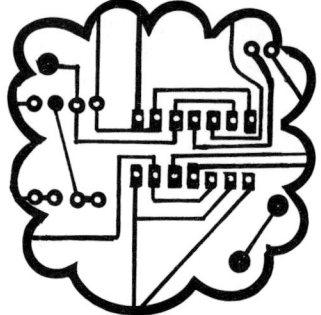

PART OF A PCB

There are two main methods of making a **Printed Circuit Board (PCB)**, namely:
(1) The **photographic** (or indirect) **method**,
(2) The **direct method**.
Both are described below.

PHOTOGRAPHIC METHOD

It produces professional results and the **mask** can be re-used.

(1) Planning the circuit (if needed)
Plan the circuit on 0.1 inch spaced graph paper (not metric size) which is the standard spacing for chips etc. You cannot cross over using copper tracks but can bridge the tracks using the components. Plan in pencil as if **looking down on the components**. Double check that the sizes and hole positions are correct. Alternatively, use a PCB program on a computer.

Plan out on 0.1 inch grid graph paper

(2) Making the mask
Place a sheet of OHT plastic (acetate) over the PCB design. Rub on PCB transfers to make a re-usable **mask** of the circuit diagram with all the information you require on it.

Tape holding acetate sheet over the pcb design

(3) Photographic process
Invert the mask and place it underneath a piece of photosensitive PCB, removing the protective layer first, then expose it in an **ultraviolet light box** for 2 to 5 minutes.

Photosensitive PCB

Acetate mask

LIGHT BOX

(4) Developing the photosensitive PCB
Develop the photosensitive PCB in sodium hydroxide (1 molar strength) for about 1 minute. The circuit's image will appear faintly. **DANGER**: Handle with care.

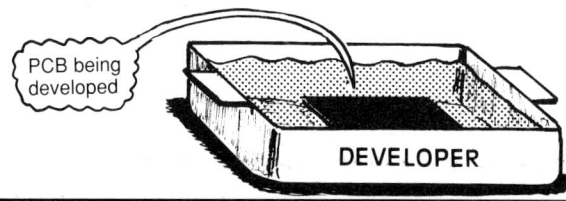

PCB being developed

DEVELOPER

(5) Etching the PCB
Etch the board in the **bubble etch tank** containing ferric chloride until the unwanted copper has dissolved. Check regularly to monitor progress. **DANGER**: This chemical is corrosive and any splashes will ruin clothes. Wash the etched board with plenty of water.

Lifting the pcb out to check

ETCH TANK

(6) Drilling the PCB
Drilling the PCB using the correct size drill – usually 0.1–1.5 mm.

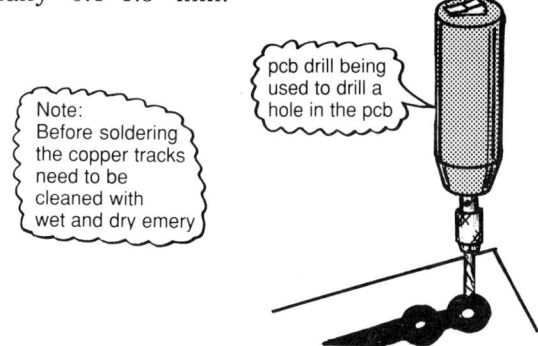

Note: Before soldering the copper tracks need to be cleaned with wet and dry emery

pcb drill being used to drill a hole in the pcb

(7) Painting the top of the board
Paint using car spray, then add a **legend** if required using permanent pen or rub–on transfers. Finish off by protecting transfers with clear car lacquer.

DIRECT METHOD

This method is only suitable for making one PCB at a time. Results are quicker but not as professional as the photographic method. The process is carried out as follows:

(1) As the photographic method (see opposite)

(2) Transferring the design onto the PCB
Place the PCB **design** drawing (inverted) on top of the **copper** side of the PCB with **carbon paper** between, then trace the design onto the copper.

If a simple circuit, it can be drawn straight onto the copper with a pencil.

(3) Applying the transfers to the PCB
Add PCB **transfers** or use a black permanent pen to draw the circuit diagram out neatly using the carbon paper track outlines made to help you.

(4) Not needed, go to stage 5.

(5) to (7) as the photographic method.

PCB CIRCUIT EXAMPLES

CORNER OF A PCB

Some useful PCB **circuit masks** are provided on this page. The components and circuit diagrams are as indicated. The PCB **masks** are as seen from the copper side of a PCB. Pin 1 of the chips and where components go are indicated by the thin lines. To check the PCB mask against the circuit diagrams, photocopy the page and then look at the mask from the reverse side.

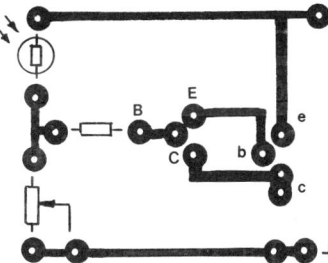

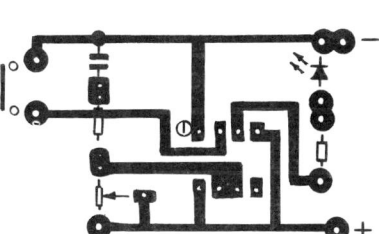

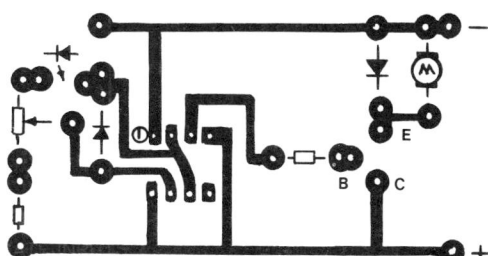

D.C. DARLINGTON PAIR CIRCUIT
See '**Sensitive switching**', page 40, for circuit and components

TIMER
A variable timer based on a 555 timer chip. See page 51, '**Timer**', for component details.

MOTOR SPEED CONTROL
Precise control of a d.c. motor is possible. See page 50, '**Good motor control**', for details.

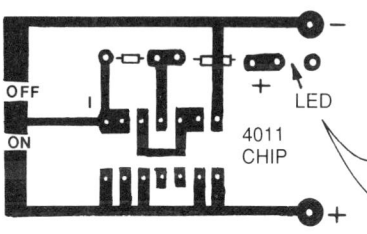

TOUCH LATCHING CIRCUIT
Made using a CMOS 44011 NAND gate chip, see page 62, '**Touch latching switch**' for details.

The component legends for the circuits below can be seen on '**Symbols to cut out**' page 69, and photographs of made PCBs are illustrated throughout this book.

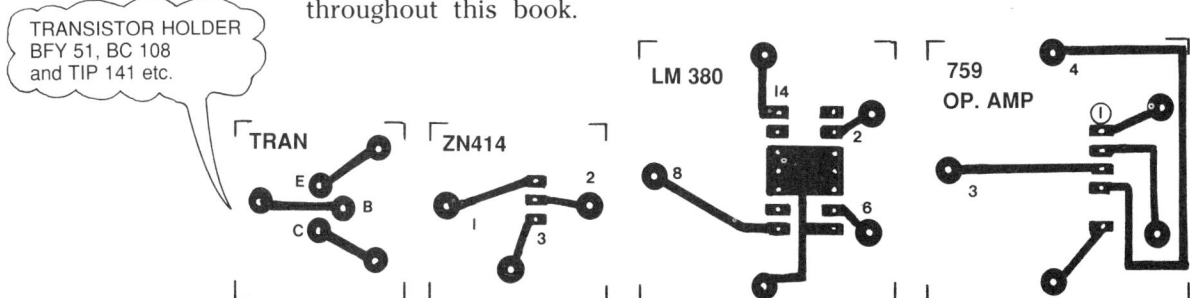

TRANSISTOR HOLDER
BFY 51, BC 108 and TIP 141 etc.

GENERAL PURPOSE CHIP HOLDER (14 pins) Suitable for NAND, NOR, OR, AND, NOT gates etc. The NAND gate legend is shown on the '**Symbols to cut out**', page 69, but any appropriate legend can be added.

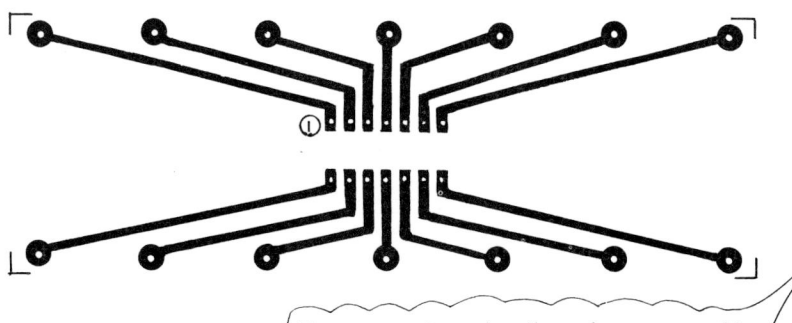

The components used are those shown on page 64, '**A counting circuit**'.

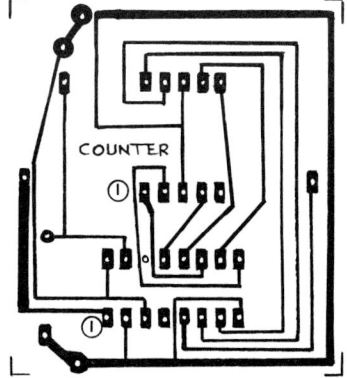

0–9 COUNTER
Drawn as '**Seen through the board**' (ready for use on acetate).

ADDRESSES
PARTS USED
BITS ETC

APPENDIX

EQUIPMENT USED IN THIS BOOK

Note: 'Any supplier' means any electronic supplier

Connecting wire 0.6 mm dia. JPR code 01 0350
(Wire must be 0.6 mm if using EZI–DUN kits)

Bulb 6 V (Must be 0.6 A type)	Any supplier
MES bulb holders	Any supplier
Diode IN4001	Any supplier
Switch (push-to-make)	Any supplier
DC Motor 1.5–4.5 V	Any supplier
Motor holder (plastic clip)	DIY plumbing
(supplied in 100s)	
1 kΩ Potentiometer	Any supplier
Light dependent resistor (ORP12)	Any supplier
Buzzer 6 V (with socket wires)	Any supplier
Crocodile clips (red and black)	Any supplier
Reed switch	Proops
Magnet	Proops
Worm gear (fits on motor)	EZI–DUN
Pulley pack	Any supplier
BC108 transistor	Any supplier
BFY51 transistor	Any supplier
Resistors 680 + 100 kΩ + 2M2	Rapid
Resistors 1 kΩ 10 kΩ	Rapid

(Must have 0.6 mm wires if used with EZI–DUN kits.)

10 kΩ Enclosed preset	Any supplier
100 kΩ Enclosed preset	Any supplier
Thermistor (negative type - TH3)	Any supplier
Capacitors 0.01mF, 0.1mF, 1mF	
10 mF, 100 mF	Any supplier

(Must have 0.6 mm dia wire ends if used with EZI–DUN kits.)

555 Timer	Any supplier
741 Op. Amp.	Any supplier
555 Timer	Any supplier
4011 NAND Chip	Any supplier
LED (red)	Any supplier
Relay 6 V DPDT	Any supplier
EZI–DUN Board for B- and G-Kits	Commotion or EZI–DUN
EZI–DUN Boards for E-Kits	EZI–DUN
(It has fewer sockets than the B- and G-Kits)	
Spare sockets	EZI–DUN
Printed circuit board	Any supplier

For the radio:
ZN4142 Radio chip, Ferrite rod,
150–300 pF tuning capacitor,

Crystal earpiece	Maplin

For 0–9 counting display:
470 kΩ resistor + 4026 CMOS chip

+ common cathode display	Code 57 0115 Rapid

For 2 Watt Amp:

LM380 chip + 35 Ω speaker	Any supplier

For Light Follower:

759 Op. Amp. chip	Any supplier

For Thyristor Latch:

Thyristor type TIC 106D	Any supplier
Darlington pair of transistors TIP 141	Any supplier

NON CIRCUIT PARTS

Electrician's solder (with flux)	Any supplier
Automatic wire-stripper	Commotion
Geared-down motors	Commotion
Propellers (for motors) 2 mm shaft hole	EZI–DUN
4 mm bolts, 15 and 25 mm long (used to bolt other parts on)	

Computer Control Interface:
The Barnet box interface from Commotion comes with a good Logo-based program. The interface can also be used with other programs.

USEFUL ADDRESSES

Commotion
Redburn House, Stockingswater Lane. Tel. 01-804 1378
Suppliers of EZI–DUN construction kits and technology equipment for schools: Computer control, construction systems (such as LEGO®· Plawcotech), motorisation, drawing equipment, tools, electrical components etc.

Collins Educational
77–85 Fulham Palace Road, Hammersmith, London W6 8JB
Publishers of books by Stewart Dunn
Electronic Projects Made Easy
An Introduction to CDT
CDT for GCSE

Rapid Electronics Ltd
Hill Farm Industrial Estate, Boxted, Colchester, Essex CO4 5RD. Tel. 0206 272730. Economical electronic suppliers, worth phoning for a catalogue, used by the author for many of the electronic parts.

JPR Electronics
Unit M, Kingsway Industrial Estate, Kingsway, Luton, Bedfordshire LU1 1LP. Economical electronic suppliers.

Maplins Electronic Supplies Ltd
PO Box 3, Rayleigh, Essex SS6 2BR. Comprehensive electronics catalogue. Also sell to the public (useful if pupils want to order direct).

RS Components
PO Box 99, Corby, Northants NN17 9RS. Very comprehensive catalogue but not as competitive as some suppliers.

Technology Teaching Systems Ltd
Penmore House, Hasland Rd, Hasland, Chesterfield S41 0SJ. General technology supplier including Meccano (limited electronics) .

Technology Supplies
6 Stoke Court, Market Drayton, Shropshire TF9 2DY General technology suppliers including 4mm nuts and bolts.

Proops Distributors Ltd
Heybridge Est, Castle Rd, London NW1 8TD. Reed switches, magnets and various job lots.

EZI–DUN
56 Malvern Drive, Stony Stratford, Milton Keynes, Bucks MK11 2AE. Stewart Dunn, author of this book and inventor of the EZI–DUN construction system, can advise on difficult-to-obtain parts and EZI–DUN construction kits. Send an SAE to the above address.

PROJECT LIST

Alarm, latched	36,46
Amplifier, 2-watt	57
Amplifier, 741	56
Amplifier, sound	55,56
Amplifier, operational	42
Badge	9,32
Boat	18
Buggy, computer	26
Buggy	10
Buggy, parts	14
Buggy, steerable	13
Car, alarm	54
Car park barrier	27
Computer buggy	26
Computer show	24
Conveyor belt	41
Counter, 0-9	65
Counting circuit	64
Crane	15
Dimmer light	3
Display ideas	53
Disco, sound operated	58
Disco effect	54
Display containers	58
Display	50
Door, garage	41
Door opener	45
Fan timer	52
Flashing eyes	53
Flashing light	11
Flashing lights	47,48
Flashing transport	53
Helicopter	3
Intercom, 2-way	57
Jewellery	32
Lap counter	66
LDR-sensing circuit	37
Light follower	43
Light seeking buggy	43
Light sensing	61
Lighthouse	11
Liquid level indicator	39
Magnet controlled buggy	10
Motor control	50
Motor reversing	35
Multivibrator clocks	46
Mulitvibrators, astable	46
Multivibrators, bistable	46
Multivibrators, latch	46

Multivibrators, monostable	46
Music organ	50
Organ	50
Pendant	32
Plant waterer	45
Pulser	46
Quiz game	16
Quiz indicator	54
Racing track counter	66
Radio, badge	32
Radio, 414	59
Record player	50
Relay, motor reversing	34
Relays	33
Ring, main	5
Robot	20
Room alarm	9
Sensing circuit	37
Sensitive switching	40
Seven segment display	64-67
Siren	54
Sound amplifier	56
Spotlight	3
Stage	24
Steerable buggy	13
Stop watch	67
Switches, membrane	7
Temperature sensing	61
Thermistor, temperature	37
Thermometer	42
Time delay	52
Timer, 555	49
Timer	50-52
Touch latching	62
Touch operated timer	52
Traffic lights	19
Train	12
Vehicle reversing	34
Vehicle, simple	12
Vehicle, 'tip up'	12
Vehicles	12,34,50
Very sensitive switching	41
Walking robot	19
Washing machine	20
White line follower	43
Window opener	45

INDEX

A

A.c. amplification 55
Alarm, latched 36,44,46
Amplifier, 2-watt 57
Ammeter, see multimeter
Amplifier, 741 56
Amplifier, sound 55,56
Amplifier, operational 42
AND gate 60
Appendix 73
Astable 46

B

Badge 9,32
BASIC language 21
BASIC programs 21-26
Batteries, series 31
Bistable 46
Boat 18
Buggy, computer 26
Buggy 10
Buggy control 21
Buggy parts 14
Buggy, steerable 13
Bulbs, parallel 5
Bulbs, series 6

C

Cams 19
Capacitors 28
Car alarm 54
Car park barrier 27
Chip types 60
Clock 63
Components xi
Computer buggy 26
Computer control 21
Computer interface 22
Computer show 24
Conducting 2
Contents iii
'Control it' logo 21
Conveyer belt 41
Counter (0-9) 65
Counting circuit 64
Crane 15
Current 30

D

Darlington pair 39,40
Demodulate 59
Developer 71
Digital electronics 60
Dimmer light 3
Diodes 17
Display ideas 53
Disco, sound operated 58
Disco, effect 54
Display containers 60
Display 50
Door, garage 41

Door opener 45
Door protection 41

E

Electronic symbols 68
Etch tank 70

F

Fan timer 52
Ferric chloride 71
Ferrite rod 59
Flashing eyes 53
Flashing light 11
Flashing lights 47,48
Flashing transport 53
Frequency, music 49

H

Helicopter 3
Hull shapes 18

I

Illuminated card 9
Insulators 2
Integrated circuit 60
Intercom, 2-way 57
Intercom 56
Introduction vi

J

Jewellery 32

L

Lap counter 66
LDR sensing circuit 37
LDR 4
Light box 70
Light follower 43
Light seeking buggy 43
Light sensing 61
Lighthouse 11
Liquid level indicator 39
Logic 46
Logic gates 60
Logo programs 21-27
Logo sequence plan 25
Logo, intro 21,22
Logo 21,22

M

Magnet and reed switch 10
Monostable 46
Motor control 50
Motor reversing 34
Motor reversing, light operated 35
Multimeter 29-31
Multivibrator clocks 46
Multivibrators 46
Multivibrators, astable 46
Multivibrators, bistable 46
Multivibrators, latch 46

Multivibrators, monostable	46
Music	49
N	
NAND gate	60
NOR gate	60
NOT gate	60
O	
Octave	49
Operational amplifier	42
OR gate	60
Organ	49
Oscilloscope	49
Outputs	28
P	
PCB examples	72
PCB making	70
PCB	71-72
Pendant	32
Piezo sounder	63
Plant waterer	45
Polarity tester	17
Potential difference	29
Potential divider	37
Power supplies	vi
Preface	vi
Pulser	46
Q	
Quiz game	16
Quiz indicator	54
R	
Racing track counter	66
Radio, badge	32
Radio, 414	59
Radio	59
Record player	52
Reed switch	9
Relay, motor reversing	34
Relays	33
Ring, main	5
Robot	20
Room alarm	9
S	
Sensing circuit	37
Sensitive switching	40

Seven segment display	64-67
Siren	48
Soldering	70
Soldering shapes	70
Sound amplifier	56
Spotlight	3
Stage	24
Stop watch	67
Switch, reed	9
Switch, reversing	15
Switch, types	8
Switches, AND type	8
Switches, OR type	8
Switches making	7
Switches, membrane	7
Symbols to cut out	69
Symbols	68
T	
Temperature sensing	61
Thermistor, temperature	37
Thermometer	42
Thyristor	44
Time delay	52
Timer	50-52
Timer, 555	49
Touch latching	62
Touch operated timer	52
Traffic lights	19
Train	12
Truth tables	60
Tuner	59
Tuning	59
V	
Vehicle	12,34,50
Vehicle reversing	34
Vehicle, simple	12
Vehicle 'tip up'	12
Very sensitive switching	41
Voltage, control	3
Voltage divider	37
Voltage, measuring	29
Voltmeter	29-31
Volts	29
W	
Washing machine	20
White line follower	43
Window opener	45
Worksheets	xiii